KP

THE BIOGRAPHY
OF A REBEL

KP
THE BIOGRAPHY
OF A REBEL

Marcus Stead

JOHN BLAKE

Published by John Blake Publishing Ltd,
3 Bramber Court, 2 Bramber Road,
London W14 9PB, England

www.johnblakepublishing.co.uk

www.facebook.com/Johnblakepub   facebook

twitter.com/johnblakepub   twitter

First published in paperback in 2009
This edition published in 2013

ISBN: 978-1-78219-431-6

British Library Cataloguing-in-Publication Data:

A catalogue record for this book is available from the British Library.

Design by www.envydesign.co.uk

Printed and bound by CPI Group (UK) Ltd, Croydon, CR0 4YY

1 3 5 7 9 10 8 6 4 2

Papers used by John Blake Publishing are natural, recyclable products made
from wood grown in sustainable forests. The manufacturing processes
conform to the environmental regulations of the country of origin.

Every attempt has been made to contact the relevant copyright-holders,
but some were unobtainable. We would be grateful if the
appropriate people could contact us.

MARCUS STEAD is a freelance news and sports writer and avid cricket fan who regularly contributes to a range of printed and web-based publications. His previous books include *Arise Sir Frankie Dettori* and *In Bod We Trust*, a biography of rugby union legend Brian O'Driscoll.

CONTENTS

1
A GOOD START IN LIFE

From the very start of his life Kevin Pietersen was surrounded by competitive people. Born on 27 June 1980, his upbringing was both privileged and tightly disciplined. He was the third of four children, all boys, and his childhood was mainly a happy one. He grew up in Pietermaritzburg, the capital of Natal Province, a sleepy town lying in the shadows of the more cosmopolitan and lively Durban, which is about an hour's drive away. It is often mocked by Durban people who refer to it as 'Sleepy Hollow'. The writer Tom Sharpe, who once lived in Pietermaritzburg, loved to say it was half the size of New York Cemetery and twice as dead.

The greatest historical event to take place in the town happened in the early life of Mahatma Gandhi. In May 1893, when Gandhi was travelling by train to Pretoria, a white man objected to him sitting in a first-class carriage.

Gandhi had a first-class ticket and believed he had the right to sit there, but was ordered to move to the van compartment at the back of the train. He stood his ground and was thrown off the train at Pietermaritzburg. Shivering through the winter night in the waiting room of the station, he made the momentous decision to stay in South Africa and fight the racial discrimination against Indians which existed there.

Out of the struggle emerged his vision for non-violent resistance, called Satyagraha, which much later became an influence for Martin Luther King. Today, a bronze statue of Gandhi stands in the Pietermaritzburg city centre. The party capital of South Africa it certainly was not, but it provided the stable environment in which Kevin spent his formative years.

His father, Jannie Pietersen, is an Afrikaner and has worked as a director of a civil engineering firm for most of Kevin's life. Until the late 1980s he worked locally in Pietermaritzburg, and then in Durban where he has remained ever since. Kevin's mother, Penny, first arrived in South Africa aged 18. She is originally from Canterbury and emigrated to South Africa, when her father, a coal miner, got a job there. She met Jannie while he was in the army doing his national service in Pretoria.

Kevin's eldest brother, Tony, is now married with two children and works as a minister in his own church in Durban. Next up is Gregg, who is also married, and manages an import and export company which involves travel all around the world. His younger brother, Bryan, now lives in England and used to run a bar in Nottingham before moving to Southampton a few years ago.

Jannie has been a huge influence on Kevin's life and shares many characteristics with his son. He is full of energy, commuting long distances to and from work each day, and when he gets home he usually spends several hours in the garden. He only sits down to go to sleep, when his energy is completely spent. Sitting around watching television just isn't for him. Sport has always played a huge role in Jannie's life. In his younger days he played first-division rugby in South Africa and he and his wife both play squash to a good standard.

With Jannie having such a good job it meant that Penny could concentrate on raising the children and maintaining the home where they enjoyed a comfortable upbringing – their house was spacious and there was a large pool in the back garden – but this did not mean they were in any way spoilt as children.

As the man of the house, Jannie ran a strict regime with his children. All four boys lived in fear of his cane, called an army stick. If any of the children misbehaved at home or at school they could expect to be beaten with it. When Kevin was growing up his father's choice of punishment seemed harsh, but as he matured he learnt to respect Jannie for it. Today, Kevin believes caning should be allowed in homes and schools He's gone on record saying that children in Britain get away with too much, while being brought up to fear the cane does them good. Despite the strictness, Kevin found the family home a loving and warm place in which to grow up. Jannie and Penny's marriage has always been rock solid and none of the children have ever seen them have a serious argument.

Kevin's parents are devout Christians and, as with many South Africans, the Sabbath is strictly observed in their house. The whole family would attend church on Sunday mornings and again on Sunday nights throughout Kevin's childhood. The children were lucky because their home was surrounded by green-belt land, and their health-conscious parents encouraged them to live the outdoor life. From their earliest years they would run and walk in the nearby forest.

The boys were always close, yet Jannie installed a competitive edge amongst the siblings that was to have a profound effect on Kevin far beyond his childhood. Even as small children they would be up at the crack of dawn and would race a certain number of lengths in the pool, which would be followed by a run around the local neighbour-hood, after which they'd go out on their bikes.

When Kevin was just five years old he broke his collarbone, but only a fortnight later he was out of a sling and back jumping in the swimming pool. This resilience to fight injury, and a determination to get back to being active as soon as possible, was a characteristic that would shine through again and again in the years ahead. All of this met with his parents' approval. Sitting in front of the TV or spending endless hours playing computer games wasn't encouraged. They both wanted the boys to get into good habits at a young age, and all the boys embraced this lifestyle.

Kevin's first school was Clarendon, his second was

Merchiston, and his senior high school was the prestigious Pietermaritzburg College. All were fee-paying and for boys only. He attended his first two schools during the apartheid era in which children were labelled as 'white', 'coloured' or 'black', according to their ethnicity. Kevin's schools were for whites only. This was the political system in which Kevin was forced to grow up, and things only began to change when he reached his early teens. Fortunately, the experience of his early years did not lead him to believe in segregation and he regularly mixed happily with coloured and black children outside school.

All of Kevin's schools maintained strict regimes which mirrored that of his home life. From the start the children were expected to be punctual, which instilled a hatred of lateness into Kevin which has stayed with him to this day. Everyone knew their place, and respect was expected to be shown to teachers, other members of staff and those in senior forms.

Nobody would get away with taking advantage of anybody else, and being cheeky or abusive was not tolerated. The children lived in fear of the cane, and there was absolutely no nonsense of any kind. Kevin knew that if he received the cane at school he would very likely be caned again at home when his father found out what he'd done.

That said, the strict regime made for a safe and happy time at school and it gave Kevin the opportunity to lay the foundations for the rest of his life, as well as forcing him to get into good habits that would stand him in good stead in his future career.

His love of sport was well-established in his first few years at school and although he was good academically, eventually gaining three A-levels, sport was always his passion. Every Sunday, Kevin would accompany his parents and his brothers to church, which he always loved doing, even though he didn't fully appreciate the religious aspects of it until he was much older. The main reason he enjoyed church so much was because the Pietersens would meet up with their best friends, the Cole Edwards family, and Kevin and his brothers would get to play soccer with the children. Their father was the minister of the church, and the two families have remained close.

His enthusiasm even got to the stage where Kevin would ask his parents if he could go to church early so he could spend some time playing soccer before the service started. Each week after church they would come home and enjoy a Sunday roast, before returning to church for the evening service. As time went on they joined with the Cole Edwards to play in a soccer team called the Savages. While all the Pietersen boys were showing an interest in competitive games, his parents had by now realised that it was Kevin who was the most enthusiastic and the most likely to make a career as a sportsman.

The school year in South Africa was divided into terms for rugby, cricket and athletics, and Kevin was keen on all three. He was good enough to represent Natal Schools at rugby, squash, swimming and cross-country, but although he also represented the province at cricket, there were no obvious signs during his junior years that this would be the game in which he would excel.

A GOOD START IN LIFE

Kevin's father promised that he would buy him his first cricket bat when he made his first 50, and the moment came when he was eight, playing mostly against ten-year-olds. He was being coached by Digby Rhodes, father of Jonty, who was the first big hero in South African cricket after the readmission of the national team to the international stage following the apartheid years.

Jannie took his son to King Sports and purchased a Duncan Fearnley colt bat. This meant a huge amount to Kevin and it became a treasured possession – because treats like this were very rare. Jannie always taught his children to be careful with money and to buy what you need, rather than what you want. He never bought them branded trainers when cheaper, un-branded ones were just as good. The lesson he was teaching them was that material things aren't that important in life, and that you should always be careful with money because you never know when you may really need it.

Kevin's game developed gradually, but as his teenage years approached there were no obvious signs that he was going to be an outstanding international cricketer. At the age of 12 he suffered a serious setback when he broke an arm after falling five or six metres from a piece of gymnasium equipment. For once his enthusiastic attitude had cost him dear, and the injury set him back almost a year. He hated being sidelined for so long and found the wait to return to action deeply frustrating. For the time being, his sporting life was on hold.

But no sooner had he got back to fitness than disaster struck again. Playing rugby for the first time after recovering

7

from the gym injury, he was tackled as he caught a high ball at full back, breaking his arm in exactly the same place. This time, when they took his arm out of the cast, it still hadn't set properly and the doctor had to break it yet again – and put plenty of pins in it. Kevin thought it would never get better and his sporting career would end before it really began. It took a long time, but eventually his arm healed and is now very strong because of all the pins in it.

Kevin was a late developer in cricket but during his last year at Maritzburg College he was starting to excel. However, he was not selected for the first team because the coach, Mike Bechet, seemed to think more highly of a lad two years younger called Matthew Cairns, who Kevin regarded as something of a teacher's pet. It was only when Matthew emigrated to New Zealand that Kevin got his chance in the first team, but unfortunately for Kevin there were just five games left before his days at the college were over.

Bechet, whose former pupils include Jonty Rhodes, now considers Kevin one of his protégés. In his end-of-year summary for 1997, Bechet wrote, 'As an off-spinner Kevin bowled with intelligence and aggression – as he did with his batting. Bowlers screaming in his face didn't faze him. He would tell them they'd better get ready to fetch the next ball straight out of the trees – just like the last one he'd hit for six.'

Evidently the arrogance and in-your-face attitude we have come to associate with Kevin Pietersen was starting to come through. Yet Bechet's change of heart seems not to have altered Kevin's view of his former coach. He hasn't forgiven him for overlooking him for so long. Bechet has even asked Kevin's mother for mementos such as shirts Kevin has worn in matches, but the cricketing star has little contact with him.

Although his time in the college team was short, Kevin soon began to excel. He had a point to prove and knew that time was running out if he was to get himself noticed. Fortunately he had done well enough to be selected for South Africa Schools, where he formed a good working relationship with Graham Ford, the former coach of South Africa, who helped take his game onto the next level.

Throughout his time at school Kevin never really knew what he wanted to do when he left. He was pretty good at so many sports but there was never one that shone out above the rest as his best. And despite doing well academically he knew that office life wasn't really for him. During his later years in school he became more and more keen on cricket, but he had serious doubts about whether he could forge a career in the sport.

Then at the age of 17 he decided to give cricket a real go and see if he could make it, although at that time there were very few signs of how good he would eventually become. The brash and cocky persona was there, but he was far from world-class batsman material. Spin bowling seemed to be his forte, something that had not changed since his early teens. He was a competent lower-order batsman but he lacked upper body strength, and hitting fours and sixes didn't come easily to him.

After completing school he signed for Natal B, which gave him his entry into first class cricket, as well as joining the club side Berea Rovers. When playing at first class level it quickly became apparent that, while he was fairly good as an off-spinner and fielder, his lack of physical strength was going to be a problem which would hinder any natural ability as a batsman. He knew something drastic had to be done to put this right. He spent the winter training in all aspects of the game with his friend, Grant Rowley, as well as maintaining team practices. To build his muscle strength he had two stints on Creatine, the muscle-building drink, which is perfectly legal to use.

For the first time, Kevin's commitment to cricket was absolute. He would think about it day and night. Everything was now geared towards a career as a professional cricketer. He was a decent off-spinner, a good fielder and his batting was now beginning to improve. The following season he earned a first-team place in the Natal side, touring Western Australia with them and taking his first five-wicket haul as an off-spinner in a match at Lilac Hall. Kevin was beginning to believe in himself, his career was starting to gather pace, and he was seriously thinking that he could make a career from professional cricket.

Kevin knew that experiencing a good standard of cricket in another climate would stand him in good stead for his future career, when he would have to play on very different pitches. Natal colleague Doug Watson, who had played cricket for Cannock – a club side in Staffordshire, England – a few years earlier, suggested that he would find the experience of playing there hugely beneficial. With the help of Paul Greenfield a five-month stint at the club was arranged. His parents backed him all the way – they believed he was good enough academically to make a decent career for himself if things didn't work out, but knew that in his heart he wanted to make it as a cricketer. Jannie made it clear to him before he left that spending a period in another country would help him to grow as a cricketer and as a man, but if things didn't work out for whatever reason, he would always be welcome to return home. Kevin's parents probably appreciated the emotional rollercoaster he was about to experience more than he did himself at the time.

Kevin was excited at the prospect of playing in such a different environment, but he could not have imagined the huge culture shock that would engulf him. When he arrived in the town he was taken to the cricket club and was greatly impressed with the quality of the facilities there. Everything seemed so exciting and he couldn't wait to get down to work. However, he received a reality check when he was shown the room he'd be staying in for the duration, which was very different to what he'd been used to back home. It was situated directly above a squash court and was tiny by comparison to the room he had in his parents' house.

Everything was so different to what he'd been used to. Cannock was a small town and there was very little in the way of nightlife. Besides, he hadn't yet made any friends to spend his free time with. There were no wild parties and there seemed few opportunities to have fun. Others pointed out to him that if he expected to go on long winter tours to places like Pakistan in the future, the lack of the sort of social scene he was used to back home was something he'd have to get used to.

Kevin had to learn to cope with these huge changes to his life. From the spacious and relatively luxurious surroundings of his parents' home, he found himself boxed in to a claustrophobic room. He had no mobile phone, so he couldn't just call his parents or his brothers whenever he felt homesick. Yet this was one of many sacrifices he would have to make if he was to develop his game and achieve his dreams.

Despite struggling to get to grips with the Black Country accent, he did manage to make some firm friends around the area and took a job at the clubhouse bar to help pay his way. Even so, homesickness was a real problem, and it didn't seem to get any easier as he settled in. He yearned for his old life in South Africa and found being separated from his parents and brothers for long periods difficult to get used to.

Jannie became increasingly concerned to discern from their phone conversations that Kevin wasn't happy in England and wanted his family to be around him. He decided that he and Penny would fly out to England for a week to try and help him through this difficult patch. When they arrived they took him down to Bournemouth and spent some time just being a family again, and Jannie took the opportunity to have a heart-to-heart with his son. He reassured Kevin that he was behind him and Cannock was exactly where he needed to be at this point in his development.

The week with his parents appeared to help Kevin a lot and he seemed much happier for the remainder of his stay. That said, not everything went as smoothly as he would have liked. Kevin wasn't entirely happy with the direction in which the club were taking his cricket. He was still a bowler who could bat a bit, and, as far as he was concerned, bowling was going to be his forte. The club captain, a slow bowler called Laurie Potter who had played county cricket for Leicestershire, didn't choose Kevin to bowl as often as he would have liked. This was to prove a blessing in disguise, because it forced him to raise his game as a batsman.

Off the field there were a few isolated problems too, including a problem concerning disputed earnings Kevin claimed were due to him for bar work. But, all in all, he had little to complain about. Once he'd adapted to his new environment he found himself surrounded by mostly decent people who looked after him. What's more, Cannock went on to win the Birmingham and District Cricket League that season. By the end of his time at Cannock he had had enough of the place, but knew it had been a character-building experience.

Being forced to deal with the more negative aspects of live in Cannock – such as living in a small room in a small town – proved to be character-building and helped turn him into the person he is today. It taught him to be more inquisitive and to stand up for himself when he needed to. The experience of living in such cramped conditions made him realise that he could travel anywhere in the world and cope without some of the luxuries of home without it affecting his cricket. After his Cannock experience Kevin was a less materialistic person and didn't allow himself to be affected by outside distractions when there was a cricket match to be played.

Kevin had grown up and now had the maturity to make it

at the highest level, although there was still a great deal of work to be done before he was the finished article as a player. Yet something was about to happen that would completely change the course of his cricketing career.

2

THE HARDEST CHOICE OF ALL

The previous year Kevin had played in a match for Natal against the touring England side. The game was one he'd look back on with pride, as he managed to take four top-order wickets and scored 61 not out from 57 balls, despite batting at number nine.

The England side was captained by Nasser Hussain, who was new to the job and clearly wanted to make his presence felt. Kevin was impressed with the professional and diligent way in which Nasser went about being captain, and took time after the game to have a chat with him. He walked in, bold as brass, and clearly wasn't star struck at meeting such a big name in world cricket.

He knew his mother's nationality could potentially open doors for him, but at this stage he just wanted to find out a little more about English cricket from Nasser, and wasn't looking to make any big commitments. Kevin thought that because of his British passport he might like to play county cricket as a non-overseas player some time in the future, and he wanted to test the water a bit by having a chat with the England captain. Nasser gave Kevin the phone number of his brother, Mel, who played for Fives and Heronians in the Essex League.

Nasser would later curse his luck, because he had got completely the wrong end of the stick. He thought Kevin had wanted to play club cricket, and that's why he gave him Mel's number. His mind was elsewhere and it didn't occur to him that Kevin might have been looking to play for Essex in the not-too-distant future. He would later regret an opportunity missed – and a few people at Essex didn't let the matter drop too quickly once the story got out.

At this stage Kevin could not possibly have envisaged what was about to happen. South Africa was a rapidly changing country, the years of apartheid were over and a painful process of creating a racially equal society was underway. Inevitably this brought about controversies of its own, not least in sporting circles. A quota system was introduced into South African cricket to positively discriminate in favour of players of colour as a means of speeding up the process of racial integration.

In Kevin's mind this whole process was unethical and he has no qualms about publicly describing it as bullshit. As far as he was concerned everyone should have been treated equally, regardless of the colour of their skin, and the ridiculous quota system process was inevitably going to create exactly the sort of divisions it intended to confine to history. He also believed that it did no good for the person who was being selected because of the colour of their skin, rather than because of their ability as a cricketer.

Natal was no exception to this process. There had to be three non-white players in the team and Kevin was told that his place was being taken by a young off-spinning batsman called Gulam Bodi, starting with the match against Northern Transvaal at Kingsmead. Kevin could not hide his rage when he learnt he was being dropped. He threw a water bottle across the Natal dressing room and announced to everyone present that he was leaving. He knew Gulam was nowhere near as good as he was and was chosen ahead of him purely because of the colour of his skin. Kevin had nothing against Gulam as a person and – needless to say – nothing against his colour, but he was outraged and deeply hurt that he had been replaced by an inferior player. To date, Gulam has made a few appearances in one-day internationals for South Africa, but nobody would put him in the same class as Kevin Pietersen.

Once he had calmed down from the initial shock he picked up the phone and called his father, sobbing as he told him the bad news. Jannie immediately dropped everything to be with his distraught son, and tried to find a way forward for him. Together they insisted on a meeting with Philip Russell, a former county cricketer with Derbyshire who had just become the Natal coach, taking over from Graham Ford. While Kevin had developed a huge respect for Graham, he thought Philip was less independent of mind, and he wasn't optimistic that a way back into the team could be found.

Philip told Jannie and Kevin that the reason he had been

dropped was simply because of the quota system. From what Kevin could gather, no attempt to find a way around it had been sought. It seemed pretty clear to him that if one of the better non-white players had not been an off-spinning batsman, he would never have been dropped. Kevin knew that the time had come to consider his options. His mother's nationality could potentially be used to his advantage, and his British passport would allow him to play for an English county as a non-overseas player.

When he was at Cannock he had built up a rapport with Clive Rice and had gone to Trent Bridge to practise with him a few times. The two men got along extremely well: Kevin found Clive to be an excellent coach, but had a strict, no-nonsense approach that reminded him of his father. He also didn't believe in mincing words and told everything like it was, and this was exactly the sort of advice Kevin felt he needed at this time.

Kevin had a chat with Clive not long after being dropped, just to test the water. Clive had been a South African selector and knew the way events were heading, and had advised Kevin to leave long before the Natal controversy happened. Clive's advice was typically blunt. He told Kevin he had no future in South African cricket and wanted him to start a new life with Nottinghamshire. Although he didn't know Kevin especially well at this stage, he had seen enough to be sure that it wouldn't be necessary to send him for a trial at Trent Bridge, and in the winter of 2000 Kevin received a contract offering £15,000 for the 2001 season – far more than he was getting at Natal.

THE HARDEST CHOICE OF ALL

Clive had been the first South African captain when the country was readmitted into the international fold following the end of apartheid, but by now he was deeply suspicious of the direction in which his country's cricket was going. His advice to Kevin was exactly the same as the advice he would openly give to any young South African cricketer – get out of the country as soon as possible. His fears were justified. As he pointed out, the under-19s had even lost to Tibet, and hardly any cricket followers knew they even played the game in Tibet.

'They say they don't have quotas in South African cricket now,' said Clive, 'instead they have targets.' And that, he said, was the same thing by a different name, describing it as both bad and incestuous. To his mind, all Natal had done was pick a player who was not as good as Kevin in his place. To put it bluntly, as far as he was concerned the quota system was encouraging and creating mediocrity, and he thought Kevin was above that sort of system. This situation was proof enough for him that cricket in his beloved homeland was in self-destruct mode, and the long-term consequences could be potentially disastrous.

Clive was aware that Kevin wasn't always the easiest person in the world to get along with, yet this really didn't matter to him. All he was interested in was the fact that Kevin could play cricket, and it was his job to give him the coaching, discipline and structure to bring his talents onto the next level. He had worked alongside people he regarded as difficult characters when he was a player at Notts – such as Eddie Hemmings, Derek Randall and Chris Broad – yet however difficult they could be for him, as long as they were performing on the field he didn't care. This would be the same approach he wanted to take with Kevin. His offer to the young protégé was certainly generous.

Even so, Kevin still had a lot of thinking to do. A move to England would mean making a fresh start in more ways than one. He had no family and few friends there, and this was an important factor, taking into account how lonely and homesick he had often felt during his time at Cannock. He had a chat with Graham Ford, who he still held in high esteem because of the way in which he had helped him along at South Africa Schools and Natal. Graham was also adamant that Kevin should make the move to Nottinghamshire. He then asked one of his mentors, Harry Brown, and he said the same. He also asked Shaun Pollock, the captain of South Africa, for whom Kevin had the utmost respect because of his achievement and status in the game. Surprisingly, Shaun was equally enthusiastic in his belief that Kevin should make the move.

There were other people whose opinions he valued and who wanted him to stay, but as far as Kevin was concerned Natal had forced the issue. They knew full well he had already spent a summer in England and had built up a good relationship with Clive and others at Nottinghamshire. Natal were aware of the problem, and knew that if Kevin left he would be a loss to South African cricket, but those with any authority did nothing about it and merely blamed the system.

However, there was one more chance for South African cricket to hold on to Kevin, and he was still open to persuasion to stay, should certain assurances be made about his future. Dr Ali Bacher, the chief of the United Cricket Board and the most powerful man in South African cricket, wanted to see Kevin. Dr Bacher played a big part in setting up the rebel tours of the early 1980s while South Africa was isolated from the rest of the cricketing world due to sanctions, and he was the man who had been head of the UCB since the old black and white cricketing authorities had merged in the early 1990s. In this capacity he had brought South African cricket back from the wilderness and played a vital part in getting them readmitted to the international fold. This was a man who could make or break Kevin's future in South African cricket.

Jannie and Kevin flew up to Johannesburg for the meeting with an open mind, yet both understood the importance of what was about to take place and they knew that they would probably leave the meeting with a firm decision one way or the other.

For the majority of the meeting Jannie did the talking while Kevin stayed quiet. Dr Bacher claimed that the quota system would end fairly soon and that selection would be done on merit. Kevin piped up and asked whether, say, in a year's time, the black and coloured players weren't good enough, Natal would field an all-white side. Dr Bacher's reply told Kevin all he needed to know. He gave a firm 'no' and said that they will be good enough and they will play. This gave Kevin the insight he needed. He tapped Jannie's leg, the two nodded at each other and they both knew this was the turning point of the meeting. At the end, they thanked Dr Bacher for his time and as soon as they were out of his earshot Jannie told Kevin he was going to Notts, and that the quota system would never finish.

They flew back to Durban and immediately phoned Clive Rice to accept his offer to play for Notts. Kevin then pulled out of the Natal squad, as this was a requirement for him to be able to play for Notts as a non-overseas player. He did so knowing he would never play for the side again.

In Kevin's mind everything was going wrong with South African cricket. When he was a child he had two cricketing heroes: Hansie Cronje and Allan Donald. He especially admired Cronje for his strong and aggressive batting style and had a high regard for his ability as a captain. Kevin had played against him when South Africa played Natal in a warm-up match. Cronje scored 50 not out, and the following day the story broke that he had been involved in match-fixing. It was a controversy that shook South African cricket to its core. Kevin picked up no hint the day before it came out that anything was untoward, but in the weeks and months that followed the sheer enormity of what Cronje was being accused of further discredited an already sorry state of affairs in South African cricket.

In retrospect, Cronje still remains a hero in Kevin's mind. He was a truly great player who made a terrible mistake, and his death in an air accident two years later was a tragedy. Kevin is firmly of the view that Cronje's achievements in the game outweigh the one hugely foolish mistake he made, and he has forgiven him for the shame he brought upon himself and South African cricket as a whole.

THE HARDEST CHOICE OF ALL

Kevin had made a decision that would affect the rest of his professional life. This wasn't a case of playing in England for a year, and if things didn't work out he could go back home. Kevin was, to all intents and purposes, emigrating. From this moment onwards his loyalty would be to English cricket. As a child he had been overjoyed at seeing South Africa readmitted to the international cricketing community, and as he got a little older had dreamed of playing for the national team and emulating his heroes. But this was a country that seemed happy to see him frozen out due to what he regarded as a dubious and unethical way of integrating the races.

The scandal played no part in Kevin turning his back on South Africa, but it further highlighted to him how far cricket had fallen. Kevin now believes that if he'd chosen to stay, his career would have been blocked by the system and he would not be playing cricket at all now. Maybe he would have achieved fame and success in another sport, but we will never really know.

From now on, neither Kevin nor any member of his family would support South Africa against England again. Both his parents were completely supportive of his decision, and fully appreciated that this was not a decision he had taken lightly or without a considerable period of thought. Deep down, they knew there was no other way forward. From this moment on, Kevin Pietersen was an England man.

3
LEARNING THE HARD WAY

Kevin Pietersen arrived at Heathrow airport in April 2001 with just a suitcase for baggage and a head filled with dreams. A bed-and-breakfast in Nottingham was his first port of call. He was told that practice would be at 10 o'clock next morning. After unpacking his few belongings he drove around the town, getting lost trying to find places. Here was a young South African lad who didn't know what to expect, chucked into a boarding house with a lady he didn't know. He was a long way from family and friends, and couldn't talk to anyone about anything. He went to bed that night, his head spinning with worry, wondering what the next day would bring. Added to this was the pressure of having no safety net. He knew he had to make a success of this. There was no going back. It was a case of adapt or die.

The fact that his younger brother, Bryan, moved to the Nottingham area to run a bar at around the same time certainly brought a degree of home familiarity to his life. He was also relishing the prospect of working closely with Clive Rice, who had become something of a paternalistic figure to him. Very early on, Clive had told Kevin that he would aim to get him playing for England in four years.

It wasn't long before Kevin moved to his own flat in Nottingham – the place he would now call home. His objectives for the season ahead were very clear: to better himself as a player and as a person, and to learn enough to become a serious contender for a place in the England team by the time he qualified late in 2004.

It didn't take too long before all the feelings of homesickness began to subside. He would still get to see plenty of his family, especially Bryan, and he felt he was at a club, and indeed in a country, where his talents were genuinely appreciated and he had a means to develop and progress. The same could not be said of South Africa, and he knew England was the place he had to regard as his home from now on.

Kevin was especially pleased that Nottinghamshire signed Greg Smith at the same time that he arrived at the club. Greg, like him, had a British passport and was eligible to play as a non-overseas player. They also picked up a young fast bowler from Northamptonshire called Richard Logan, who quickly became a very close friend.

Notts were playing second-division cricket in the County Championship that year, and this was a level that Kevin felt comfortable at competing. He debuted as a number six batsman and felt he could still become an all-rounder. In the nets, he continued to work hard at off-spin bowling. In the months that followed his bowling would become less and less of a priority as Clive realised that Kevin was something very special as a batsman.

That first year at Nottingham was a very successful one for Kevin's batting career. He scored 1,275 Championship runs over the season, scoring at a rate of 82 every 100 balls. Even then it was clear that he wasn't going to be someone who messed around, and had an in-built penchant for quick scoring. He scored four centuries and topped the Notts first-class averages at 57.95 per innings. The team's achievements were less successful. They reached the semifinals of the Benson & Hedges Cup but their hopes of promotion in the Championship dwindled away and they finished a disappointing seventh.

At the end of the season Kevin felt he had made good progress towards the goal of being the best player he could be. There were occasional moments when he would sit in his flat missing his old family life in South Africa, but these were few and far between. He never seriously questioned his decision to leave South Africa and knew that the whole process of living in England and fending for himself was part of growing up and vital if he was to achieve his ambitions.

Kevin was also beginning to form strong views on the state of county cricket in England. He felt that English domestic cricket was the best in the world, but there was so much cricket being played that it could dampen the players' enthusiasm to win. He also thought that there was a lot of mediocrity in county cricket and a lot of players who were lucky to be earning a living from the game. To his mind, not every player shared his ambition to make tough sacrifices and work hard to be the best player they could possibly be.

He believed that the function of county cricket was to produce players for the England team, and there were some counties who had their share of players who were never going to compete for England places, instead being happy to cruise along in pursuit of their pay cheque and ultimately a benefit year. This was something he regarded as a serious negative trait in the English game, and did nothing for the pursuit of excellence.

Clive was a great example of someone Kevin regarded as having the right attitude towards county cricket. In Kevin's view, Clive had inherited a lot of players who seemed happy to earn their money while not working hard to maximise the potentials of themselves or the team as a whole. Clive wanted to get rid of all the players who fitted into that category and bring players in who were achievers and had the right mental attitude to the game.

Kevin had been delighted with the way in which Clive had brought his game along during that first year. He quickly treated him with huge respect and as a father figure, but as the year progressed he really began to appreciate how good Clive was. On taking over as coach, he had already been one of the county's greatest ever players and captains, and now he was beginning to make real long-term progress with the squad. However, he wasn't afraid to upset a few people along the way. These were people who, in Kevin's view, badly needed upsetting.

Nevertheless it came as a devastating blow to Kevin when

Notts decided to sack Clive. He was especially sickened by the manner of his sacking. Clive had gone back to South Africa two weeks previously to visit his dying father for the last time. Everybody at the club knew about the sad situation in which Clive found himself, but they still decided this was the right time to get rid of him.

This decision had a huge impact on Kevin's state of mind. He began to question whether this was the sort of club he wanted to be part of, and if he wanted to be surrounded by people who behaved like this. He had lost his mentor, the man who had brought him to the club, the man who had helped him through those tough times when thinking over his future in South Africa. This was also the man who had helped him settle in at Notts and had brought his game on in leaps and bounds during his first season.

Kevin's mood was made worse the very next day when it was revealed that Mick Newell would be taking over as coach. He had been working with the second team and therefore he already knew the players, but Kevin wasn't impressed with the fact that Mick's playing career had hardly been exceptional. This wouldn't be the last time Kevin criticised a person's ability to coach a team based on their own playing record.

Immediately upon his appointment, Mick took the decision to drop Kevin to the second team. Kevin was initially shocked, considering his record as a batsman had been so good the previous year, and felt as though Mick had something against him. This was as big a blow to Kevin's morale as Clive's departure the previous day had been.

LEARNING THE HARD WAY

When he asked for an explanation, Mick told him that he hadn't been playing as well as he should have been, that he was below par, and that he wasn't going to play in his team on reputation alone or based on what he'd achieved in the past. Considering his track record in the previous season had been impressive, Kevin was upset by his decision. He felt that Mick wanted to put him on some sort of trial.

His first one-day game for the seconds was away against Yorkshire at Headingley, where he was bowled for a low double-digit score by an off-spinner. This was proof enough for Kevin that his head wasn't right, and he still hadn't come to terms with what had happened to Clive. This wasn't the way Kevin usually handled off-spinners, and it was rare for one to bowl him. The next game was another one-dayer away at Durham, where Kevin found himself playing against Steve Harmison, who was coming back from injury. Kevin knew this wasn't a bad team to be facing and treated them with due respect, but managed a creditable score with the bat, which earned him a return to the first team.

Meanwhile, Kevin had by this stage had enough time to form a considered opinion of Mick, and had decided that he was no match for Clive. In his mind, Mick wasn't the right person for the job and was the exact opposite of Clive, in that in was more prone to placate people. Clive, on the other hand, always spoke his mind and had the same methods as Kevin.

Kevin certainly made his presence felt on his return to the first team, scoring four consecutive centuries. He was able to put the problems he was having with Mick to the back of his mind and get on with the business of playing to the best of his ability. Good fortune plays a part in every sportsman's career and cricket is no exception. Players are never far away from a fall that can lead to a long lay-off, or a career-threatening injury, and, in cricket especially, bad luck has a disquieting habit of striking at the worst possible time.

With four consecutive centuries under his belt, Kevin couldn't ask for things to be going much better. He headed to Colwyn Bay for a match against Glamorgan, eager for more of the same. Fate dealt him a bitter blow when he dived for a ball when fielding, causing him to fracture his leg, and it was clear that the injury was bad enough to keep him out for the rest of the season. It was a bitter blow, but one he could do nothing about. Nevertheless he managed to finish the season at 61.41 – the highest average for a Notts batsman. He had proved to himself that batting was his forte, and was now doing considerably less bowling. There was no doubt in his mind that he had what it took to make it as a Test batsman.

However, this sense of personal progress was tainted with a growing belief that all was not well at Notts. The team were playing well and ultimately gained promotion to the first division, but he didn't think that Mick's ability as a coach had a lot to do with it. To him, the arrival of Australian Stuart 'Stuey' MacGill had been one of the main reasons for the team's success in the latter part of the season.

Stuey had arrived at Trent Bridge in early August and went on to take 40 wickets in six first class matches. Nobody who has seen him at his best could deny his ability as a world-class leg spinner, but he had the misfortune to be part of the same generation as a certain Shane Warne, meaning his opportunities to play for Australia were extremely curtailed. Had he been born in another era, or been eligible for another country, his track record suggests that he would surely enjoy greater recognition as one of the all-time greats of world cricket.

Stuey was a thoughtful, intellectual man, who had a sense of individuality and a balanced life outside cricket. He had once read 24 novels during a tour of Pakistan and had a reputation as a bit of a wine connoisseur. A few years later he was the only Australian player who refused to join the tour of Zimbabwe on moral grounds, deeply unhappy at the way in which President Robert Mugabe was oppressing his people. Stuey immediately hit it off with Kevin, and their friendship would become a huge source of comfort in the difficult times that lay ahead.

At the end of the season, Stuey asked Kevin what he was doing that winter. Kevin said that he hadn't made any definite plans, so Stuey firmly insisted that he join him in playing grade cricket in Australia. Stuey got him a place playing alongside him for Sydney University, in a team that also included Greg Matthews. He was following in illustrious footsteps, as previous players for the side included the likes of Imran Khan. Kevin stayed in a pleasant part of Sydney at the top of George Street, a short walk from the university.

Grade cricket was a whole new experience for Kevin and taught him the value of protecting his wicket. The way it worked was that one week you would be batting, and the following week you'd be fielding. This meant that if one week the game was rained off, there could be a very long gap between your opportunities to bat, and it was in the batsman's interests to make the most of the chance to impress when it came along.

This was a vast contrast to county cricket, where batsmen who make a mistake can usually put it right within a few days. The standard of play was decent – it was better than club cricket but not as good as county cricket. Kevin also liked the hard-working culture that existed there, and was impressed by the loyalty of many Australian international cricketers, such as Shane Warne, who made the effort to turn out for their old teams from time to time, keeping them in touch with their roots.

Kevin was the club's top scorer and helped them to win the first grade title for the first time in around 100 years. This had been a worthwhile and important part of helping him become a more rounded player, and got rid of some of his more reckless tendencies with the bat. The value of playing here was heightened by the fact that he didn't rate Mick as a coach back at Notts, and didn't feel his game had developed as it would have done if Clive had still been there. Kevin's life off the field was starting to become settled and largely happy. He had begun dating Cate Pugh, an Australian advertising art director who he'd met during his time at Sydney, and they soon settled into a stable relation-ship that was to last for several years.

In 2003, Kevin's love affair with Notts began to sour. He was still less than impressed with Mick's ability as a coach, and as the season developed he became increasingly concerned that some of his team-mates were more interested in themselves than the overall good of the team. In other words, he thought their main aim was to do enough to keep their place in the side, and nothing more.

Kevin was also greatly unimpressed with the captaincy of Jason Gallian. Great things had been expected of Jason when he first came on the scene as a youngster, and he was thought likely to be a major player for England. Whilst he had the talent, it appears he lacked the temperament to make it at the highest level, and ended up playing just three Tests for England. Now he was an experienced cricketer captaining his county, and Kevin didn't see any proper leadership or ambition from him. Many respected pundits predicted Notts could finish in the top three in the first division of the Championship, but Kevin just couldn't see this happening.

On a personal front, the season represented yet more progress. Kevin topped the Notts averages for the third year in succession, scoring 1,488 Championship runs at an average of 51.31, including four centuries. He had proved he could handle the step up in quality, following Notts' promotion to the first division, and that he was able to perform consistently well at this level. His one-day game was also heading in the right direction, scoring 776 in the National League, one of the best tallies in the history of Notts.

As the season progressed, Kevin's relationship with his team-mates got worse and worse. One bad result followed another and Kevin let it be known to his colleagues and the press that he felt he was carrying the team. Things became so bad that he would sometimes warm up on his own. The only two members of the team he still got on well with were Stuey and Richard Logan. Relationships were civil with a few of the others, but between the rest they were ice cold. In the end, Notts were relegated from the first division. It was a situation few would have predicted at the start of the season, but the disagreements between the players and the lack of harmony at the club meant that team spirit hit rock bottom, and they were unable to produce good cricket on the field.

On the final day of the season, his rift with Jason Gallian came to a head. During the game, Kevin told Jason he wanted to leave. After the game they spoke in the dressing room and Kevin left to have dinner. He admits to saying some things he probably shouldn't have, but the exact details of who said what are unknown. While he was gone, he received a phone call from Bilal Shafayat, telling him that Jason had trashed his equipment and thrown it over the balcony at Trent Bridge, and had said, 'If he does not want to play for Notts he can f*** off.' Kevin was outraged by Jason's behaviour. Here was a captain, a man who was supposed to lead by example, behaving in a childish and unprofessional way. What made it worse was the fact he'd done it when he wasn't there, which Kevin believed showed a lack of guts on his part.

Kevin looked seriously into the possibility of taking legal action to release him from the one year that remained on his contract. Notts felt like a completely different club to the one he had joined a few years before, and it wasn't a place he felt deserved his talents or level of dedication. That dedication and love of cricket were as strong as ever, but his morale had now hit rock bottom.

Since his arrival in England, Kevin had been aware that those involved in the England Academy were keeping an eye on his progress. David Graveney, the England chairman of selectors, had told him that when he first arrived in 2001 they considered him 'one to watch' for the future. The knowledge that he was being watched by such influential people was something that helped him get through the last few difficult months at Notts.

At the end of the season he received a phone call from Rod Marsh, the former Australian wicketkeeper who was now in charge of the academy, who asked him to spend six months at Loughborough with the probability of a tour to India at the end of it. This was a wonderful opportunity for Kevin to help develop his name, and to show the important men in the England setup just how good he really was.

Kevin was instantly impressed with what he saw at Loughborough. The training facilities were absolutely superb, but there was far more to the experience than that. One of the aims of the centre was to prepare upcoming players for the full pressures of life as a professional cricketer. In the months ahead Kevin and his fellow academy members would be briefed by journalists from both the print and broadcast media, teaching them how to cope with and handle interviews.

Working with computers was also part of the course.

Kevin was already pretty computer literate and it came as a shock to find so many young people there who didn't have a clue. For a modern cricketer, computers are vital for analysing your own game and sussing out how your opponents play. They also allow cricketers easily to keep in touch with their family and friends when on long tours to the other side of the world. Kevin was amazed at how little some of the players knew about computers. After all, they were from the same generation as him. They would need to make the most of the opportunity to put this right.

Early on, Rod Marsh, along with his assistants Nigel Laughton and Richard Smith, let Kevin know exactly where he stood with them in relation to the situation at Notts. They said that they'd heard certain things about him, and didn't believe them. They were going to judge him on merit and it was up to him to make the most of this opportunity. This came as a huge relief to Kevin. It was perfectly normal for these important men to have concerns based on what they'd heard, but he was glad he was being given a clean slate and wasn't being prejudged.

Kevin's time with the academy was demanding, but largely happy. He commuted from Nottingham each day, which he found especially difficult during the winter months. He would have to be up at 5am, several hours before it became light, and it would be dark again by 4pm. He'd normally leave the academy by 6pm, and by the time he got home there wasn't really much time to do anything.

In spite of the tough schedule, his time at the academy was a great success. He quickly warmed to Rod Marsh, who he regarded as disciplined and shared his belief in working hard to make yourself the best player you can possibly be. During his time at the academy he also soon built up a strong friendship with Simon Jones, and also got on well with Michael Lumb and Matty Prior, who would eventually break into the England team. Others there included his Notts team-mate Bilal Shafayat, and Kabir Ali.

Kevin relished the gruelling routine at the academy, and those he was closest to also put in the hours, but there were also a handful of players there who he felt weren't as dedicated as they should have been. He knew they had the talent to be in the academy, but also that they weren't willing to work hard to make the most of the opportunities that were put in place. He has never named names, but it's fair to say none of those he blames have made it into the England setup, whereas others, such as Jones and Prior, were to soon get their reward for their hard work.

That winter was a truly happy time for Kevin and gave him the chance to really take his mind off the situation at Notts and reflect on his future. He started 2004 by going on the representative tour to India with his fellow academy graduates. This was the first time he and Cate had been apart for any length of time since they had been together, and it was an experience that was tough on both of them. Cate decided to go and spend the period with her parents in Sydney, while Kevin was made to appreciate just how difficult life as an international cricketer would be, and the extent of the sacrifices that would have to be made.

The team stopped off in Malaysia first, to acclimatise. In

the three games they played, Kevin failed to get into double figures and when they arrived in India they played some one-day games in which Kevin didn't really feature. Rod decided to ask Kevin to open the batting in the next game in Bangalore. Kevin didn't think he was a natural opening batsman and had never tried it before, but had enough respect for Rod to just do what he asked. He took the view that he had to bat at some stage, so it might as well be at the start. It was a smart move on Rod's part and boosted Kevin's confidence no end. He went on to make 131 from around 80 balls in a superb innings.

From then on there was no stopping Kevin. He scored another century in a four-day game against India A in Chennai. After this, he scored two centuries in their first Duleep Trophy matches against the South Zone, and followed this up with a 94 in the next game with East Zone in Amritsar, which was one of the worst places he'd ever seen. The team as a whole wasn't performing well, losing both Duleep Trophy matches. This was hardly a surprise, considering the strong quality of the opposition, the lack of any senior players in the side, and the fact they hadn't played much competitive cricket together before, but Kevin still felt very happy with life. He was perhaps trying a little too hard to score runs on some very difficult pitches in those early games in Malaysia, but once he'd told himself to relax, things couldn't really have gone any better.

Playing in India was a worthwhile aspect of his education. It gave him the chance to play against some superb spin bowlers on wickets that suited their game. He knew playing against spin was one of the most difficult challenges a batsman can face, and a completely different experience to facing fast bowlers. Playing spin bowlers required a huge amount of mental strength and was comparable to a chess match.

At the end of the tour Rod told Kevin he was now ready for international cricket. Hearing this from a man of Rod's stature meant a huge amount to him, even though it would be another year before he was eligible to play for England. This didn't matter; he had achieved, and even excelled, his aims that winter. In his mind, Rod now featured alongside Graham Ford and Clive Rice as the coaches and mentors who had helped develop his cricketing ability and given him the mental strength necessary to make it at the very highest level.

Kevin returned to Notts with a glowing report from Rod. He hadn't made any enemies during the winter and had got on well with all the people that mattered. As far as he was concerned this was proof that he wasn't the monster some people at Notts had made him out to be. The Kevin that returned to Notts in the spring was tougher, more mature and savvy. He decided that he had to just keep his head down, be professional and get through the next season, after which he'd be free to move to another county and would be eligible for the England setup. Kevin had three firm friends within the Notts team who helped him get through that season. They were Stuey, Richard Logan and the Australian David Hussey, who had joined as an overseas player. He was on reasonable terms with a few of the others, but his relationship with Jason and Mick remained icy, and he had lost respect for several others in the team.

His motives for doing well were now more selfish. He didn't feel the obligation to perform for his team-mates like he had done during his time with the academy or in years past at the club, but he knew it was important to still play to the best of his ability to stay in contention for England. On the field, Kevin had another good season with Notts, scoring 965 runs with an average of 53.61. This wasn't quite as good as the previous few seasons, but it was still pretty decent and had helped get the team promoted. At one stage Kevin even hinted he would be prepared to stay at Notts. They had put some of their troubles behind them and were playing as a team.

At the end of the season the club made Kevin an offer that would have made him their highest paid player. Kevin told them that he didn't care what other people earned, but felt he deserved more than they were offering, considering his massive contribution to the side over the past few seasons. He asked Mick what his plans were for the team, and was told that they'd be sticking with the players that got them promoted. A few days later he found out that his two best friends in the team, Stuey and Richard, had been released by the club. He found this decision baffling. They were getting rid of one of the best spin bowlers the world has ever seen, and were also letting go of a very decent young cricketer.

Kevin couldn't work out why they would want to do this. He thought maybe the club wanted to split them up, thinking they had formed a cabal that was dividing the dressing room. This episode was the final straw, so he rang his agent and told him in no uncertain terms that it was time to move on.

4

MAKING
THE GRADE

Kevin had offers from several counties eager to sign him up, but he wanted to look at the full picture before making a firm commitment. His preference was for a move south, but he was also keen to play for a county that was professionally run and had ambition. He had formed the view that county cricket teams were now businesses and had to be run as such.

Hampshire was one of several counties that were interested in signing Kevin, so a meeting was arranged with some influential people at the club. It was run by Rod Bransgrove, who was a successful businessman in his own right. The work he had done in rejuvenating Hampshire had been extraordinary. When he took over, the club was in dire financial straits. The building of the new Rose Bowl ground had gone massively over budget and it seemed likely they wouldn't be playing first class cricket at all in 2001.

However, Rod's ambitious and forward-thinking approach helped turn the club around, and within a few seasons they had gone from mediocre also-rans to a highly professional outfit that could compete for serious honours. Kevin knew from Rod's reputation that this would be a man worth meeting, and this was the sort of person he admired. He wasn't to be disappointed.

The meeting taught Kevin that Hampshire was a progressive, modern and purposeful club that he wanted to be a part of. He liked Rod from the outset and knew this was a man he would want as his boss. Further meetings were arranged with the coaches, Paul Terry (the First Team Manager) and Tim Tremlett. Paul was a former fast bowler who had played two Tests for England in 1984 and had gone on to have some success in coaching the Melville Cricket Club in the Western Australian Pennant cricket competition, and ran a cricket academy in Perth. Paul immediately hit it off with Kevin: they shared a philosophy and cricketing outlook.

The whole experience was positive, and Kevin found he got on with absolutely everyone he met. Another massive incentive for joining the club was the prospect of playing under Hampshire's captain, the great Shane Warne. Few would dispute that Shane was the greatest leg spin bowler of all time. He had come through at a time when spin bowling in general was in danger of dying out, and has put this great aspect of the game back on the map. Furthermore, everyone knew about Shane's competitive and no-nonsense approach to cricket, and Kevin realised that playing alongside a man of his stature was a tremendous honour, and an opportunity that few cricketers ever receive.

Hampshire seemed to tick all the boxes. It was in the south. It was somewhere with a cricketing outlook Kevin could relate to and liked. The people there were fantastic, and there was nobody he didn't get on with. The facilities were new and of the highest standard. However, there was one drawback: the wicket at the Rose Bowl. At a time when Kevin was trying to impress the selectors, he knew getting big scores here wouldn't be as straightforward as at Trent Bridge.

On the other hand, he wanted to challenge himself. He had perhaps become a bit too comfortable at making big scores at Notts on a comparatively easy wicket, and needed a greater challenge in bread-and-butter cricket to help make him become a better batsman on the international stage. The money being offered was significantly more generous than Notts had offered him. There was nothing more to think about, and the deal was done. Kevin would be joining Hampshire for the 2005 season.

The end of the 2004 season gave Kevin something else to celebrate – he was now eligible for England, and this thought was now never far from his mind. After the deal with Hampshire was done he decided to take a break in Majorca. One day he was sitting by the pool when he received a phone call from David Graveney, the chairman of selectors. It was good news: he had been selected for the short one-day tour of Zimbabwe. Kevin was naturally delighted with the news, but it didn't come entirely as a surprise. He was aware that several players who were in contention for places had asked to be rested for the tour, in some cases because they had ethical objections to going. One slight dampener was that he wouldn't be on the main winter tour of South Africa. There had already been a great deal of debate about how he would cope in his country of origin, and he felt ready to face the challenge, but the selectors clearly felt this was a step too far and wanted to protect him.

He phoned his parents straight away and told them the good news. They were over the moon and couldn't hide their excitement at the fact that the huge gamble their son had taken a few years earlier had paid off. Jannie, in particular, felt a sense of relief as well as pride. He had been there when Dr Bacher effectively told his son that he had no future in South African cricket, but this snub had turned out to be an enormous blessing in disguise. This was one of the happiest moments of Kevin's life so far, and he celebrated the news in style with a bottle of champagne at the Majorca pool side.

The tour would begin with a few warm-up matches in Namibia before going on to Zimbabwe. There was no escaping the serious moral and ethical controversies that surrounded the tour. The country, which had once been one of the most economically prosperous in Africa, was now in a state of collapse. The Mugabe regime had caused widespread poverty and disease across the nation, and political opponents had been beaten and killed for daring to speak out. There was no free speech, no democracy, and all opposition was suppressed by government forces.

Steve Harmison had written a column in a Sunday

newspaper saying he wouldn't be joining the tour as a matter of conscience, and BBC reporter Ralph Dellor gave similar reasons for staying at home. Andrew Flintoff, a close friend of Harmison, was also known to be having serious reservations about going, but he ultimately decided to take part.

Kevin felt he knew more than most about the real situation in Zimbabwe, having lived most of his life in neighbouring South Africa. He felt that it was his job to play cricket, and the issue of whether it was right to go politically was a matter for his employers. He had been to Zimbabwe before and had seen people living on the streets, and felt he knew more than many people in the England setup about the reality of the situation. As far as he was concerned the poverty the England players were about to see on the streets of Harare was no different to what still goes on in many parts of South Africa to this day.

He didn't feel as though he would be in any physical danger by going, and he personally thought it unlikely that the Mugabe regime would look to make political capital from the tour. Having been brought up as a Christian, he believed that when your time was up there was nothing anyone could do about it. This was the start of his England career. Staying away wasn't an option. He still had a lot to prove. But this was no ordinary tour and Kevin fully understood the potential for a whole range of non-cricketing factors to make the experience go badly wrong.

To help Kevin and the other newcomers settle in, a 'buddy' system was introduced whereby they would be paired up with a more experienced player who would help them feel settled and give them someone to practise and exercise with. Kevin was paired with Ashley Giles, and the two immediately hit it off and formed a friendship that was to last. Kevin knew how lonely it could be when travelling, and having someone like Ashley around made him feel a lot more comfortable. One man Kevin would be spending a lot of time with was the former Glamorgan and England batsman Matthew Maynard, who was now the batting coach. As a player, he liked to dominate bowlers and had a very similar mind-set to Kevin – positive, aggressive and in-your-face. Also, like Kevin, he was no stranger to controversy.

In 1989, when he was a fringe player for England, Matt ran foul of the cricketing authorities by agreeing to go on Mike Gatting's controversial tour of South Africa, when the country was still banned from international sport due to the policy of apartheid. His justification for going was that he was desperate for a taste of international cricket, having just been dropped from the official England team. For this he served a three-year ban from Test cricket.

Matt also had leadership qualities, which came to fruition when he led Glamorgan to the County Championship title in 1997. However, there were some key differences between the two men. Matt had a reputation for liking a drink, and his love of partying got him into trouble from time to time. He was also a heavy smoker. This contrasted heavily with Kevin's clean-living approach which had seen him make many sacrifices to get to this level.

Matt's appointment as England batting coach had been controversial. Former England captain Michael Atherton had made comments about him being unsuitable for the job because he had gone on the rebel tour in 1989. The ex-England coach Keith Fletcher said that Matt's reputation for partying might not set a good example to the younger players (the truth was that Matt had cleaned up his act a great deal in the previous few years).

Nevertheless, Matt and Kevin got on extremely well. They were both rebellious, anti-establishment figures who weren't afraid to speak their minds, and had both gone through their share of controversies in cricket. This, combined with a similar playing philosophy, resulted in the two working very closely at England level during this tour and for the next few years.

Matt told Kevin that for as long as he put cricket first, he could become one of the greatest batsmen in the history of the game. Even at this early stage he knew Kevin was something special and had told coach Duncan Fletcher that they must let him play in the upcoming one-dayers. He was in no doubt that Kevin was more than capable of making the leap from superb county batsman to world-class player. In the past, players such as a young Graeme Hick, and even Matt himself, had shown so much promise at county level yet had never quite managed to adjust to the international game. Matt was certain Kevin had what it took to avoid that trap.

In Matt's view, Kevin's attitude was spot-on. He was like a sponge, soaking up new information, and was forever full of life, always looking to improve the way he played his shots. His approach to practice and sense of personal discipline were exactly what was required. Matt couldn't have asked any more from Kevin in the lead up to the matches in Zimbabwe.

The warm-up games in Namibia didn't go as well as Kevin had hoped. His first innings was particularly bad, and saw him being given out, slogging, to a very bad decision. In the next match he did slightly better. Despite only scoring in the 20s, he hit a good boundary through the covers, followed by a six straight over the bowler's head in the next. The experience gave his confidence a much-needed lift, with the important matches against Zimbabwe getting ever-nearer.

Kevin felt ready to take on Zimbabwe and show the world just how good he was. However, politics reared its ugly head shortly before the squad was about to leave for Zimbabwe. It transpired that 13 of the travelling press corps had been refused entry to the country. If this situation prevailed, there was no question of the England team playing cricket there.

The players just sat by the pool in their hotel and waited for news. Many of the older players would have preferred it if the tour was called off there and then, but such a scenario would have been hugely disappointing for Kevin. This was the moment he had waited years for, when, finally, after all the sacrifice and tough decisions, he would be able to go out and play for his adopted country. And now it all seemed to be in very serious danger of not happening at all, because of a political situation way beyond his control.

After what seemed like a lifetime of hanging about waiting for news, the players were told that the press would be allowed in after all and the tour would be going ahead as planned. The worst part of it for all the players was the uncertainty and the hanging around, but Kevin was more relieved than most, because his dreams of playing for England would be coming true after all.

Once they knew the trip was definitely going ahead, the players were briefed by management on how to deal with the off-field problems they may encounter once they entered Zimbabwe. Kevin thought these were likely to be more challenging than anything they'd experience on the field, because the side they were facing was severely weakened for political reasons and was not likely to be a major threat to the England side.

In the lead up to the matches Kevin became aware of just how good a captain Michael Vaughan was. Being new to the squad, Kevin didn't really know what to expect from him, but soon realised in these difficult times that Vaughan was a man who commanded the respect of the entire dressing room. He wasn't a shouter and certainly wasn't a dictator. Instead, he would ask a player a question so they could think about what he'd suggested and work it out for themselves. Kevin responded well to this approach and knew that this was a man whose leadership and guidance he would come to value and deeply appreciate in the times ahead.

England would be playing four one-dayers in all, the first of which took place in front of a decent-sized crowd in Harare. Things went very smoothly, with politics being kept well away from the cricket. Kevin scored 27 not out as England won by a comfortable five-wicket margin.

Kevin really made his presence felt in the next game, scoring an unbeaten 77 from 76 balls, earning himself the Man of the Match award in the process, and playing a real part in England's 161-run victory. Despite the fairly weak quality of the bowling attack, Kevin was naturally happy that his England career had got off to a solid start. There would be more important, more challenging matches around the corner, but, for now, Kevin had made his presence felt. Failure here could well have seen his England career truncated before it really got going. Kevin didn't play in the third match, and when he returned to the side in the fourth and final match in Bulawayo he experienced his only disappointment of the tour when he was out first ball. Unsurprisingly, England won both matches easily, and Kevin considered it a job well done.

In the days that followed the tour, a number of journalists and pundits began to question whether Kevin was too leg-sided a player to succeed against the world's greatest bowlers. They predicted this could be a real vulnerability, and could leave him susceptible to lbws. Kevin wasn't unduly concerned by this, and remembered that Mark Waugh was very much a leg-sided player and had become one of the world's greatest ever batsmen. Duncan Fletcher seemed happy to let Kevin carry on as he was, and Matt Maynard would definitely have passed comment if he felt Kevin needed to adjust his technique. Matt told Kevin that he'd spoken to Duncan about his progress, and they'd both agreed that he was very much part of the fold for the future.

It was nearly time for Kevin and the other members of the squad who weren't going on to the Test series in South Africa to fly home. Before he did, he had a chat with Duncan, who told him he would try to get him into the squad for the one-dayers that followed the Test series after all. Kevin was elated to hear this from the England coach, and it sent his confidence through the roof. This meant he had established himself in the England one-day squad, and had impressed the people that mattered during the short tour of Zimbabwe. There was another reason to celebrate, because this opportunity would give Kevin the chance to settle a rather important old score. Come January, he would seek to show South Africa what a huge mistake they'd made in letting him go.

5
HOME IS WHERE THE HEART IS

Once he arrived back in England after the tour of Zimbabwe, Kevin was still slightly anxious as to whether he'd actually be going to South Africa. He didn't doubt Duncan's sincerity when he said he'd do his best to get him into the one-day squad, but the decision wasn't entirely his to make. So it came as a huge relief to Kevin when, in early January 2005, he received a call from David Graveney, the Chairman of Selectors, confirming he'd be on the plane to South Africa for the one-dayers.

Kevin knew from the time he'd arrived in England nearly four years earlier that his adopted country was due to tour South Africa soon after he became eligible, and Clive Rice had advised him to use this as motivation, an extra incentive to get into the England squad. Kevin was initially disappointed not to be included for the Test series, but understood the selectors' reasons for leaving him out, considering his inexperience at international level and the problems he'd face from hostile crowds in South Africa.

Once he knew he'd definitely be going, Kevin trained hard at Loughborough to get into the best possible shape for the upcoming matches. It was around this time that the South African captain, Graeme Smith, started making some personal comments in the press about Kevin. They went along the lines of how Kevin had turned his back on his home country and how he would try to ensure that he wouldn't get any runs in the upcoming series. This only made Kevin even more determined to make a big impression in South Africa, but it was also the beginning of one of cricket's most open rifts.

Graeme's comments had taught Kevin a lot about the South African captain's character. The aspiring England squad member didn't mind people making fun remarks in the papers to try and wind up the opposition – he'd seen Australian players do it often enough – but when *they* did it, it was in a humorous way and was often original and witty.

Certainly, Graeme was a great batsman and a world-class cricketer, but inheriting the captaincy at 22, in the wake of the Hansie Cronje scandal, had given him a great deal of power, which Kevin didn't think he was using wisely. The upcoming matches would be the opportunity Kevin needed to put Graeme in his place.

On a more positive note, the lead up to the one-day series gave Kevin the chance to spend some time with Darren Gough. They quickly hit it off and found they had quite a bit in common. Darren was a man with a similar personality to his, and someone he looked up to for his achievements in the game. Knee trouble had put paid to Darren's Test career in 2003, but he was still a force to be reckoned with in one-day cricket and was still very much a part of the England squad in the shorter format of the game.

Darren, who was by now an experienced cricketer, gave Kevin some advice about his international career. He told him to just play his natural game, to just be himself and enjoy the experience, and to do this no matter how fierce the opposition or surroundings may be. Darren was a man who was never afraid to show his emotions, and often looked as though he was enjoying life on the field. This was the advice Kevin needed, and it was exactly what he wanted to hear from a senior team-mate. In a sense, Darren was telling Kevin to carry on doing the same things, and that there were no problems with his attitude or approach.

Kevin travelled to South Africa with the other players who had only been selected for the one-day series. As he arrived in Johannesburg he felt a lot more nervous than usual. He knew from living in the country that he was likely to experience some highly vocal, unforgiving crowds. Given the exceptional circumstances that surrounded him, having turned his back on South Africa four years earlier, he did not really know how bad things would be. This was uncharted territory, and it wasn't as if he could turn to a senior team-mate or member of the coaching staff to ask them what to expect.

They were arriving at a time when the England Test team were completing what proved to be a successful series against South Africa. The Test players were staying at the Sandton Sun Hotel, which was in commuting distance from Centurion where they were playing in the final Test of the series. Kevin checked in along with the rest of the one-day players and was greatly touched by the warm welcome he received from the rest of the squad. This confirmed in his mind that he wasn't a second-class member of the side. He was one of them, and the fact he had only lived in the country for a few years was an irrelevance. This helped him feel a lot more comfortable at the prospect of facing the country that had rejected him.

There were ten days to go until Kevin would be playing in his first match of the tour, so he took the opportunity to have a night out with Darren in Sandton, the upmarket suburb of Johannesburg. It was a great night and a chance to enjoy the social side of cricket. Darren had proved to be good fun after a drink, but, on this occasion, he wasn't exactly a paternal influence on Kevin.

They arrived back at the hotel at around 2am and had both made a lot of noise as they retired to their bedrooms. Kevin was completely unaware that he had done anything wrong. As far as he was concerned, there were still ten days before he'd be needed and having a bit of fun this far away from a game was acceptable. What he hadn't taken on board was that he was sharing a hotel with a group of players who had to be on top form the following morning because they needed to win a Test series.

The next day Kevin and the other players who weren't involved in the Test were training at Centurion Park when

HOME IS WHERE THE HEART IS

Matthew Maynard told him that Duncan Fletcher wasn't happy because some players from the one-day squad had been making a noise in the early hours of the morning. Kevin knew full well he was talking about him and Darren, but chose to lie low for the time being.

Darren told Kevin he was going to own up, but Kevin said they might get away with it if he didn't say anything. Darren, being more experienced, was wise enough to know better and told Duncan, who in turn worked out Kevin had been involved. Duncan took Kevin to one side and asked him what time he'd got in the night before. He told him that he couldn't remember because he'd been drinking, which was the truth.

Kevin was smart enough to realise it was in his interests not to lie to Duncan about what had gone on. Duncan warned Kevin that his behaviour wasn't acceptable and that he'd been brought to South Africa as a reward for his good performances in Zimbabwe. He told him to remember this fact and that he had an obligation not to let people down. It was a slap across the wrist but Kevin quickly realised that it was a good lesson. He had found out that messing with Duncan was not a good idea and now knew what standards of behaviour were expected from him as a member of the England squad.

Both Kevin and Darren apologised to Duncan for their behaviour. Kevin knew there could be no repeat of this incident, and if it happened again he could be considered a disruptive influence amongst the squad, which might jeopardise his England future. However, Kevin remained determined to enjoy himself, but recognised that there was a time and a place. He believed that one of the benefits to being an international cricketer was making so many friends all around the world, and being able to enjoy socialising in different cultures. He understood the importance of such friendships in opening doors for him once his playing career was over. There could be opportunities in coaching, the media and in business as a direct result of the relationships he built up during his playing days, and this was not something to be undervalued.

The night before the first game, all the nerves Kevin had experienced before he landed in Johannesburg came back. He was now just hours away from his confrontation with the South African team, and had no idea what sort of a reaction he'd get from the crowd. For the first time in his life he sought the advice of a sports psychologist, a man called Steve Bull who was employed by the England setup. Steve asked Kevin some simple questions, such as, what did he do in county cricket? What process did he go through when batting? Did he watch the ball at the start of the bowler's run? Kevin told Steve that he never stopped watching the ball until he had either played it or left it. Steve's advice was clear: he had to do exactly the same thing the next day. He had to shut out the crowd, just play his natural game, and not worry about anything.

The match at The Wanderers Stadium was a day-nighter, so Kevin had a bit of time to kill in the morning. He just remembered Steve's words from the night before, but did not underestimate the importance of this day. Unusually for a cricket match, both national anthems were to be played before the game got under way. As Kevin lined up with the rest of the England team his parents watched from the stands, and Jannie admits that during those moments he did wonder whether his son was lining up for the right team. These doubts didn't last long.

Kevin sang 'God Save The Queen' at the top of his voice, word-perfect, and with more enthusiasm than many of his team-mates. This meant a massive amount to him – he now felt like a full Englishman, and believed he had been completely accepted as a member of the team. Jannie observed that the England players actually looked like a team as they stood there, linking arms, whilst the South Africans looked like a group of disjointed individuals. He now knew his son was playing for the right country.

Once the anthems were over, England captain Michael Vaughan called his players into a huddle. He knew full well the significance of this game for Kevin, and wanted to make a few things clear to the side. He told them that if Kevin got any abuse from the South African players they were to stand by him. To abuse one player was to abuse the whole team, and they were to abuse them back. Kevin was greatly touched by Michael's words, and knew he was playing under a truly great captain.

The match started well for Kevin and he eased some of his inner tension by taking an early catch to dismiss Herschelle Gibbs off the bowling of Matthew Hoggard. Not long afterwards Michael sent Kevin to field on the boundary near the most hostile section of the crowd. This really was going to be a test of Kevin's character.

He was quite used to having a bit of banter with the supporters of opposing teams when fielding on the boundary. Normally it's just good fun and helps break up the tension of an important game. But this was very different, and the abusive remarks were not being made in jest. He was being called a Judas and a racist for leaving the country because of the quota system. Michael probably asked Kevin to field there to throw him in at the deep end and get this stuff out of the way. South Africa ended the innings with a disappointing 175 for nine from their 50 overs. Kevin knew this game was very winnable, and it was up to him to make a decent contribution as a batsman to help England reach their target.

The innings didn't start well for England. Kevin watched as, early on, South Africa took the wickets of key England batsmen for only a handful of runs. He realised that the reaction he'd get when the time came for him to come out and bat was unlikely to be pleasant. With the score at 44 for three, his time had come.

He walked out of the Wanderers pavilion to an enormous wall of noise, with thousands of South African fans booing him as he made his way down the steps. The onlookers had never heard anything like it. This was by far the nastiest and most hostile entrance any batsman in world cricket has had to face. It showed no sign of relenting as he entered the field and approached the middle. Jannie felt upset at how his son was being treated. Kevin's mother burst into tears and couldn't understand why anyone would feel so much hatred towards her son. The usually ultra-confident Kevin felt nervous and sweaty as he prepared to face the first ball. It was to come from a man whose face was familiar to him: Andre Nel, one of cricket's most colourful and flamboyant characters.

Andre was a larger-than-life giant of a man, and an extremely good fast bowler, who Kevin knew he had to treat with respect. Andre claims he has an alter ego, called Gunther, who he turns into the moment he gets onto the pitch. Gunther has his own life story. He lives in the mountains in Germany, and when he was a child there was a lack of oxygen going to his brain, so something went wrong in his mind, making him the crazy, over-the-top character we see on the pitch. Turning into Gunther helps give Andre the extra competitive edge he needs to perform at his best, but people who meet him away from the field soon realise he is a gentle giant. He has a reputation as a man who makes time for everyone, and won't turn down a request for an autograph if he can help it. In fact, it's said he once gave one of his team-mates such a big hug in the dressing room that he cracked one of their ribs, but he's not saying who it was.

Kevin was good friends with Andre, and he knew that any abuse that came his way from him was done with a twinkle in his eye. When he turned into Gunther, Andre was too competitive for some people's tastes, and he certainly played up to his reputation during his first delivery to Kevin. Even so, Kevin knew him well enough to be aware that he was a thoroughly decent person off the field and one of life's true gentlemen.

The booing intensified further as Andre began his run up

for that first ball. Although Kevin was his friend, he wanted to make an extra special effort to send him back to the pavilion for a duck. Fortunately for Kevin, the ball swung away from him and went just outside off-stump. He felt a sense of immense relief. His England career could've been over in a flash if he'd been out first ball. The tension was eased by the fact that the man batting at the other end was his captain, who was batting brilliantly so far. After that first ball they had a quick chat, and Michael told Kevin to just watch the ball – it was white and it was heading his way. That's all he had to do.

Kevin played in a surprisingly conservative way during the start of his innings, taking 11 balls before hitting his first runs. However, after he'd settled in he was in his element. He took quite a bit of pleasure from hitting his first boundary off Andre's bowling, when he hit the ball through backward point. He was pleased with the spirit in which the South African players were treating him. Andre was having a bit of harmless fun with him, and there was no business from the rest of the team; they were all just getting on with their jobs, which was to stop Kevin doing his. All of them, that is, apart from one – their captain, Graeme Smith.

Kevin felt hurt and insulted by Graeme's remarks in the build-up to the game and wasn't surprised that he was likely to be one of the men in the South African team who would have a dig at him on the field. Graeme kept asking him how much he'd paid himself for the 'kevinpietersen.com' logo on his bat. Kevin hit back by asking Graeme who he thought he was. One of the greatest rivalries in world cricket had begun.

Here were two men who clearly appeared to be hardly enamoured of each other, but would be seeing plenty of each other in the days, even years, ahead.

Michael and Kevin were starting to turn the match around, and made the scoreline a respectable 103 for three after 25.1 overs, when the heavens opened. The storm that followed was massive, and it soon became clear there was no possibility of a resumption of play. England won via the Duckworth Lewis method, and whilst Kevin was delighted with the result, he did feel a sense of personal disappointment that he was stuck on 22 not out. He would have preferred to finish the match to its full conclusion and maybe make the big score he had been dreaming of for weeks, which had become an even stronger ambition following the hostile reception he got from the crowd. Once the match was over, one of the umpires, Ian Howell, apologised on behalf of South Africa to Kevin for the reception he'd received, describing it as both disgusting and disgraceful. It was a gesture Kevin deeply appreciated.

As Kevin looked back on the day's proceedings he realised this had been one of the most important occasions of his life. He had survived the nastiest reception any batsman in world cricket had ever received, and knew that there were millions more people around South Africa watching on television who would happily have joined in if they'd been in the stadium. Yet he'd got through it, and he realised this had been an enormous character-building experience. Getting through this meant he could survive any mental challenge thrown at him when playing at international level.

Back at the hotel he talked things through with his parents and brother, Bryan. They were all feeling emotional after a tough day and all felt extreme pride in the way Kevin handled himself before, during, and after the game. A reflective Kevin truly understood for the first time the enormity of the decision he had made four years earlier, and how profoundly it had affected the South African public. Kevin woke up the next morning to find his picture plastered all over the South African newspapers. His contribution to the match in playing terms had been relatively minor, so the only reason for such full coverage of his performance could be the furore that surrounded him representing England.

Although he had done all he could in the game, and hadn't made any major mistakes, he still didn't feel he had done enough to make his presence felt in the England team. For this reason, the next game couldn't come quickly enough. He travelled to Bloemfontein with the rest of the squad and slept through most of the journey. He'd had a decent night's sleep before setting off, but the emotional pressure he'd been under had left him feeling drained.

Once he'd checked in to the hotel, Kevin received a welcome surprise which gave his morale a major boost. His brother Gregg and his wife Nicky had paid him a visit on their way from Cape Town to Johannesburg. Kevin hadn't seen as much of some of his brothers as he would've liked in recent months, so this unexpected opportunity to spend an hour with Gregg was much appreciated. Later that day Kevin began to wonder what sort of a reception he'd receive when he took to the field in Bloemfontein. This was in the heart of Afrikaner country, and the thought of receiving an even worse welcome than in Johannesburg began to play on his mind.

The pressure was showing as he took part in an absolutely dreadful net session the day before the game. He wasn't moving his feet properly and one net bowler got the better of him three or four times. Kevin didn't know what was happening to him, considering he'd been batting so well both before and during the first game. All of a sudden, his confidence was gone and his head was in a mess.

On the day of the match Kevin went to the ground early so he could have an extra net session with Matt Maynard, which went much better. Kevin hoped the problems he'd experienced the day before were just a blip caused by the emotional strain taking its toll. Now he felt in control of his mind again, and remembered some advice his old mentor Clive Rice had given him when he first arrived in South Africa – to use any stick he received to his advantage.

Kevin came out to bat with the team once again after the loss of three early wickets. There was the predictable booing from the crowd, but this time it didn't feel as intense as it had in Johannesburg. He noticed the message on the large electronic scoreboard which read, 'Welcome home, Kevin Pietersen'. Was it meant as a friendly gesture or was it drenched in sarcasm? Kevin had no way of knowing for sure, but it was more likely to be the latter.

Once again, Kevin's partner at the start of his innings was Michael Vaughan. He had built up a huge respect for his captain over the relatively short period they'd been working together, and found him to be a calming influence, which was exactly what he needed at this particular moment. Early on in his innings, Kevin hit Shaun Pollock for six, smashing the ball over square leg. This was a huge moment for him, as Shaun had been one of his boyhood heroes. It meant as much to Kevin as when he had first played for England, and saw his mental confidence go through the proverbial roof. He now felt that he could do anything on this day, and all the doubts and nerves that he'd experienced in the lead up to the match had suddenly disappeared.

Perhaps he got a little too carried away, and began to show signs of overconfidence, which became a trademark of his game that was to resurface from time to time, and was not one of his better qualities. He was trying to hit Jacques Kallis and Andrew Hall over mid-off, but the ball kept on landing near third man. This was dangerous, and bowlers of their calibre deserved to be treated with more respect. Many people felt he was fortunate to get away with playing some of those shots, which were considered by some to be irresponsible.

The fact he kept on getting away with it saw Kevin's confidence surge further – everything seemed to be going right for him now. Once he'd reached 60 he knew that this would be a great opportunity to make a century. He felt invincible. Everything was going right.

Kevin wanted to spend as little time as possible in the 'nervous nineties', even if that meant continuing to take risks which could be considered reckless. Makhaya Ntini bowled Kevin a yorker which he hit to deep square leg, giving him his first senior international century. Kevin had landed on the international stage and he celebrated in style, waving his bat exuberantly to the England dressing room and to his parents in the stand. This was another massive moment for him, and he felt a huge weight of expectation lifted from his shoulders. Kevin was now a man who had proved to the world he could make it on the international stage, and had done so in circumstances very few cricketers had ever experienced.

Some observers felt Kevin went too far with his wild release of emotions following his century, especially when he kissed the three lions badge on his shirt. It was felt in certain quarters that this was intended as a direct insult to the big shots in South African cricket, but Kevin was determined to make the very most of this special moment. He was celebrating not only for himself but for his family, his friends, the entire England playing and coaching team who had made him feel so welcome, and for the mentors who had advised and encouraged him in his career to date. Certain people had received criticism for sticking by him and encouraging him to quit South Africa, and Kevin thought of all these people as he let himself go.

What Kevin didn't realise at the time was that the whole South African crowd had turned their backs on him. There wasn't very much applause either, but Kevin was so carried away in celebration that he didn't notice until he saw the television highlights later that day – not that it would have bothered him in the slightest.

England went on to reach a respectable 270 for five from

their 50 overs, with Kevin scoring an unbeaten 108 from 96 balls. The innings also included a partnership of 92 from 79 balls between Kevin and Paul Collingwood. Kevin knew that if England won the match from here, he wasn't a bit-player as he had been in Johannesburg. This time, his contribution had been vital, and people would be talking about him, not because of where he was born or the country he now represented but for his outstanding contribution with the bat, which was exactly what he wanted.

England had achieved a decent score with 270, but the South African batting line-up was strong, and if they were on form it was a very reachable target for them. The England bowlers had to be on top form and it looked likely to be a close run-chase. Jacques Kallis and Herschelle Gibbs were at their best, scoring 63 and 78 respectively, and the match went down to the final over. South Africa needed just seven runs from six balls. Few people thought England stood a chance.

Michael Vaughan had gone off the field suffering from an upset stomach, so it was left to Marcus Trescothick to show leadership on the field. He charged the inexperienced Kabir Ali with bowling the all-important final over. Bob Willis, who was commentating for Sky Sports, was less than impressed with the acting captain's choice of bowler, remarking, 'He's bowled like a camel and fielded like a drain.' Kabir's most recent over had been carted for 13, including a vast straight six from Justin Kemp.

Kabir's first delivery was a waist-high no-ball that Mark Boucher swatted for four through square leg, and the game seemed to be well and truly in the bag. Kabir's first ball had been characteristic of his bowling in the match to date. His confidence was clearly in tatters, and his body language didn't suggest things were going to get any better for him. Three runs needed from six. Surely there was no stopping South Africa now.

His next delivery was another full toss, but this time Boucher hit it straight in the air before Ashley Giles caught him at deep midwicket. The game was back in the balance, and Kabir's confidence rose. He now walked with his head held high, and clearly believed he could salvage something from the game. He conceded just a single from his next two balls. He then delivered a perfect length to the new batsman, Ashwell Prince, that he could only squeeze between midwicket. There was confusion and hesitation between the two batsmen, giving enough time for the ball to reach Kabir, who took the bails off to run out Prince.

South Africa needed two from two. This was now edge-of-your seat cricket. Shaun Pollock grabbed a single from the next ball to level the scores. The home team needed to snatch a single from the final ball. If not, the match would be a tie, only the twentieth time that had happened in 2,219 one-day internationals. Kabir delivered a full-length to Andrew Hall, but the batsman lost sight of it and chopped it down late. Wicketkeeper Geraint Jones got hold of the ball and quickly stumped Hall to tie the match.

Kevin couldn't believe what he had just witnessed, and he immediately ran up to Geraint and lifted him up off the floor, hurting his own back in the process. The rest of the team surrounded Kabir – he had become a hero in that last over after bowling dreadfully for most of the match. The whole England team were loud and jubilant, and celebrated as though they'd actually won. This was a victory in all but name, and an important one at that.

In contrast, the South African crowd sat in a stunned silence. They had assumed that victory was theirs, but the team had blown it at the crucial moment. To make matters worse, it was the player they so passionately hated who had cost them the game. They had booed Kevin as he entered the field to bat, and had done everything they could to make him feel like an unwelcome traitor throughout his two matches to date. But it was Kevin who was having the last laugh. Their abuse had made him even more determined to play to the best of his ability. He recalled Clive Rice's advice to use any stick he received to his advantage, and he had done exactly that. It was a bit like when batsmen made 'sledging' comments at Shane Warne before he bowled to them. All it did was make him even more focused and determined to get them out.

The result was even more special for Kevin when he was made Man of the Match. Without his contribution with the bat, England wouldn't even have been in contention, let alone been in a position to take the match into a tense final over. Even so, Kevin was quick to heap praise on Kabir for his incredible bowling in that final over – this was his day too. Spirits in the camp were high after that result, and the squad travelled on to Port Elizabeth for the next match believing that they could win the series. The only worry was their captain, whose upset stomach looked like staying with him for a good few days.

HOME IS WHERE THE HEART IS

Clive Rice had witnessed Kevin's performance in the last match, and while he was naturally delighted that his protégé had made such a massive contribution with the bat, he was concerned by his reckless streak and felt it could cost him dear if it wasn't stamped out. He contacted Kevin in Port Elizabeth and came to see him for a chat on the morning of the game. He started with a positive, telling Kevin to keep going out to show people how good he was. He knew himself how good Kevin was, and wanted everyone to see it, particularly those who were making his life difficult during the tour. Then Clive repeated his motto that Kevin had heard so many times before: don't get out, stay unbeaten.

Clive firmly believed that a batsman should never give his wicket away because it helps his average or stats. His philosophy was that if the opposition can't get you out you will retain your superiority over them. Clive left Kevin by repeating those words, 'Don't ever throw it away.'

Kevin obviously had a huge respect for Clive and would always make time for his opinions and advice, but at the present moment he felt invincible and thought he could take on the world. He hadn't taken time to contemplate how dangerous some of his shot selections had been during his century in the previous match, and how lucky he'd been to survive them. If he carried on playing like this, his luck was likely to run out, probably sooner rather than later. Clive had done his bit to encourage Kevin to exercise a little more caution, but once he was at the crease he was on his own, and it was up to him to take it on board.

In the match at Port Elizabeth, England batted first but,

crucially, they would have to play without Michael Vaughan because his upset stomach had not improved. This was a considerable blow to the side, which would have to do without his hugely respected leadership as well as his contribution with the bat. Kevin made a good start, making 33 from 36 balls. His confidence remained high, and everything was going to plan.

Then, without warning, his luck ran out. His friend Andre Nel was bowling, and Kevin played a silly and unnecessarily adventurous shot that handed Gibbs an easy catch. Kevin was angry with himself because he knew that he should really have made a bigger score after such a confident start. In truth, Clive's advice before the match had been spot-on and it was only a matter of time before Kevin's overconfidence got the better of him. Without his captain batting out there with him to remind him of the importance of staying in, Kevin had handed his opponents his wicket on a plate. This was his first serious error in international cricket.

The captain's absence had left as big a void in the team as some commentators had feared, and left many of England's batsmen disappointed on the day, with only Vikram Solanki putting in a decent score. England's strong batting line-up should have made far more than 267 for eight in their 50 overs on a pitch that favoured the batsmen.

Kevin had the chance to make amends in the field, but this wasn't to be his day. Early on, he messed up a chance to run out his bitter rival Graeme Smith, only for the South African captain to go on and play a match-winning innings of 105, the first century by a South African captain in a one-day international.

HOME IS WHERE THE HEART IS

Kevin was feeling angry and frustrated with himself and with the way the match was heading. Without guidance from their captain, the England team, which had previously seemed like such a solid unit, was now disjointed and erratic. A rare positive moment came when Kevin caught Jacques Kallis, but the manner of his celebration left a lot to be desired. On catching the ball, he turned to the crowd and waved a defiant fist in the air. This was the first time Kevin had let the inevitable crowd abuse get the better of him. He seemed able to cope with it when he was playing well, but as soon as his form experienced a dip, he let down his guard in the spur of the moment, although he never intended it to be as malicious as it may have looked at the time.

Umpire Steve Bucknor came up to Kevin and gave him a friendly warning after seeing what he'd just done. He told Kevin that it was hard enough for him over here, and not to make it any harder for himself. Kevin told Steve that he was just having a bit of fun, and they both agreed to laugh it off. Inevitably, the match was lost. Poor batting combined with some sloppy fielding had cost England and the disjointed side crumbled. The sooner Michael Vaughan was back where he belonged, the better. Any team can have one bad match, but playing like this was not a habit England could afford to get into.

The squad flew on to Cape Town for the next match of the series. During the flight, Kevin mentioned to Darren Gough that his hair was getting a bit long and he felt like doing something different with it. Darren couldn't resist the opportunity to lead Kevin astray once again, and suggested he do something stupid with it. Kevin's haircuts had always been fairly conservative until now, but Darren had planted a seed in his mind. They checked in to the Cullinan Hotel, and Kevin was adamant that he was going to go through with it. There was a hairdressers within the hotel complex, and Darren insisted on going with Kevin to make sure he was true to his word.

They pondered what exactly they should do to make Kevin stand out. Darren eventually told Kevin he should put a line through his hair. Kevin liked the sound of that, but the lady working there had never done anything like it before. This was going to be a nerve-racking experience for her. It didn't help when Kevin reminded her that he was going to be on TV the next day and needed to look good. The poor lady was in uncharted territory, but fortunately for her there was no mirror there, so Kevin wouldn't really know what she'd done until he got back to his room.

Kevin went through with it, and noticed people giving him funny looks on the way back to his room. When he arrived there he headed straight for the bathroom mirror. It was certainly different, but he wasn't exactly elated with what he saw. The line was a shade of dark orange, and nothing like the blonde and blue colours cricket fans would become used to seeing within the next year. The reaction he got from the England setup, though, was good. Some liked it, others found it funny, but nobody said anything seriously negative as though it would somehow damage his ability or reputation as a player.

Even Duncan Fletcher saw the funny side. He started

calling Kevin names like 'skunk' and 'raccoon', and generally made a running joke of it, which proved good for team spirit and brought a smile to many faces. Kevin had drawn attention to himself in a fun, but not entirely original way. Jimmy Anderson had beaten him to it with a red streak through his hair several years earlier. Despite being a Lancastrian, Jimmy was an Arsenal supporter and had probably taken inspiration from Freddie Ljungberg, who had done something very similar.

The Cape Town match took place at Newlands, with breathtaking scenery as a backdrop. The South African team had something of a new look for this match. Herschelle Gibbs was moved down to number four in the batting order to make way for AB de Villiers at the top. Gibbs was relieved of the pressure opening the batting brings, and found it easier to play his natural game at number four. It turned out to be a masterstroke by the South Africans and Gibbs made a century to help his side to 291 for five from their 50 overs. This was a solid total, but one that could be reached if the England batsmen performed to their best.

The batting that followed from the England team was, to put it mildly, diabolical, with Kevin being the only saving grace, scoring 75. England completely fell apart and were all out for 183. This was certainly very embarrassing, but the England total would've been utterly shameful if it hadn't been for Kevin's contribution.

Kevin sensed that many of the players, especially those who had played in the Test series, were suffering from fatigue. Winning the series had been the main objective of the tour, and in that sense it had been very successful, but it was becoming clear that a gruelling series of seven one-day matches over a relatively short space of time was taking its toll on quite a few of the players. Kevin still felt relatively fresh, as he was one of a handful of cricketers who hadn't been part of the Test squad and had coped reasonably well with the mental pressure he faced. He had a lot on his mind, and generally only managed around five hours sleep per night, but still felt he would click into gear when the matches arrived. None of the players wanted to end the tour on a flat note, so it was important to keep morale high for the remaining matches.

With England 2-1 down in the series, the boys made their way to East London in the Eastern Cape Province for the next match. The backdrop there was nothing like as spectacular as the one in Cape Town, but it certainly provided the setting for an enthralling game of cricket.

The night before the match it had rained heavily, leaving the pitch saturated. This was going to provide an unusual challenge that few of the players had experienced before. Large patches of sand were placed around the outfield to make fielding safer, but this wasn't likely to be a conventional game of cricket.

The England bowlers struggled to get anything out of a difficult pitch, and Justin Kemp took maximum advantage of the favourable conditions, making 80 runs from just 50 balls. He wasn't hanging about, and neither was Graeme Smith, who scored a century to help South Africa to 311 for seven. Kevin knew Graeme was a superb cricketer despite having mixed feelings about him as a person, and as he watched the South African batsmen make such high scores, he knew the pitch favoured aggressive batting. He realised he would have a golden opportunity to make a big score of his own later on.

This was a huge target for England, and Michael Vaughan led by example with the bat, but by the time Kevin joined him at the crease it looked like being an enormous task to salvage the game. For once, Kevin had an excuse to bat aggressively and take risks. It was do-or-die, this wasn't the time to protect your wicket or minimise the chance of getting out. It was a high-risk strategy but there was a big part of Kevin that relished the opportunity to play, what was to him, his natural game. Clive Rice, and many others, had tried very hard to discourage Kevin from playing this way, but on this occasion there was no other option.

He was very nearly stumped on 16, but the fact South Africa messed up this opportunity seemed to send Kevin's confidence through the roof. Once again he felt invincible and thought he could get away with anything. They say confidence breeds confidence, and for Kevin, everything seemed to be coming off the middle of the bat. He tried whacking the ball as hard as he possibly could, and no-one tried to stop him or told him to ease off a bit. Batting out there was fun and he had a plan for every bowler. He knew that in one-day cricket the ball generally stopped swinging around after about the 12th over, and batting down the order played into his favour, especially on a pitch like this. There was no point in trying to stop him, this was England's only hope of winning the game, even though winning was still a very long shot.

During this slot, one of Kevin's most famous traits – the whip shot to leg – made its debut. For him, this meant that every ball on or outside off-stump could be hit through mid-wicket by playing this shot, and there would normally be at least two runs in it. It would be an absurd risk in most situations in test cricket, but soon became an important part of his one-day armoury.

It eventually became clear during the final over that despite Kevin's ambitious and aggressive batting, victory was beyond England. He found himself on 94 with just one ball left. The game was gone, but a century would be possible with a six from the last ball. By now he was batting with Darren, who told him he might as well go for it. Andre Nel bowled Kevin a full toss which he smashed high into the stand for his fourth six of the innings.

Kevin had made his century from just 69 balls, the fastest ever by an Englishman in a one-day international and the tenth fastest of all time. Despite this remarkable personal achievement, Kevin wasn't in the mood for celebrating. He immediately came back down to earth with the realisation that England could not now win the series. He would rather have scored just one run and contributed to an England victory than scored a century but end up on the losing side. The century he scored might not have done his average or career stats any harm, but he certainly didn't feel like celebrating that night.

The next match of the series was going to be an

emotionally charged occasion for Kevin. It was to be played in Durban, and would see him return to his old home ground of Kingsmead for the first time. Pietermaritzburg, the town where he grew up, wasn't too far away. He had no idea what sort of a welcome he'd get, because this time he wasn't only faced with the prospect of a hostile South African crowd, but also with the reality that he'd be coming face-to-face with some people he'd known since childhood, and had no idea how they'd react to him and the decision he'd made to change national allegiances.

Soon after they arrived in Durban, Darren decided to try and lighten Kevin's mood by tying some 'welcome home!' balloons around his wrist. As they arrived at the hotel, they were greeted by genuine warmth from the staff, who played music and even sang to them as they checked in.

Kevin began to feel a lot more at ease after such a kind welcome from the staff. However, this no longer felt like home. Yes, he knew exactly where he was and knew his way around the area like the back of his hand. But despite the familiarity of it all he now felt like an outsider looking in. Even though he knew everything so well, he felt like a visitor. It gave him an entirely new perspective on being in the town.

The feelings he experienced in those hours after checking into the hotel made Kevin feel even more English than he had done to date. Yes, there were plenty of friends and family still based in the area, but this really wasn't home any more. He now felt a more integrated member of the team than ever – there was to be no sense of split loyalty during his short stay in the area.

Kevin knew that he was unlikely to be given a warm welcome by the Kingsmead crowd when he came out to bat. After all, this was the ground where he'd played for Natal, and had been the place where his chances of getting on in South African cricket were ended when he was dropped and replaced by an inferior player, simply because of the colour of his skin.

England were fielding first, but the start was delayed by rain. When play was possible, it was the bald, towering figure of Alex Wharf, playing in his first match of the series, who made an immediate impact with the ball for England. Much to Kevin's delight Alex bowled Graeme Smith for just one run, and then surprised Kallis with a bouncer to leave South Africa with an embarrassing one for two. Gibbs went on to hit his second century of the series to give some respectability to the South African score, but England maintained their advantage and would be chasing an adjusted target of 213 from 48 overs.

For most of the South African innings Kevin was fielding at cover point or on the boundary and was pleasantly surprised by the reception he received from the local crowd. He recognised some of the faces sitting directly behind him from his college days and enjoyed some good and entirely friendly banter with them. For once, fielding on the boundary in South Africa was a happy experience.

More bad weather followed, which meant that Kevin never did find out what sort of reception he'd get from the Kingsmead crowd as he came out to bat. Even more disappointing was the fact that the no-result meant South

HOME IS WHERE THE HEART IS

Africa had won the series, having a 3-1 lead with just one match to play.

However welcoming people had seemed inside the ground, Kevin soon got a reminder that there were probably plenty of people in Durban who weren't best pleased to see him. Normally, after each game Kevin would go for a few beers with some of the guys (especially Darren). This would typically start in a local bar before moving on to a club. The social side of cricket meant a lot to Kevin, as this is where he'd make lifelong friends, and it gave him the chance to unwind and let go of the tension that big games inevitably bring. But on this occasion going out wasn't such a good idea.

Faisal, a senior security guard, insisted Kevin didn't go out that night, believing there was a heightened risk of somebody wanting to start a fight with him in his home town. Kevin was adamant that he be allowed to at least have a few drinks and let his hair down. Eventually, a compromise was reached and they agreed to go to a quieter bar rather than a club. Even then, Faisal arranged for six security guards to go with them.

The final match of the series was played at Centurion in Johannesburg. For the players this meant a return to the Sandron Sun Hotel where the one-day tour had begun. Kevin checked in feeling reasonably happy with his lot. The tour had been a successful one for him as a cricketer, even though it had obviously been a disappointing series for the England team. After the largely positive reception he'd experienced at Kingsmead, he began to think that maybe he was starting to win round the South African crowd, and they were beginning to respect him for his cricketing ability, if nothing else. A reality check was around the corner.

While he was warming up, Kevin received some of the worst abuse he'd experienced throughout the tour. He suspected the culprits were locals who had come to the Sunday morning start direct from their Saturday night out, and were still heavily intoxicated with alcohol. They were relatively few in number but made up for it with the vile abuse they threw in Kevin's direction. The series was lost, and this match was about giving some respectability to the scoreline, as well as sending the supporters home with a smile on their faces. South Africa batted first and reached 241 for seven, with Ashwell Prince making his maiden half century, finishing on 67 not out, and Graeme Smith scoring 47.

Kevin was becoming used to going out to bat with England in trouble, but he had never known it as bad as this. England looked dead and buried on 68 for six as Kevin made his entrance. It was now up to him and Ashley Giles to salvage something from this game. Kevin knew that smacking the ball around wasn't an option on this pitch. It was a time for remembering every word of Clive Rice's advice and protecting his wicket at all costs. There were no more reliable batsmen to follow once he was out.

He started cautiously, reaching 50 off 80 balls, but then felt able to step up the pace and added another 50 in just 24 balls. Kevin had scored his third century in five innings, and the mature way in which he'd reached it showed he had a good cricketing brain and knew how to adapt his game to the circumstances. As he reached his century his dignity took something of a dent when he gave the crowd an unintentional moon after accidentally colliding with Ntini.

This time there was no booing from the crowd, no back turning, and no bad language. After everything he'd been through, Kevin received a standing ovation. Finally, the South African people had accepted him for who he was – a brilliant cricketer who had shown character and come through everything they'd thrown at him on previous occasions. Kevin took off his helmet and acknowledged all corners of the crowd with his bat.

During those moments an array of emotions went through his mind. He thought back to his original decision to turn his back on South African cricket with a heavy heart, and all the negative press coverage he'd received in his home country when he returned as an England player. Now, at last, he had conquered what seemed like the biggest mountain of all – to get the South African public to accept him. Kevin was ultimately bowled by Andrew Hall for 116 and England fell just two runs short of winning the match when they ran out of wickets in the penultimate over. Once again Kevin had given the England batting total respectability, but for him this was a case of three centuries in five innings, and not a victory to show for them.

His role in saving England's face was rewarded when he was awarded both Man of the Match and Man of the Series. Kevin had begun the series as an unknown quantity. Nobody knew for certain if he had what it took to make it at international level. Just seven one-day internationals later the whole cricketing world knew exactly who he was. He was without doubt the most exciting batsman in the world, who could have cricketing fans sitting on the edge of their seats like no other player. He was a unique character, a maverick with a tough personality able to cope with all kinds of adversity. All this without having even made his Test debut.

Kevin felt like celebrating that night, and there was good reason for the rest of the squad to join him. It felt like a long time ago now, but the Test series had been a massive success, and there were a number of positives within the team that could be built upon to make the one-day side a success in the months ahead. It was the eve of Valentine's Day, and Kevin somehow ended up with a bunch of roses which he handed out to the ladies in Sandton that night. This was a night for celebrating, and most of the boys let themselves go by drinking copious amounts of local champagne.

As the evening went on, Kevin got talking to Darren, and the subject of tattoos came up. At the start of the tour Darren had the three lions tattooed on his arm, and Kevin had told him at the time that he was thinking of having it done himself. The press had somehow found out about this and from time to time during the tour various journalists would ask Kevin if he was still planning to have it done. It became something of a running joke, but very few people seriously believed he'd go through with it. His parents found out about the plan and were not at all happy with the idea of their son having a large tattoo on his arm. Jannie even told Kevin that Darren had better sort his knee out and get some sprinting practice, because he'd be after him for putting the notion into his son's head.

Once again it was Darren who led Kevin astray that night. He brought the subject up, and kept saying to Kevin, 'Bet you don't do it.' After a few drinks, Kevin insisted he'd go through with it. He was being serious, but Darren just thought it was the drink talking. The following morning Kevin got up at 9am after just two hours' sleep, and went down to the tattoo shop in the Sandton mall. Although he'd had a few drinks the night before he knew exactly what he was doing and had no doubts about going through with it.

While the tattoo was being done, Kevin rang Darren on his mobile and told him to listen to this, before placing his phone next to the needle so he could hear it. Darren couldn't believe Kevin had gone through with it. His initial reaction was to say, 'Are you in some bird's room?' When Kevin assured him this was for real, he came down and joined him. Darren hadn't been feeling too well and had missed the last match with a stomach bug, but he had to witness Kevin having the tattoo and rushed down to see for himself the three lions being drawn.

Having the tattoo was Kevin's way of confirming, beyond any doubt whatsoever, that he was now an England man. Throughout the tour he'd felt like a full member of the squad, and considered himself to be 100 per cent English. There were no split allegiances, and no real soft spot for his home country. England was the nation that had taken him in, welcomed him and helped him to develop his game. Returning to the area where he grew up had been a largely pleasant experience, but he now felt like an outsider there, and this didn't feel like home at all any more. The one-day tour had been largely successful for him, if not for the team as a whole. He had scored 454 runs from 430 balls in six innings, with an average of 151.33. He had made the world sit up and take notice of him and had left much of the South African cricketing fraternity kicking themselves for letting him leave and making him feel worthless a few years previously.

Having the tattoo was painful enough, but the really hard part would be plucking up the courage to tell his parents what he'd done. Someone had leaked to the press that he'd gone through with it, but for now Kevin denied it, and made every effort to cover it up when he was out in public. His secret was safe – for now.

6
IN AT THE DEEP END

ollowing the South Africa tour Kevin took a well-earned
week's holiday in Australia. Unfortunately, he hurt his
foot running on the beach, which set back his preparations
for the new season. Even so he was feeling very good about
the way his cricket was developing, though he was aware of
the danger of getting carried away. There was still a long
way to go if he was to become the best cricketer he could be,
and there was an important season ahead.

Kevin was really looking forward to making a fresh start
at Hampshire after the misery he had experienced in his final
years at Notts. Soon after he returned to England he moved
to Southampton and was joined by his brother Bryan, whose
arrival was an enormous comfort to him. Bryan had moved
to Nottingham at roughly the same time as Kevin, and the
two brothers had always been there for each other when
the going got tough. Bryan shared his brother's love of

cricket and had played for Nottinghamshire and Worcestershire Second XI sides. Finding a club side in the Hampshire area would be a priority for him when he joined his brother in Southampton.

More good news was to follow when Richard Logan and Stuart MacGill both signed on the dotted line for Hampshire. This was an enormous source of comfort for Kevin. It was like he'd taken the best bits of being a Notts player down south with him. These had been his two key allies in the dressing room during those dark days at Notts, and they had become very firm friends. Now they'd continue to play together at their new club. From the very start, Kevin found Hampshire to be every bit as impressive as he was led to believe when he agreed to join the club the previous autumn. In Chairman Rod Bransgrove, he found a man who had business connections throughout the world, and ran the club in a modern, forward-thinking fashion.

Joining Hampshire felt like a breath of fresh air after all that had gone on at Notts. This was a club where every aspect of a player's welfare was looked after. Time was taken to discuss with players whether everything was okay in their personal lives, and if they were settled and happy in the area. There was a support system in place for when the players were away, and Kevin found it easy to build up a rapport with everyone at the club, including the people who served the food and worked behind the bar.

They were also big on doing small things that mean so much to the players, such as sending congratulatory texts from the chairman, coach and captain when a player did well for England. In Hampshire, Kevin found a club that was forward-looking, as well as having a family atmosphere where everybody from the chairman to the man who swept the stand all played their part in making the county a success.

Kevin quickly learned that Shane Warne was every bit as great a captain as he had been led to believe. Shane was a legend of the game in his own right, but Kevin soon discovered that he also had excellent people skills, and knew how to deal with members of the team to get the best out of them. Shane's deputy was Shaun Udal, a veteran off-spinner who was already in his mid-thirties. Shaun had clearly learned a lot from playing under Shane and it gave his game a new lease of life at an age when most cricketers are in the autumn of their careers. In Shaun, Kevin found a man who shared the captain's positive attitude, and knew the captaincy was in safe hands when Shane was going to be needed by his country later in the summer.

One of the reasons signing for Hampshire appealed to Kevin was because playing at the Rose Bowl would force him to become a better batsman. The Trent Bridge wicket at Notts was sympathetic to batsmen like him, whereas the Rose Bowl would present him with new challenges and force him to work harder for his runs, which in turn would do his game no harm at all when he was playing international cricket.

The foot injury Kevin sustained in Australia forced him to miss the start of the season and when he did eventually make his debut he found it difficult to regain his previous form, and gave his wicket away cheaply during his first few games. Despite this, he found that his team-mates and the coaching staff weren't treating him any differently. The whole ethos of the club was to have a positive attitude, and nobody put any undue pressure on him to perform, knowing that it would take time for him to fully recover from his injury and adapt to his new surroundings.

Nobody wanted Kevin to make a good impression at Hampshire more than Kevin himself. After everything the club had done to make him feel so welcome, he thought that the least he could do was pay them back by making some big scores of his own. Inevitably, it wasn't long into the season before people at the club started wondering just how much of Kevin they'd be seeing during the summer, due to possible England commitments. There was no doubt at all that he'd be called up for the one-day internationals, but there was a question mark over whether he'd feature in the Test team for the upcoming Ashes series.

Kevin wasn't convinced he'd get a call-up. Every one of the Test batsmen had played their part in winning the series in South Africa the previous winter. For Kevin to be given a place in the team, somebody else would have to be dropped, and there was currently nobody in the England batting line-up who didn't fully deserve to be there.

The international summer started with a two-Test series against Bangladesh. With all due respect, it was always likely to be a rather one-sided affair, with all of the leading England batsmen putting in big scores. The debate taking place in the media was about whether it was time to drop

Graham Thorpe in favour of Kevin. There were those who felt Graham still had a great deal to offer the England side, and he was a safe pair of hands, having been a fixture in the England side for well over a decade.

There were those who felt that Kevin's attacking style of batting wouldn't fare well in Test cricket, and it was better to use him primarily as a one-day batsman. However, this logic didn't stand up to scrutiny. His record in four-day cricket was better than his record in the one-day game at this stage, and some people automatically assumed he played both versions in the same way. Kevin actually felt that his style favoured the longer version of the game. There were more gaps in the field, which allowed him to play more attacking, natural shots, even if his technique didn't look particularly orthodox.

Kevin's confidence returned with a century at Canterbury, followed by another at the Rose Bowl. This was an important psychological milestone for him as he had proven to himself and to the team that he could play on this much tougher wicket. Soon after that match came a phone call from David Graveney to tell him that he had just missed out on selection for the series against Bangladesh. It wasn't a huge surprise. He simply hadn't put enough runs on the board in the early part of the domestic season, and there was no reason for the selectors to take any unnecessary risks with the batting line-up, when every single one of them had performed well in South Africa. In the event, the Test series against Bangladesh was every bit as one-sided as the pundits expected. England eased to victory in the first Test by an innings and 261 runs. The second Test was Graham Thorpe's 100th, and he scored an unbeaten 66, which, combined with a century from Ian Bell, helped England to another monumental victory.

An ageing Graham Thorpe was always the most likely candidate to drop out of the Test team in favour of Kevin. Normally batting at number four, he was barely needed in the series against Bangladesh, but when he was eventually called upon, he showed he was still able to put in a big score. In 2002 Graham had taken a break from the international game due to some well-publicised personal problems. From the time he returned in 2003 until the end of the series against Bangladesh he had scored 1,635 Test runs at an average of 56.37.

Kevin fully understood that with Graham putting in such impressive figures, there was every reason to suspect that the door to the Test team would be closed for the time being. Graham was a vastly experienced cricketer who had seen it and done it all before. He knew how to play Glenn McGrath and Shane Warne, and how to deal with the tough mental challenges that come with every gruelling Ashes series. It's true that Graham didn't play as aggressively or score his runs as quickly as Kevin, but he also very rarely gave away his wicket cheaply or took unnecessary risks. For the time being, Kevin would have to concentrate on making runs for Hampshire, and getting himself ready for the upcoming triangular one-day series against Bangladesh and Australia, which would see him making his home debut for England.

The Twenty20 format of the game was starting to take the

cricketing world by storm. It was originally conceived as a replacement for the Benson & Hedges Cup, and the England and Wales Cricket Board (ECB) wanted to try something experimental. It had its critics – there were those who considered it to be barely a form of cricket at all. To some purists its target audience was people who didn't really understand cricket. Nevertheless, its early years as a county-based competition had been an enormous success, with huge crowds and plenty of positive, attacking cricket. The whole world was beginning to sit up and take notice, with similar competitions being organised in other countries. As an international form of the game, it was still in its infancy, but there was to be one Twenty20 game played at the start of Australia's tour in the summer of 2005. The venue was the Rose Bowl, and Kevin knew that this would be a chance to make a major impression on his home ground.

This was a massive day for Hampshire, too, as it was their opportunity to impress the ECB in their bid to host a Test match at the Rose Bowl in the summer of 2009, the next time Australia were due to tour England. The setting was perfect – this was a modern, state-of-the-art arena suitable for international cricket at the highest level. The Hampshire public came out in huge numbers for the game. There were plenty of people in fancy dress, lots of families and activities to keep the children occupied. This was a cricketing arena fit for the 21st century.

Kevin warmed up and could see the likes of Ricky Ponting, Brett Lee and Glenn McGrath getting ready for action. He wasn't frightened of them, but kept asking himself what on earth could they do to beat them? This was a team full of legends of the game. Some of them were getting on a bit, but they were all established, brilliant cricketers in their own right. This was going to be a long, hard summer.

Playing positively is not an optional extra in Twenty20 cricket. It simply doesn't suit the more defensive batsmen, no matter how good they are. Somebody like David Gower, a superb Test batsman in his own right, would need to make enormous adjustments to his game if he was to be successful in this format. As an attacking batsman, this was an opportunity Kevin relished, even more so considering it was being played on his new home ground.

He batted pretty well, making a contribution of 36 as England went on to make a total of 179. Yet it was the England bowlers who were the heroes on the day. Darren Gough and Jonathan Lewis just charged through the Australian batsmen. They seemed to understand that they would only be bowling for short periods, so they might as well throw themselves fully into it, with there being no need to conserve energy for later on. They were far too good for Australia. Darren was on a hat-trick at one stage but chose to bowl an aggressive bouncer with the vital ball. Later, Australia were on 31 for seven and were eventually all out for 79. Kevin had taken three decent catches and was voted Man of the Match by Sky Sports viewers.

It was a wonderful night for Kevin, for Hampshire cricket, and for England. They had started the summer as they meant to go on, proving to Australia that they were no respecters of reputation and would give as good as it got in the contests ahead. Michael Vaughan was quick to play down the significance of the win, saying it was only a Twenty20 game, and he was right in that there were more important contests ahead. This was a one-off game and this format was not yet truly established at international level in the way it would be in years to come. Even so, England had laid down a marker for the summer.

The one-day series soon followed, and after such an impressive winter series in South Africa, Kevin's place in the side was secure. The first match saw Bangladesh take on Australia in Cardiff, while the England players got some practice in for their match against the Aussies in nearby Bristol the following day.

News came through to the England players in Bristol that, half an hour's drive down the M4, one of the biggest shocks in cricketing history had just taken place. Incredibly, Bangladesh had beaten Australia in their match in Cardiff. This was the same Bangladesh who put up little resistance against England in their short Test series against England just a few weeks earlier, and, to put it politely, still had a long way to go before they could be considered serious players in world cricket.

This was a far more significant result than England's victory over Australia in the Twenty20 game. Kevin knew from this that Australia weren't infallible, and that it would be possible to beat them this summer if he and the rest of the England boys played to their potential. For the first time the England squad really believed they could beat Australia, not only in the one-day series, but in the Ashes itself. Some pundits believed that Australia's biggest weakness was in the fact that many of their leading players were getting on a bit. Yet with age comes experience, and there was a strong argument that even if a few of them had reflexes that weren't as sharp as they once were, they more than made up for it in knowledge of how to play cricket at this level.

Nevil Road in Bristol is a tight, compact ground with short boundaries, which makes for a great atmosphere on international days when 16,000 fans get behind their team. Australia's day started badly when the squad turned up at the wrong entrance. It seemed as though nothing was going right for them. The setting could not have been better. The sun was out and it was a proper summer's day, with the temperature reaching 30 degrees inside the ground, something that doesn't happen too often in England. As expected, the crowd came out in huge numbers and the Australian players knew they were in for another tough day.

Australia batted first and began their innings well and were showing signs of a return to form. This all changed when Paul Collingwood took a superb catch to dismiss Matt Hayden, and from that moment on the match turned in England's favour. By the time Kevin came out to bat, England needed around 150 to win. This was his first 50-over international in England, and he knew the pitch favoured his style of play. The boundaries were short and there were likely to be plenty of opportunities to hit some big shots.

Sledging is a fact of life in cricket, and nobody does it

better than the Aussies. No sooner had Kevin arrived at the crease than he heard Damien Martyn shouting, 'You can do it in Twenty20 cricket, let's see if you can do it now in the big stuff.' Clearly, Damien hadn't done his research and checked Kevin's stats from South Africa. Kevin knew that there was no malice in Damien's comments, and it was all part and parcel of facing Australia. There was no doubt he'd be hearing more of this sort of thing in the weeks ahead, but all it did was make him that little bit more determined to put in a big score, and this was definitely the right reaction.

His innings started well but while England were running out of overs, he began running out of batting partners. By the time Jon Lewis came out to bat, Kevin knew that drastic action was needed. Jon was playing in his first one-day international, and his job was to hold the fort while Kevin whacked the ball around.

Jon showed a great deal of maturity for a man with so little international experience, while Kevin knew that getting ten runs an over on a pitch with such short boundaries was more than possible. He hit a few good shots off Jason Gillespie, but the most impressive moment came when he hit a six out of the ground off Brad Hogg. After that, there was no looking back, as Kevin guided England to their target, making 91 not out in the process. Kevin had passed his first major test against Australia – this was a major confidence boost. Psychologically it was important, because when the going got tough later on in the summer, he would remember this innings and realise he could bat against the world's strongest bowling attack.

England's next match of the series against Bangladesh in a day-nighter at Trent Bridge was a one-sided affair, with the home side winning by 168 runs. As he was due to come in at number seven, Kevin wasn't required to bat, and this was to be Paul Collingwood's day in the limelight. He made 112 to help England to a total of 391 for four, helped further by 152 from Andrew Strauss. Paul then took six for 31, making him only the second man to make a century and a five-wicket haul in a one-day international, the first being Viv Richards.

Despite being a bit-part player in this match, it was still a day Kevin would remember for the rest of his life, though perhaps not only for the cricket. Four months had now passed since he had that tattoo engraved on his arm, and he had gone to great lengths to stop his parents from finding out about it. The press had occasionally asked him if he'd gone through with it, but he'd always denied it. He'd carried out other precautionary measures, like always wearing long sleeves in public, and he'd succeeded in keeping it a secret from everyone apart from his England team-mates, his girlfriend, and a few other close friends – until this day.

He was sitting on the balcony, watching Andrew Strauss and Paul Collingwood pile on the runs for England, without a care in the world. Unfortunately for him, he was wearing a vest and the TV cameras soon spotted his tattoo. The truth was, he had completely forgotten about it and he had let his guard down at the worst possible time. The media frenzy that followed was to be expected, but he knew the reaction from his parents was likely to be far worse. That night he received a text from his mother saying, 'What is that on your arm? Dad says he is not happy and is after Goughy!' Fortunately for Kevin, and indeed Darren, his parents were back home in South Africa, so there wasn't really much they could do about it. They did eventually accept it, knowing that their son had a stubborn streak, and if he wanted to do something, he'd do it.

Inevitably, it was only a matter of time before Australia got their act together and began playing at something like their best. It happened at the next match, which was a day-night game at Chester-le-Street, County Durham. England started terribly with the bat, with Marcus Trescothick and Paul Collingwood both getting out for ducks, while Kevin only managed 19 before being caught by Mike Hussey off the bowling of Andrew Symonds. Australia won by 57 runs, but there was still a positive mood in the England camp and they managed to have a bit of fun during the game.

Darren had a laugh at the expense of Australian all-rounder Shane Watson. The Australian team had been staying at the Lumley Castle Hotel that overlooks the ground, and the papers had carried stories about some of the Australian players having paranormal experiences during their stay. Watson didn't like being left alone in his room, believing it to be haunted, and Darren saw an opportunity to exploit the situation. When Watson came out to bat, Darren crept up behind him before shouting, 'Boo!' at the top of his voice, causing him to jump out of his skin. Watson forced a smile, but it was clear he was a tad embarrassed at falling for such a lame attempt to scare him.

Both England and Australia breezed past Bangladesh in their next matches, before the big two met again in a bad-tempered encounter at Edgbaston. At one point, Simon Jones accidentally struck Matt Hayden with a full toss and the two men briefly squared up to each other. It wasn't a gentlemanly scene, and went against the spirit of the game, but what was important, from the England point of view, was how quickly the rest of the players rallied around Simon. The message was that if you took one of them on, you took all of them on. The match was eventually rained off, but the side won some important psychological points that day. They weren't going to be pushed around, or act in a subservient manner when faced by the Australian team.

The series final at Lord's inevitably featured England and Australia in what was by far the most important match of the contest to date. England won the toss and put Australia in to bat, and bowled them out for 196, thanks largely to some excellent work in the field. In response, the England batsmen seemed to become complacent, scoring 33 for five, with Kevin making only six runs.

Freddie Flintoff, Paul Collingwood and Geraint Jones began a substantial fight back that left England needing 19 from the last two overs to win. This was going to be a tight finish. Come the final delivery, Darren and Ashley Giles were at the crease, and they needed to get three runs from Glenn McGrath's bowling to seal a famous victory. In the event, they managed to scramble two and the match was tied, just as it had been in Bloemfontein a few months earlier, and the NatWest Trophy was shared.

IN AT THE DEEP END

Kevin knew this wasn't the worst result for the team, but he was becoming increasingly concerned about his personal form. After a strong start, he hadn't really shone in the series and he knew he'd missed a real opportunity to make a proper contribution to England's cause in the series final at the most famous cricket ground in the world. He also realised that he hadn't really done his cause for being selected for the Ashes series any good.

Both sets of players were ready for the Ashes now, and the consensus amongst supporters of both sides was that they were ready for battle to commence. The one-day series had given them a lot of high-quality cricket, and they were now ready for the main course. But before they could get down to the really serious business, there was the matter of the NatWest Challenge and three more games against Australia.

It seemed bizarre to many to have a separate one-day series against Australia so soon after the last one, but the main purpose of this seemed to be for the ICC to use it as an opportunity to experiment with the concept of 'super-subs', whereby a team could replace any of their players at any point during the match. Kevin was never too keen on the idea, saying it all seemed a bit artificial to him. The trial wasn't a success and the concept was abandoned in 2006.

The short series got off to a great start for England when they inflicted a nine-wicket defeat on Australia at Headingley, one of the heaviest in their history. Paul Collingwood with the ball and Marcus Trescothick with the bat were the key stars for England, while Kevin's main contributions were to take two catches from the bats of Matt

Hayden and Ricky Ponting. Although Kevin was obviously delighted with such a resounding victory over Australia, it was a matter of some frustration for him that he wasn't required to bat. He needed an opportunity to make up for a string of matches where he was a bit-part player, and this wasn't to be his day.

In the next match at Lord's, Australia got their revenge with a seven-wicket victory, while Kevin disappointed with the bat yet again, making only 14 before being bowled by Brett Lee. In the final match at the Oval, Kevin finally made a real impression, making 74 to give a slight respectability to a disappointing performance by the England batsmen, making a total of just 228. The Australian batsmen, Adam Gilchrist especially, were starting to find some decent form and the visitors won this final one-day match by eight wickets, with 91 balls remaining.

Although Kevin had made amends in that final match, his form had been inconsistent throughout the one-dayers. It didn't help that he wasn't required to bat in several matches, and he found it especially disappointing that he didn't get to partner Freddie Flintoff more often. Freddie had missed the one-day series in South Africa due to injury, and cricket fans everywhere had been looking forward to seeing two of the most exciting batsmen in the world playing together during this series.

Kevin knew that his innings in that final one-day match at the Oval was hugely significant if he was to have any hope at all of being selected for the Ashes. Without a big score there, it would be a no-brainer for the selectors; they would have to stick with the tried and tested Graham Thorpe. During that impressive final innings, Kevin was taunted by the Australian fielders, who kept saying, 'This is what Test cricket is like. Can you handle it?' This was just another psychological battle, but one Kevin actually enjoyed. It only served to make him even more determined to make a big score there and bring himself back into contention for the Test team.

His technique still gained a lot of column inches. There were plenty who thought he was too leg-sided to make it at Test cricket, and that the world's greatest bowlers would find him out. Yet Kevin knew that his track record in county cricket was greater in the four-day version of the game than in the shorter formats, and was confident that he could adapt to cricket's greatest challenge. At the press conference after the match at the Oval, he left reporters in little doubt that he thought he was ready for Test cricket. The Kevin that spoke to the press that evening was him at his most confident and brash. He was speaking from the heart – he felt he had stood up to whatever the Australians had thrown at him that day, and now felt ready to move his game on to the ultimate platform.

Kevin ended the series not knowing how close he really was to being called up for the first Test at Lord's. Without that big score at the Oval, he would have had little chance. Kevin knew he couldn't get ahead of himself, and understood that there was a fair chance he would be spending the rest of the summer playing in front of small crowds at Hampshire rather than facing the toughest Test cricket team in the world in the sport's most prestigious series.

Despite Graham Thorpe being a safe pair of hands, there was speculation he was suffering from back problems, and he had just announced he was going to coach New South Wales in the winter. This announcement effectively meant his England career would come to an end after the Ashes, regardless of how well he performed, and Kevin considered the possibility that the selectors might want to start looking to the future sooner rather than later.

A few days later, Kevin was relaxing in his flat in Southampton, which he shared with his friend Richard Logan. It was about 9pm, and he had drifted off to sleep, when the phone rang. It was David Graveney and he had some good news – Kevin was in the side for the Test match, which was now only a matter of days away. David told Kevin that he'd been selected because he'd done well being positive, and there was no need to change his game.

Kevin was ecstatic at hearing this and immediately phoned his parents in South Africa to tell them the good news. It was gone 11pm there and the phone call woke them up. They were overjoyed for their son, and neither they nor Kevin would get much sleep that night, as there was plenty of celebrating to be done. This moment was amongst the happiest in Kevin's life. He had certainly come a long way since making that tough decision to leave South Africa five years earlier. It was now up to him to make the most of this opportunity and repay the selectors' faith in his ability.

Kevin had to be at Lord's for a press conference the following morning. He didn't manage to get much sleep the night before, he spent a good part of it celebrating with

Richard, and his mind was racing too much to rest after that. When he arrived at Lord's the realisation of what had happened set in. He had been picked to play for his country (and yes, England was now most definitely his country) in the most prestigious series in world cricket. Nothing could wipe the smile off his face that morning as he answered questions from the British and Australian press.

The build-up over the next few days was very relaxed and Kevin found he fitted in well with the setup. He already knew most of the guys from the one-day squad, and even if he hadn't played with them, he had seen them around often enough. This was an environment he felt comfortable in from the start, and there was no adjusting to be done in that sense.

In the days leading up to the first Test, the Australians gave the impression they were on a high after their success in the one-dayers. Adam Gilchrist talked about how stories had been made up about them, with pictures in the papers of the players carrying handbags. He said that people had been laughing at them, but it was now the time to forget all that stuff because the Ashes was very near. He talked about some of the ways in which people in and around the England camp had scored psychological points over Australia. Both he and the England squad knew that none of that mattered now, and it was time to start the serious business of the summer.

7

LET BATTLE COMMENCE!

Thursday, 21 July 2005 had arrived, and Kevin was feeling more excited than nervous. Yes, there were a few nerves, which was a good thing going into such an important contest, but he was still thrilled to be finally playing in the Test team after years of hard work and dedication, as well as setbacks and disappointments.

He arrived at Lord's at around 9am, where a breakfast was laid on, beginning a routine which was the norm for all Test players in England. After that, he made his way to the dressing room, to find everything laid out for him. However, it was his responsibility to make sure that five days' worth of whites were clean and in good order to represent his country. He then went to see the doctor who gave him a cocktail of pills he needed for his bad back. They were a mixture of painkillers and anti-inflammatories, and this was something he had to do before every day's play. Most of the guys needed a combination of pills from the doctor for one ailment or another and Kevin was no exception.

Getting all his kit together for the day would take 10 or 15 minutes, while the bowlers and the keeper got their ankles and fingers taped to help them cope with the long and demanding day ahead. Kevin took a look at the famous honours board near the Lord's dressing room, which contained a list of every England batsman who had ever scored a Test century there, as well as every England bowler who had taken five wickets in an innings, or ten in a match. He was slightly in awe of all those names, and hoped his own would be joining that prestigious list someday, maybe not before too long.

It took around 20 minutes for the pills to take effect, by which time he was ready for the warm-ups. Out in the middle, Ricky Ponting won the toss for Australia and chose to bat under the cloudy skies. Back in the dressing room word had got around that Glenn McGrath had repeated his claim that the only result he could see was 5-0 to Australia. Michael Vaughan's reaction was to say that the England team didn't fear playing Australia, but were looking forward to the challenge. Kevin knew why Glenn made those remarks, and he wasn't going to fall for it. He knew all he had to do was play his natural game and not get hung up over these psychological battles that had been going on in the media all summer. That said, it would be a different story if the Aussies started playing mind games on the field.

As he sat in the dressing room waiting for the bell, Kevin

thought back to the last Ashes series in Australia. He had been playing grade cricket in Sydney at the time and he thought back to how England were annihilated by Australia. He remembered how the England team had become figures of fun in Australia at that time, with jokes being made at their expense on chat shows, in adverts, by stand-up comedians, just about everywhere. He was secretly hoping the British media would do the same, should England get off to a good start.

The pre-match team talk revolved around some familiar themes. Duncan Fletcher and Michael Vaughan spoke about the need to play positive cricket and get in the Aussies' faces straight away, as they had done in the Twenty20 match. Kevin's parents had flown over to witness their son's Test debut. David Graveney handed Kevin his Test cap before the match. It was now up to him to make his parents, the England selectors, and his country proud.

Outside the door of the dressing room a guard of honour had formed that stretched all the way down the stairs. As the players entered the Long Room they were greeted by loud cheering, and as they left the pavilion the normally-reserved and conservative MCC members began clapping and shouting, giving the England boys that extra bit of encouragement before battle commenced.

Kevin was proud to be representing his country and it clearly meant a great deal to him that his Test career was beginning at the world's most famous ground in cricket's most prestigious series. He walked out with his shoulders back and his head held high. Michael Vaughan tried to stop his men becoming nervous after such an overwhelming welcome, and reminded them of the important points upon which to focus.

Steve Harmison was given the task of bowling the first over, and for him it was a case of starting as you mean to go on. None of the England team especially minded Australia winning the toss and batting first, because the conditions looked difficult. With his second ball, Steve hit Justin Langer's right arm just below the elbow. Later on he struck Matt Hayden and hit Ricky Ponting on the helmet, leaving him needing treatment. This was all part of the plan. Duncan Fletcher called it 'getting in their space', and the captain told his players to show some anger early on.

To many cricket fans, this whole attitude went against the gentlemanly spirit in which cricket has traditionally been played, but this was Steve's way of showing his opponents he meant business. Some might describe it as meeting fire with fire, but for the traditionalists, things were going too far. Cricketing convention dictates that when a player gets hurt you should always make sure he is OK. England didn't abide by this on that first morning; in fact they even kept their distance from the Australian batsmen. It was their way of telling Australia that they wouldn't be getting any sympathy from them.

The match had got off to a perfect start for Kevin, but he was about to make his first major error, dropping Ponting in the gully. Catching had until now been one of his great strengths, but it would soon become a major talking point and be perceived as a significant weakness in his game.

Fortunately for Kevin, Steve soon bowled Ponting and the damage was minimal.

By lunch, Australia were 97 for five. However, the Australian lower-order was full of batsmen who could hold their own at the crease and they dragged themselves up to 175 for six during the afternoon, with Freddie dismissing the dangerous Gilchrist, which was followed by that famous roaring celebration. Steve Harmison then hit a purple patch to take the remaining four wickets to see the Aussies all out for 190. Steve's name was duly added to the Lord's honours board for taking five wickets in an innings. It was a great start to the match, but there was still a long way to go.

During the press conference on the day Kevin was brought into the Test squad, Tim Abraham from Sky Sports News asked David Graveney whether Graham Thorpe would be a better option coming out to bat if England were 50 for three on the first day at Lord's. David's answer was that England had been in trouble in several one-dayers in South Africa when Kevin had come out to bat, and he was sure he could do the same in the Tests. Little did Tim know that when Kevin actually did come out to bat, England were in even more serious trouble at 21 for five, thanks to a phenomenal spell from Glenn McGrath.

Walking out to bat, Kevin experienced nerves for the first time. There was a great deal of pressure on him, not just to answer Tim Abraham's point in the press conference, but also because there had been plenty of people who thought he was weak on the off-side. Kevin got off to a slow start, making only 29 runs. His priority was to protect his wicket and edge the England score to somewhere near the Australian total if at all possible.

The following morning was a different story. Kevin hit McGrath into the middle tier of the pavilion, and then began the first of his now-famous tussles with Shane Warne. By this stage, Shane had become a friend as well as his county captain, but Kevin knew just how much he wanted to get him out. However, this didn't mean that he knew Shane's game especially well. Because Kevin didn't do much bowling at Hampshire, he didn't get to see Shane practising in the nets too often. The other factor was that the way Shane bowled for Hampshire was nothing like the way he bowled for Australia. It would have been impossible for him to maintain those extraordinarily high standards he set for Australia all of the time, and at county level he quite often held a lot back.

Kevin understood that the most successful batsmen against Shane were those who had played positively against him, such as Brian Lara, Sachin Tendulkar and V.V.S. Laxman. Kevin knew this was a time for playing the sort of game that came most naturally to him. So focused was he, that at one stage when he was batting with Geraint Jones, the two players met in the middle for what should have been a chat at the end of an over. Instead, Kevin just said to Geraint, 'Sorry, China. Can't talk now. Too pumped.'

Kevin had just reached his 50 when he let Shane know that he was up for the challenge and hit him for six straight into the second tier of the grandstand. He winked at Shane, who patted him on the bum and said, 'Well batted.'

Perhaps Kevin became a little too at ease and let his guard down slightly, because he tried doing exactly the same thing with Shane's very next ball, but this time he was caught by a diving Damien Martyn just inside the rope. Kevin was out for 57, which was a respectable achievement under the circumstances, but he was annoyed at himself for not making a few more runs to get England a bit closer to the total.

Following a shaky start in the field during Australia's first innings, Kevin did better in the second when he ran out Justin Langer from point early on, but it wasn't long before he made what he considers his worst fielding mistake of the summer. Michael Clarke had made 21 runs when he drove the ball in Kevin's direction off the bowling of Simon Jones. It should have been a straightforward catch, but after touching Kevin's palm, he somehow managed to drop it. This time there were consequences, as Clarke went on to score another 70 runs in a strong partnership with Martyn.

Kevin couldn't work out why his fielding had gone to pieces in this match. It was normally a major strength, going back to his days at Natal, but now some dreadful errors had somehow crept in which had cost England dear. Of course, the Australians wasted little time in pouncing on the chance to tease Kevin, and he soon earned the nickname 'Cymbals'. Doubts started to creep into Kevin's mind but his typically positive attitude meant that not once did he become scared of fielding or wished catches wouldn't come in his direction. It was up to him to study the videos after the match and work to put it right for next time.

LET BATTLE COMMENCE!

Australia managed to get to 384, and Kevin's mistake had made the task of winning the match a whole lot harder for England. The openers got off to another poor start and by the time Kevin came to the crease he had to contend with the very real possibility that he would run out of partners at the other end, regardless of how well he batted. His fears were justified and it wasn't too long before it was clear that England were heading for a heavy defeat.

Kevin's last partner was his close friend, Simon Jones. They communicated well, with Kevin fancying that he was best equipped to get runs off Shane's bowling, while Simon would largely try and guard his wicket against Glenn McGrath at the other end. This arrangement worked for a while, before Simon was caught Warne, bowled McGrath, leaving Kevin as the not-out batsman on 64. Once again Kevin and Shane engaged in a friendly and highly-entertaining tussle during the second innings.

Typically, Shane would bowl to Kevin, rub his hands in the dirt, and then shout something at him. Kevin could see his image was being projected on the big screen, but he found it hard to keep a straight face. They were close friends and enjoyed a great rapport, even when playing on opposite sides. It showed that a bit of fun could still be had, no matter how intense the cricket was itself. Shane had taken four wickets in the innings and needed one more to get his name added to the honours board at Lord's. It wasn't to be, but he certainly made life as difficult as possible for Kevin out there. These battles added yet another interesting dimension to the Ashes series.

The innings was a personal success for Kevin. He had become only the eighth England player to score a half-century in each innings of his Test debut, but there was little cause for celebration, as the side slumped to a 239-run defeat.

After the match, Kevin, along with Geraint Jones and England's bowling coach Troy Cooley, went into the Australian dressing room to congratulate the players on their victory. There were great celebrations going on there, as you'd expect after thumping the home side at Lord's. Kevin mainly wanted to congratulate Shane, but he made a point of speaking to one or two of the other players. He wanted to talk to them because they were the best, and he thought he could learn a thing or two from their mental attitude out there. Several of the Australian players congratulated Kevin on his achievements in the match, but it didn't mean a huge amount to him because England had lost.

That night many of the England players went home, but Kevin went out drinking in a bar and on to a club with Shane and his old friend Stuart MacGill, who was part of the Australian squad. The two sets of players mixed quite a lot that summer, which didn't go down well with some pundits. But for Kevin this was perfectly normal. Socialising and making friends was all part of the experience of being a professional cricketer to him, and it was a chance to wind down and put the events of the last five days into perspective.

Kevin was careful not to talk too much about the England preparations to Shane and Stuey. There were still four Ashes Tests ahead, and he didn't want to say anything that would give them any kind of psychological advantage. Instead, they talked about other things in life. Kevin enjoyed this, as it was important to remember that not everything evolved around the Ashes and there were plenty of other things going on in the world. It was important to keep everything in perspective. They talked about mutual friends and just enjoyed having a few drinks after a gruelling five days.

When he reflected on the Test match, Kevin realised just how much he'd learned during the last week. He now knew exactly what Test cricket was all about, and that he could get runs against the world's greatest bowlers. The result had been a bad one and he had to accept his share of the blame for that. But the experience overall was a positive one. He loved it: the challenge, the complexities of the long format, and the camaraderie and banter between the two sets of players. He knew for certain he wanted a lot more, but there was still a great deal of work to be done if he was to become a fully-rounded Test cricketer, and if England were to win the Ashes.

8

AN EVENTFUL SUMMER

Gaining his Test cap undoubtedly meant a lot to Kevin, and it wasn't long before he headed for the tattoo parlour once again. This time he went to Selfridges in Oxford Street and had 'DCXXVI' (626 in Roman numerals) engraved underneath the three lions. He had become the 626th player to play Test cricket for England, and he decided to commemorate the landmark with this permanent memento.

People who intend having a lot of tattoos need to plan ahead to avoid their bodies becoming a random mess of assorted emblems and names, so Kevin made a firm decision. He took the view that tattoos should be deeply personal and shouldn't be something that other people would want to copy. For this reason, he decided that he would only add the names of his wife and any future children to his two tattoos. There would definitely be no Chinese writing or football badges, which probably came as a relief to his parents.

AN EVENTFUL SUMMER

The postmortem into the first Test was well underway in the British press, and they were looking for a scapegoat. Ashley Giles seemed to get more than his fair share of the blame for the defeat, which came as a disappointment to Kevin because Ashley was a close friend and had been since they were paired together in the 'buddy' system when Kevin was first called up for England.

What was particularly disappointing for Kevin was to see his friend criticised by so many ex-players working in the media. He felt that these were people who perhaps had not achieved as much as they would have liked in their own careers, or some who had no idea what it was like playing against this strong Australian side. Yes, everybody knew Ashley was no Shane Warne, including Ashley himself. Instead, he was a safe pair of hands who could bowl, bat and field consistently well and had a huge contribution to make to the England side.

The whole England team shared Kevin's view that Ashley didn't deserve this criticism, and rallied around him in the week leading up to the next Test, which was to be played at Edgbaston. Everything seemed to happen in the build-up. Two days before the match, Michael Vaughan was practising in the nets when he was struck on the elbow by Chris Tremlett, who was then an up-and-coming bowler with Kevin at Hampshire. Fortunately, the scan revealed Michael hadn't broken anything and would be OK to play, but these were anxious moments for the team.

Australia weren't quite so lucky. On the morning of the match the team was warming up on the outfield playing tag rugby when Glenn McGrath went to retrieve the ball. In doing so he slipped on a stray cricket ball and twisted his ankle. His part in this Test was over. Glenn was now in his mid-30s but had proved in the first Test that he was still one of the best fast bowlers in the world and a major threat to England's batsmen. His place was taken by the very able Michael Kasprowicz, who had taken seven for 36 against England at the Oval in 1997.

During the team talk in the dressing room Michael Vaughan reminded his players of the importance of remaining positive and getting in the faces of the Australians. He told them that there were still four games left and they were still very much in the series. There was a long way to go and one bad Test match did not make a summer.

The Edgbaston wicket looked to favour the batsmen and everyone assumed before the toss that whichever captain won it would elect to bat first. It therefore came as a great shock when Ricky Ponting elected to field first. As far as Kevin was concerned, this was advantage England. The decision was even more baffling when one considers the fact that Australia had just lost their best pace bowler.

With Michael's instructions to remain positive ringing in their ears, Marcus Trescothick and Andrew Strauss went out to open the batting for England. It soon became clear that the loss of Glenn McGrath had affected Australia psychologically and the England openers took advantage of some lacklustre bowling from the weakened Australia attack. Even Shane was struggling to get going, with Marcus hitting him for six in his first over.

AN EVENTFUL SUMMER

The first session went brilliantly, with only Andrew out before lunch. Marcus even managed to make 18 in the final over before lunch, at Brett Lee's expense. England experienced a wobbly period after lunch, when Marcus got out 10 runs short of what would've been his maiden Test century. Ian Bell and Michael soon followed, which meant that Kevin and Freddie Flintoff finally had the chance to have a proper bat together.

Kevin initially wanted to rotate the strike because Freddie seemed to be oozing with confidence and it seemed a good opportunity to just let him do his stuff and keep things moving along nicely. Kevin was happy to stand at the other end and watch Freddie play some truly breathtaking shots, particularly off Lee. This wasn't a time for the two naturally attacking batsmen to try and outdo each other, but to keep the scoreboard ticking along and just play their natural games.

Once Freddie was out, the responsibility for getting the runs fell very firmly on Kevin's shoulders, so he began batting more aggressively to try and help England along to a total of at least 400. In doing so he became only the sixth England batsman to make a half century in each of his first three Test innings.

Kevin was eventually caught Katich, bowled Lee for 71. He had been playing some high-risk shots, and it seemed likely he would fall short of his century against the best bowling attack in the world. There were those who felt he should have done more to protect his wicket, but he felt that getting runs was more important, as he was quickly running out of partners. Simon Jones and Steve Harmison followed Kevin's example by playing some positive shots to the best of their ability, and in doing so took England to 407 all out. This was only the second time England had scored 400 on the first day of a Test, and it was their highest first-day total since 1938.

Yet for some writers and commentators, this wasn't good enough. They felt England had missed a chance to get 500, but examining the scorecard, this seems a little harsh. Ian Bell was the only specialist batsman who put in a single-figure score, and it was important to play positively to show Australia that they meant business. There was also the fact that Australia had the strength in their lower-order to play for a draw if necessary, and England needed to leave enough time to see through their second innings.

Leaving the ground in his car at the end of the day Kevin saw Tony Greig and Geoffrey Boycott trying to flag down a taxi. Both men were commentating for Channel Four, and since they were staying in the same hotel as the England team Kevin decided to offer them a lift. He was especially keen to meet Tony, who had a life story that was quite similar to his own. He had left South Africa to play cricket in England but decided that his allegiances were with England even before his home country was banned from international cricket. He had a no-nonsense approach to cricket and indeed to life itself. Like Kevin, he believed in playing positive cricket, and had experienced plenty of controversies of his own during his career.

Tony and Kevin had no chance to get to know each other,

as Geoffrey dominated the conversation all the way back to the hotel. The Yorkshire and England legend wasted no time in berating Kevin, telling him he'd been stupid for throwing away an opportunity to make a century. Kevin fought back and told Geoff it was necessary to make runs quite quickly under the circumstances. Geoff responded by saying that it wouldn't have happened in his day, because he would have made sure his partners stayed with him until he made his century.

The rather one-sided discussion continued until Kevin arrived back at the hotel. Geoffrey asked that Kevin drop him right outside the front door. For Kevin, getting to know Tony would have to wait for another day, but despite Geoff's rather blunt and unrelenting criticism of his play he didn't regret giving him a lift. Geoffrey Boycott was a man who had been there and done it, and Kevin was willing to take his criticism on board.

To put the criticism into context, Geoffrey and Kevin's playing styles are poles apart. Geoffrey's friend, the late journalist Ian Wooldridge, was also one of his many, many critics. He once wrote, 'He was batting for Boycott first and England second and those of us who witnessed his cynical running-out of his opening partner, Bob Barber, in a Test match in Sydney can never be wholly sympathetic to his single-minded priorities.'

Geoffrey has many good qualities and a man of his achievements is entitled to his opinions, but there were plenty of other people who shared Wooldridge's view. There were many occasions where his style of play was ultra-defensive, which contrasted sharply with Kevin's, who would rather make one run and be on the winning side than make a century and lose. His personal averages came a distant second to the team's success, and this showed in his attitude on the day.

The following day the newspapers were heaping praise on the partnership between Kevin and Freddie, and it was a great morale boost not only to them but to the whole England side to see the game being given such high-profile coverage. They knew the importance of getting the Australian batsmen early on. Sure enough, Langer was hit on the head by Harmison and Hoggard got Hayden out with a brilliant first ball.

It wasn't long before Ashley Giles had the chance to prove just how wrong his critics had been. He took his first of three wickets when he got the Australian captain, Ricky Ponting, out, caught by Vaughan, which was followed by a massive cheer from the crowd. This was a superb moment in the match, and indeed the series. By the end of the day Australia had slipped to 308 all out, leaving England with a solid first-innings lead of 99. It was a good position to be in, but the match wasn't in the bag by any means.

The start of day three was devastating for England. Brett Lee took three wickets from nine balls to dismiss Trescothick, Hoggard (the night watchman) and Vaughan, while Shane had bowled Strauss for just six runs. This time Kevin had to make up for all of the opening batsmen who had under-performed. Luck was on his side at the start of his innings, when Lee's first ball was ruled not out, despite

Kevin knowing there just might have been faint touch on his bat.

However, his good fortune wasn't to last. It wasn't long before Kevin had to face Shane once again. He got off to a great start, hitting him for two sixes, but he was given out when umpire Rudi Koertzen decided he had made contact with the glove before Gilchrist took the catch. The replays showed Kevin had been unlucky on this occasion, but he may have been lucky once already in his short innings and knew he just had to accept it.

Being out for 20 wasn't something Kevin enjoyed, but he had to sit back and hope Freddie could work his magic without him at the other end. Things went from bad to worse when Shane took Ian Bell's wicket to reduce England to 75 for six, a lead of just 174. Freddie looked to have damaged his shoulder and there were fears his part in the innings would be over, but he bravely battled on, knowing England's fate in the match may well now depend on him.

Freddie soon got down to business and started smacking the ball around with flair and determination. He added 51 from 49 deliveries for the last wicket with Simon Jones to reassert England's authority on the match. Freddie's luck ran out by the time he made 73 when Shane's ball hit the stumps, but he received a well deserved pat on the back from the bowler and a standing ovation from the crowd as he headed back to the pavilion. Shane had taken six wickets from the innings; this was him at his very best.

Australia needed 282 to win. The match was in the balance, and anything could happen. The only thing that could be said with any confidence is that with two full days remaining, a result was very likely. Australia got off to a good start, making 47 without loss, but then Freddie showed that he could bowl a bit as well, taking the wickets of Langer and Ponting in quick succession in quite some style. Michael Vaughan said later that this was the moment when he first allowed himself to believe that England could win the Ashes.

During the afternoon, Australia slipped to 140 for seven and Vaughan decided to claim the extra half-hour to try and finish them off. Harmison got Clarke with a slower ball to leave Australia 175 for eight, but they weren't able to conclude the job that evening. Australia needed another 107 to win, with two wickets remaining, and plenty of people, including Kevin, thought England would be able to clean up on the Sunday morning. They were in for a nasty surprise.

Shane and Brett Lee batted slowly and doggedly, in an innings Geoffrey Boycott would have approved of. Kevin felt helpless in the outfield and couldn't believe what was unfolding in front of him. Time wasn't an issue for the Australians, because there were two days left. They would have been quite happy to keep nicking singles here and there to gradually wear down the total for the duration if necessary.

Eventually, Shane trod on his stumps, which proved a vital turning point in the game. It was now England's to lose, but even the Australian tail was capable of getting runs and batting reasonably well, Michael Kasprowicz included, so they couldn't take anything for granted.

With 15 more runs needed, Kasprowicz hit the ball to Simon Jones at third man. Kevin thought for a split second that the normally-reliable Simon had caught him, but his heart sank when he realised his friend had made a rare mistake. Australia were soon down to needing only a single-figure score for victory. Kevin knew that if England blew it from here, the mental impact on the team would be enormous. It would be very unlikely that they could recover from such a defeat to go on and win the Ashes.

Australia needed four to win. Brett Lee whacked the ball towards the boundary, but Simon Jones blocked it and they only got a single from it. Two balls later, and it was a case of now or never for England. Steve Harmison decided to give it one last go. The ball flew up off the dead pitch and hit Kasprowicz around his glove, and it travelled down the leg side where Geraint Jones took a superb catch. England had won, but boy, they had made hard work of it. Kevin experienced a cocktail of emotions all at once. There was obviously happiness and joy, but also relief that they hadn't blown what should've been a much more comfortable victory.

If England had blown it, most of the blame would have laid very firmly with all of the team's leading batsmen, including Kevin, who had all under-performed in the second innings. Any batsman can make a mistake, but for five of them to put in a bad score against Australia just wasn't good enough. The Edgbaston crowd erupted at England's tense victory. Freddie immediately walked up to console Brett Lee, who had done so much to nearly give his side an unlikely victory, in what became one of the enduring images of the series.

This match has been talked about as one of the greatest Tests of all time. Kevin had made a valuable contribution in the first innings, and they would have lost the match without the runs he made. Yet he had blown the chance to give England a more comfortable lead in the second innings, which meant he still had a lot to learn if he was to become the best cricketer he could be. Later, Kevin and a few of the others went for a celebration in Broad Street. He isn't normally much of a beer drinker, but that night he had his first taste of Guinness. They ended up in a bar where the Australian team were already carousing and enjoyed some fun banter, and found that their opponents had taken the defeat in good spirits.

Kevin partied well into the night and ended up wearing a headband and sunglasses. He generally made a prat of himself as the night went on, but it was all good fun. He and Simon Jones were the last to leave, and arrived back in the hotel well into the early hours. Despite all the ups and downs of the incredible match, England had won. Kevin and the boys had earned the right to let off a bit of steam.

There wasn't much time to recover from the emotion of the Edgbaston Test, and the team were soon on their way to Old Trafford, Manchester, for the next match of the series. Back-to-back Tests are something all modern international cricketers have had to get used to, due to the increasingly packed calendar, but for Kevin the next game couldn't come soon enough. He was on a massive high after Edgbaston and couldn't wait to get stuck in to the Aussies again, despite feeling drained.

AN EVENTFUL SUMMER

The boys knew that Australia could be beaten, and that the Ashes were now up for grabs. Yes, there were lessons to be learned from Edgbaston and losing that match would've been devastating, but fortunately they didn't have to think about that any longer.

The series was really starting to capture the imagination of the British public, way beyond the usual cricket fans. Obviously, the sheer drama of the cricket spoke for itself, but the characters in the England team, such as Kevin and Freddie, helped give them some extra attention, especially in the tabloid press. Both were mavericks, individuals who stood out from the crowd and weren't afraid to be different. Crucially, both played the sort of cricket that was attractive to spectators, which meant that people who only had a casual interest in cricket were now keenly watching as much of the series as they could. And, of course, what made this Ashes series so different to all the others in recent years was that this time England actually had a realistic chance of winning.

The Old Trafford pitch tends to favour spin, and this was almost certainly going to be the match where Shane took his 600th Test wicket. The England boys needed no reminding that this was the ground where he bowled that incredible ball to dismiss Mike Gatting in 1993. Shane had nicknamed Kevin 'Six Hundred' when they first got to know each other at Hampshire, because he was determined that Kevin would be his landmark victim. When they inspected the pitch on the first morning of the match, it wasn't quite the usual Old Trafford condition, and it seemed that the bowlers most likely to get something from it were Simon Jones and Freddie, who would be able to elicit some reverse swing from it.

In the run-up to the game it seemed likely that Glenn McGrath would still be out of action, injured, while Brett Lee was struggling with a knee infection. It turned out on the morning of the match that both were fit to play, but Michael Vaughan was keen to remind his players to concentrate on their own game. He was keen to put in a big score himself after a disappointing series to date. There was no doubt what would happen with the toss. Whoever won it would elect to bat and would have a significant advantage from the off. Fortunately, Michael won it and this brought a huge shout of 'Yes!' from the England boys.

Michael led by example on the first day and more than made up for his disappointing performances with the bat in the first two Tests with a score of 166. By the time he was out, England were in a very strong position at 290 for three. As it happened, Kevin wasn't Shane's 600th Test wicket; that honour went to Marcus Trescothick, but not before he put in 63 runs. The whole crowd stood to applaud Shane. This was an incredible landmark by anyone's standards, but to do it on the ground where he had bowled the 'ball of the century' to Gatting 12 years earlier made it all the more special.

With the exception of Andrew Strauss, all the England batsmen had put in good scores by the time Kevin came to the crease. This was a relief after their disappointing performances during the second innings at Edgbaston, and it was especially good news for Ian Bell, who had justified the faith the selectors had kept with him during a rocky period, making 59 runs before Adam Gilchrist caught him from Brett Lee's bowling.

Kevin decided to take the new ball towards the close of play, but was caught on the boundary, hooking, by sub-fielder Brad Hodge. This was a rare occasion where Kevin was angry with himself, as he quickly realised he hadn't played the situation as well as he should have done. He knew he had crossed the fine line between playing positively and recklessly, and knew any criticism coming from Geoffrey Boycott in the commentary box was fully justified on this occasion. England managed to make a healthy total of 444 by the time they were all out on the second day, but there was still plenty in the pitch for the Australian batsmen and it was always going to be hard work for the England bowlers.

As had been predicted at the start of the match, Simon Jones had managed to get something with his reverse swing and bowled superbly, while Ashley Giles took Damien Martyn's wicket with a brilliant ball, pitched just outside leg before flicking the top of the off-stump. This was a delivery Shane would've been proud of, and if Ashley had any critics remaining at the start of the match, they now had no choice but to shut up. Unfortunately for Kevin, his fielding let him down once again when he dropped a catch, batted by Adam Gilchrist. There were no excuses; he should have caught it but he didn't. He was starting to gain a reputation as an unreliable fielder at Test level, which seemed extraordinary considering how good he'd been in the county game.

England made good progress, and it seemed at one stage as if they might be in a position to force Australia to follow on. However, bad weather on the third day seemed to cause England to lose some of their momentum and a number of players weren't quite as sharp as they perhaps could've been in the field. On the fourth day they were determined to make up for lost time and Simon Jones was the star of the show, taking six for 53, his best Test figures.

Kevin was especially pleased for his good friend Simon, not least because it looked as if his Test career might be over after he sustained that famous nasty injury in Brisbane, and he had worked hard and fought back to become a better cricketer than ever. Although it was always great to have the upper hand against the Aussies, on a personal level Kevin felt sorry for Shane, who had batted superbly for his 90 and deserved a century, before becoming one of Simon's victims. Kevin felt that Shane had developed into a genuine all-rounder in recent years and had earned a lot of respect as a lower order batsman. However, it seemed that Shane was destined never to make a century in Test cricket, just like getting his name on the Lord's honours board was never meant to be.

Australia were all out for 302, giving England a lead of 142. England's task was now to score runs quickly and efficiently, as there was a slim chance they still had enough time left to win the game, despite so much of the match being lost to bad weather. Marcus Trescothick got the England innings off to a good start, making a decent contribution with 41, but Andrew Strauss was the star of the final session. He survived a knock to the ear from the bowling of Brett Lee, getting it bandaged before piling on the runs. Andrew had experienced problems earlier in the tour in coping with Shane's bowling, but by this stage he had clearly devised a plan and it was time to test it out.

The innings was a huge success for Andrew, making his sixth Test century with 106 before McGrath got him. Ian Bell made 65, his second 50-plus score of the match, but Kevin disappointed once more when he was out lbw first ball to McGrath. He was less angry with himself than in the first innings, because it was the sort of thing that could happen to anyone and he didn't think it was the result of a serious mistake on his part. He had simply lost the slower delivery in the air and didn't get his bat down before the ball hit his pads.

As the fourth day drew to a close, the most important thing for Michael Vaughan to do was declare at the right time. He called his batsmen in with his side on 280 for six, leaving the Aussies needing 423 to win. This was the sort of target that is hardly ever reached in the final innings of a Test match. Yet everyone knew that Australia were more than capable of batting all the way through the fifth day to force a draw, and there was still a lot of work to be done if England were to win the match.

As they began their coach journey to the ground on the final day, the England team got a very real indication of how the Ashes series had captured the public's imagination. Lancashire had offered final-day admission of £10, or £5 for children, so a decent-sized crowd wouldn't have been that much of a surprise. It seemed to take an age for their coach to reach the ground. It normally took about ten minutes, but on this day it was at least an hour as they crawled through the traffic. Kevin could see thousands of people lining the streets around Old Trafford, and had assumed that the ground had been evacuated due to a bomb scare or something similar.

In fact, people had been queuing since 3am and the gates had been closed by 8:30am. Some 23,000 people had packed into Old Trafford, while another 20,000 were stuck outside. In the city centre, people were advised not to bother making the journey to the match. Demand for tickets was massive, like nothing seen in English cricket for generations. For the first time ever, more than 100,000 people had attended Old Trafford during the five days of the Test. Kevin knew that the press was giving the series more coverage than usual, but now he had a real indication of just how much more intense the public's interest in the England team's performance had become. The crowd was awash with banners, and people wearing masks depicting local hero Freddie Flintoff.

Kevin did his warm-up in front of a packed, cheering crowd. He had never experienced anything like it, but it only served to make him more focused on the task in hand. There was a slight setback when he realised that his back was giving him more trouble than usual. An injury to his ninth vertebra had been with him for some time, which was to be something he'd just have to learn to live with and would probably never go away completely. It had flared up a bit more than usual on this important morning, but Kevin didn't even entertain the thought that it'd stop him taking to the field, and after a large intake of painkillers, his mind was very much back on the cricket.

The day got off to the best possible start when Hoggard bowled Justin Langer with the first ball. The Old Trafford crowd gave a massive cheer, and an important psychological point had been scored. But it was only one wicket, and this did not mean that the rest of the Australian batsmen were likely to collapse like a row of dominoes. Of course, all they had to do is play very conservatively and not lose their wickets. Matt Hayden and Ricky Ponting got stuck in, and they proved especially difficult for the bowlers to break down. Hayden in particular seemed to be able to find the gaps in the field where no-one was standing and built up a decent innings before the Flintoff eventually bowled him for 36.

At lunch, Australia were just two wickets down. This was proving to be very hard work, and things didn't get any easier in the afternoon session. Yes, England took important wickets, but every new Australian batsman that came in understood his job was to stay in and they executed this plan brilliantly. As the afternoon wore on there was an increasing, though still fairly remote, possibility that Australia would actually snatch the match from England, especially when Ponting reached his century.

By the time the tea interval arrived Australia were 182 for five. Adam Gilchrist struggled to cope with the reverse-swing from the older ball and he was dismissed for just four runs by Freddie. There was little chance of Australia winning now, but Ponting was still at the crease and was proving extremely hard to get out. England were now firm favourites to win, but to take the wickets of five very able batsmen in one session was a big task.

Michael Clarke came to the crease and proved to be the sort of partner Ponting needed. He stuck around for what seemed like an eternity before Simon got him with a quite brilliant reverse in-swinger. When they sent Jason Gillespie out to bat before Shane, the England team knew that Australia had given up any hope of winning the match, and that in itself was a huge boost. Just five balls later Gillespie fell victim to Hoggard and Australia found themselves on 264 for seven. Against any other country this would've been a case of just bowling out the tail-enders as quickly as possible, but there wasn't really such a thing as a tail-ender in this Australia side. There was still Shane to come, and Brett Lee and Glenn McGrath were better than the average tail-ender, and could guard their wicket effectively.

Ricky Ponting had passed his century and was joined at the crease by Shane. Cricket fans up and down the country were arriving home from work to find the match finely balanced. With 15 overs remaining, Australia were 314 for seven. Kevin was fielding at short mid-wicket when Shane hit a ball in his direction. He confidently dived after it and felt certain he'd get to it, but once more it was dropped. This time, the dropped catch might actually matter, and he knew it. However, he also knew he had to compose himself very quickly, put it to the back of his mind, and get ready for the next ball. It was in the past, and this was no time to dwell on it.

AN EVENTFUL SUMMER

With 10 overs remaining, England's hopes of victory, along with Kevin's morale, received a massive boost when Geraint took a superb catch off Andrew Strauss's thigh to dismiss Shane. Freddie celebrated with a peculiar caterpillar movement, or perhaps it was meant to be a break dance. Substitute fielder Stephen Peters, who was more used to playing county cricket for Worcestershire than playing on the biggest stage in world cricket, came mighty close to running out Brett Lee.

Soon afterwards the moment arrived that well and truly swung the match in England's favour when Harmison dismissed Ponting, thanks to some fine wicket-keeping from Geraint. There were 24 balls left and only one more wicket was needed. Glenn McGrath joined Brett Lee at the crease. This wasn't going to be easy. Simon was off the field suffering from severe cramp, while Steve and Freddie would surely be feeling drained after two gruelling back-to-back Tests.

Freddie had a decent lbw appeal declined, while Steve had tried his best to break them down, but had ultimately been unsuccessful. Australia had been let off the hook. However, Michael Vaughan once again gave an example of why he was one of the most respected captains in world cricket. He called his players together straight after the last ball and told them to look over to where the Australians were standing. He pointed out to them that the Aussies were celebrating like they'd actually won the match. When did they last do that?

He had made a very good point and had made the players pick themselves up straight away. This was the first truly competitive Ashes series for a very long time, and their reaction to a draw had shown in a way that they had learnt to respect the quality of this England side.

Michael's words were exactly what the England team needed to hear. They had emerged the stronger team from their second exhausting battle in as many weeks. It came as no surprise when the Aussies started making statements to the press saying that England had blown their big chance, but Michael made sure that every member of his team moved on to Trent Bridge knowing that they had the upper hand, and were capable of winning the Ashes.

Yet again this was a match that had everything, but on this occasion it was disappointing for Kevin on a personal level. It is too simplistic to say that dropping the catch from Shane's bat in the second innings had cost England the match, but there were plenty of respected people in the game who now openly said that his mistakes while fielding were costing England dear. This factor, combined with scores of 21 and a duck in the Test, made it a poor match by his standards. He still had a lot to prove before convincing all observers that he had the mental strength to be of value to the side in the most tense and important situations.

After two exhausting Tests, there was a week's break before the next match of the series at Trent Bridge. Kevin felt it was about time he put in a three-figure score with the bat, and was concerned by his inconsistent form at the crease. There were those who felt he should play straighter in the Test game, but ultimately he knew that he would only perform to his best if he played the game that came most naturally to him. Again, he had to judge where the fine line came between playing positively and taking unnecessary risks with his wicket.

The Australians had injury concerns of their own in the lead up to the match. Glenn McGrath had recovered unexpectedly quickly to play at Old Trafford, and had gone on to play in a tour match at Northampton without any hint of problems. Then, without warning, he was ruled out of the Trent Bridge Test with an elbow injury, which may have been caused by placing too much pressure on other parts of his body to protect his damaged ankle. Either way, he wasn't going to be playing and this had to be to England's advantage. He was once again replaced in the side by Michael Kasprowicz.

Jason Gillespie was having a dreadful series by his standards, and was replaced by Shaun Tait, a youngster who had gone through a short and unsuccessful spell at Durham. In sharp contrast, England would be unchanged for the fourth successive Test, which was a remarkable achievement in itself. If they could stay together for one more Test after this, they would become the first England team since Arthur Shrewsbury's side in 1884/85 to go through an entire Ashes series without making a change. Kevin valued the consistency in selection. It gave him the opportunity to get to know his team-mates well as players and as human beings. The days of the selectors making knee-jerk reactions every time a player had one bad match were thankfully over, and this, combined with an improvement in the treatment of injuries, meant that there was no need to make any changes to this side.

Kevin knew from his days at Notts that Trent Bridge was

very much a batsman's pitch, and he was naturally pleased when Michael won the toss and made the decision to bat first. There had been quite a bit of rain around in the days leading up to the match, which may have caused problems with the pitch, but they were proven to be unfounded once Marcus and Andrew got out to the middle. They showed this was definitely a batsman's pitch, reaching their century partnership at the incredible rate of five an over.

The partnership reached 105 before Andrew became Shane's first victim of the match, and when Michael took his place at the crease he continued to pile on the runs, making a half-century of his own. Unfortunately for England, Shaun Tait was making the most of his unexpected opportunity to play, taking the wicket of Marcus for 65 and Ian Bell for just three. When Kevin came out to bat, England had lost three wickets in 13 overs, with 146 runs on the board. Their momentum had been lost, possibly due to interruptions for rain. He knew this was his chance to make amends for the disappointing performances of late, and there could not be a better time, or a more suitable pitch, on which to make his first Test century.

Kevin's innings started well; he was playing confidently and luck seemed to be on his side as he got away with taking a few risks, like when Kasprowicz missed a chance to claim his wicket caught and bowled, and when Hayden missed a golden opportunity for a run out. After these initial scares he seemed to be bedding in for a long innings, but on reaching 45 he was caught Gilchrist, bowled Lee.

Getting caught out like this was bitterly disappointing for

AN EVENTFUL SUMMER

Kevin. Forty-five is a respectable score and significantly better than either of his performances at Old Trafford, but he had a great feeling batting out there and saw no reason why he couldn't go on and make a century. Some traditionalists considered Kevin's batting quite uncomfortable viewing at times. Yes, he had made half-centuries in the series, but he took too many risks for some people's tastes, and they argued that it was always only a matter of time before his luck ran out in every innings. The only way Kevin was ever going to answer such criticism was by scoring a century in an important innings, and he had just blown a chance to do exactly that.

After his heroics at Old Trafford, it was now up to Freddie to work his magic again. He had decided he needed a break after the last Test, so had gone for a few days' rest in France to recharge his batteries. It wasn't long before he showed the crowd that the holiday had done him good, scoring a century in a quite brilliant partnership with Geraint Jones. Kevin was naturally delighted to see the England total pass the 400 mark, but he was also pleased for Geraint, who had made 85 runs himself. Geraint had been under constant scrutiny in the press over his role in the side, which Kevin felt was unfair. Some pundits had questioned his ability as a Test batsman, but in this innings he showed just how capable he was.

England's lower order helped the score on to 477, a decent total by anyone's standards. Many cricket writers had predicted that Trent Bridge was where Matthew Hoggard would really come into his own, because the pitch tended to favour swing. Matthew had bowled well in the earlier Tests, but hadn't claimed as many big scalps as Harmison, Jones and Flintoff. Even so, he had taken important wickets at crucial times, and few would argue that the selectors were right to persevere with him.

Expectations of Matthew were high, and in the final session of the second day he didn't disappoint, taking the wickets of Langer, Hayden and Martyn, leaving Australia trailing at 99 for five at the close of play. The following morning England carried on where they left off, and the Australian wickets tumbled one by one, the highlight being Andrew Strauss's brilliant dive at second slip to dismiss Adam Gilchrist. Australia's innings seemed to be in terminal collapse, but Brett Lee added some respectability to their total with 47 runs off 44 balls. They were eventually all out for 218, and England forced them to follow on for the first time in 18 years. Simon Jones had been the star bowler on that third morning, completing his second five-wicket haul of the series, including four for 22 from 32 deliveries.

Michael Vaughan's only concern as he called the players together to discuss the follow-on option was whether his bowlers were too tired. He needn't have worried. Any lack of freshness was made up for by the high morale in England's bowlers, they felt up for it and wanted to keep the momentum going.

The 'real' Australia came through in that second innings, and they managed to get to 50 without losing a wicket before Freddie dismissed Hayden. Fate struck England a cruel blow when Simon left the field with an ankle injury, which was to end his summer and rule him out for the winter tour of Pakistan. He had been bowling superbly all summer, and winning the Ashes would undoubtedly be a lot harder without him. Simon had earned the right to consider himself one of the best fast bowlers in the world.

Australia got to 129 before they lost another wicket, when Justin Langer was caught by Ian Bell off Ashley's bowling. Their captain, Ricky Ponting, was batting well and had reached 48 when an incident happened that caused the only instance of bad sportsmanship between the two sides during the entire series. Simon's place in the field had been taken by Gary Pratt, an out-of-favour player for Durham. Gary threw the ball at the stumps, and the third umpire's verdict was required to determine whether Ponting had got his bat past the line in time. The England players were standing together waiting for the verdict when Ponting suddenly started shouting a load of angry words in their direction. Kevin didn't know what his problem was, and neither did anyone else.

Sure enough, Ponting was out, and he continued his tirade in the direction of the England balcony. His words were intended for Duncan Fletcher, who had been making some toast when he heard a commotion going on and had wandered onto the balcony to see what was going on.

It turned out that Ponting had been angry that England had allegedly been resting their bowlers during fielding sessions and had replaced them with agile fielders. What he hadn't taken on board was the fact that Simon clearly left the field in agony and was still at the hospital when the run-out happened, so they could hardly be accused of resting him for later.

The Aussies also seemed to get touchy about this after the match, making points along the lines of how only designated 12th men from the existing squad should be on the field, and how a bowler should replace another bowler. Yet this was the same Australia that allowed Brad Hodge, one of the best fielders in the squad and not the designated 12th man, onto the pitch at Old Trafford. Not only was he on the pitch, but he took a superb catch to dismiss Kevin on that occasion.

This episode transpired to be an important turning point in the series. Kevin knew that pressure had been mounting on Ponting ever since he had won the toss and wrongly put England in to bat at Edgbaston, and now, in this rather small technical matter, he had finally shown this. As for Gary Pratt, he had shown what a good fielder he was on that day, but his cricketing career came to an end when Durham decided not to renew his contract in August 2006. Yet his place in history was secure, and he developed a cult following among the England fans, as well as the honour of having the pavilion on Sky Sports' Cricket AM show named after him. He now manages a self-storage company in Bishop Auckland.

Damien Martyn's wicket soon followed, before the Australian middle order all put in decent scores. Nevertheless, England were very much on top and with plenty of time to spare, there were no excuses for not winning the match from this position, provided the weather stayed clear. Simon Katich also lost his temper when he was given out lbw off Steve Harmison's bowling. England were clearly getting to them.

Kevin's fielding was still an issue. This time, he dropped a catch from Michael Kasprowicz's bat, which made it a total of six such mistakes in the series. Again, there were no excuses; he should've caught it and he didn't. Australia put in a decent total of 387 in this innings. There were no centuries, but there were no ducks either. Everyone had contributed something to the cause, with only last man Shaun Tait putting in a single figure score.

England needed to score 129, and, with only one Test to play, if they succeeded they could not lose the series. With their batsmen having performed so well in the first innings, this should have been relatively straightforward. In fact, nothing had been straightforward in this series, and this relatively modest target was no exception.

In the team talk before they went out to bat, the instructions were to play the ball and not the situation. In other words, the batsmen weren't to do anything they wouldn't normally do. Marcus Trescothick started very well as he confidently made runs off the Australian fast bowlers. Everything was going well for England at 32 without loss, and they seemed well on their way towards reaching the target. Enter, Shane Warne.

Shane dismissed Marcus with his very first ball, and in his next over he added the England captain to his tally. He had taken two wickets for no runs in seven balls, leaving England on 36 for two. The match clearly wasn't over as far as he was concerned, and it wasn't long before he claimed the wicket of Strauss, with a highly disputable catch from Michael Clarke.

Kevin came out to join Ian Bell in the middle, and this was one of those rare occasions where he was feeling just a little nervous. Brett Lee claimed Ian's wicket with the very next ball, to leave England on a very scary 57 for four. Kevin now felt a huge weight of expectation fall on his shoulders, but it helped that the next man in was Freddie, who was on good form. Despite both men being highly entertaining, attacking, batsmen to watch, common sense prevailed as they both knew this wasn't a time for getting carried away. Between them, they got 46 runs in roughly as many minutes, and Kevin believed they were well on their way to victory when they reached 100 for four.

They had made just another three runs when Kevin allowed his restored confidence to get the better of him by attempting a completely unnecessary drive off Brett Lee, which was edged to wicketkeeper Gilchrist. Kevin felt this was his biggest low in cricket to date. He understood the stupidity of what he had just done. It had gone against everything they had agreed in the dressing room. Overconfidence had prevailed, and he felt he had let his country down at the worst possible time.

When he returned to the dressing room he didn't know what to do with himself. The match was now completely out of his hands and he sought comfort by chewing one of his rubber wristbands, which were the nation's favourite fashion accessory that summer. He was on edge, more nervous than he had ever been at a cricket ground.

AN EVENTFUL SUMMER

Freddie had helped moved the score onto 111 when he was bowled by a perfect delivery from Brett Lee. By now, Kevin wasn't the only person in the dressing room with their nerves on edge. Everyone knew the enormity of what was at stake. Lose from here, and the long summer's work had been for nothing and they would only have themselves to blame. The score was 111 for six, and 18 more runs were needed.

With the score on 116 a frustrated Geraint Jones took an unnecessary risk when he tried to hit a ball from Shane for six, only for it to reach Kasprowicz. This was a horrible situation to be in, and the entire dressing room was on edge as Matthew Hoggard went out to join Ashley Giles in the middle. Simon Jones was in no fit state to play cricket, but he was prepared to go out and bat on one leg, and have Strauss as a runner for him if necessary. Kevin was still chewing at his wristband. Steve Harmison was due in next, but he was mentally shattered by this experience.

The crowd cheered every single one of those remaining 13 runs as though it was a match winner, including the two no-balls signalled by umpire Steve Bucknor when Brett Lee stepped over the crease. To Matthew's credit, he had been working especially hard at his batting all summer and had become a reliable night watchman, but he could hardly be classed as a strokemaker. Yet with eight runs still needed, he cover-drove Brett Lee for four, in a shot which even the world's greatest batsmen, including Kevin, would've been proud to have played. The dressing room erupted with joy, but they soon came back down to earth with the realisation that four more runs were needed, and absolutely nothing could be taken for granted, especially when Shane was around.

It soon became clear that Matthew and Ashley felt far more comfortable against Brett Lee than Shane, who really was at the peak of his powers during this innings. Two singles later, and Ashley was to face Shane again. Just two more runs were needed when Shane bowled a rare full toss; Ashley struck it confidently but it went straight to Simon Katich's boot. Shane's next ball almost bowled Ashley. This was horrible for Kevin and the entire England team watching on the balcony. They could do nothing to help the boys in the middle, nor could they do anything to calm their nerves, which can't have helped whoever they intended sending out to bat next.

After what seemed like an eternity, it finally happened. Shane over-pitched on leg stump and Ashley stroked it past the infield. The ball was heading towards the boundary but they decided to run two, just to be on the safe side. The dressing room went wild this time; they had reached their target, but had made very, very hard work of what looked like a pretty small accomplishment. At the end, the team did a lap of honour for the crowd, which had clearly been through a similar range of emotions as the players.

Kevin was delighted but also very relieved. He knew he would have been in for a lot of stick if England had blown it in that second innings, because his reckless mistake epitomised everything that was wrong with England's batting, although having to face Shane at his absolute best certainly didn't make their job any easier. The Man of the

Match award deservedly went to Freddie, but Kevin was especially pleased for Ashley, who had taken so much unfair stick at Lord's. He had come through that, playing well at Edgbaston, bowling one of the greatest deliveries of spin ever seen at Old Trafford, and now making the winning runs in such a tense encounter.

England were 2-1 up and could not lose the series. Yet there was still one more Test to be played, and after four exhilarating games so far, there was no way, weather permitting, that the final match at the Oval was going to be a damp squib.

9
A NATIONAL HERO

The build-up to the final Ashes Test at the Oval began as soon as the match at Trent Bridge was over. From the moment Ashley Giles hit the winning runs, everyone watching knew the equation. Win or draw at the Oval, and the Ashes were England's. Lose, and the series was drawn, which, in this summer of high expectations, meant all the hard work had counted for nothing. It was now late summer and the football season was well underway, which normally meant that cricket would struggle to compete for column inches. Not this year it didn't. Everyone was talking about the Ashes. In the pubs, in the workplace, just about everywhere, football had to take a back seat until mid-September. Cricket was the order of the day.

For Kevin there was the matter of the Cheltenham and Gloucester Trophy final against Warwickshire to be played. In a sense, it was a welcome distraction from the intense pressure of the Ashes, and it was nice to be able to repay the faith Hampshire had shown in him by playing in this important game. His participation was not without its critics. There were plenty of people who felt that risking Kevin, along with Ashley Giles and Ian Bell, in this game was madness. The thinking was that England should always come before county, and they could sustain an injury, or tire themselves out by playing in this match. Kevin felt no such conflict of interest. He considered it an honour to play for his county and help try to give them their first piece of silverware since winning the Benson and Hedges Cup in 1992. He also found himself on the same side as Shane Watson, the Australian all-rounder who had been part of their one-day squad earlier in the summer.

Hampshire batted first and began the match well. A strong second-wicket partnership of 136 between Nic Pothas and Sean Ervine helped propel the side to a substantial total, but for Kevin, his batting performance proved to be another disappointment when he was caught by Ashley off Jonathan Trott's bowling for just five runs. Trott finished with three wickets for 35, while Neil Carter took five for 66. The Warwickshire bowlers conceded 20 runs from wides, but still managed to bowl Hampshire out with the last ball.

Chasing 291 to win, Warwickshire sent Carter out as a pinch hitter, a role he soon fulfilled, scoring four fours and one six en route to 32, and Nick Knight and Ian Bell did well keeping up with the required run rate. Just before he reached his 50, Ian suffered from cramps that limited his movements and he was caught by Chris Tremlett off the bowling of

Shane Watson on 54. This was a worry for Kevin, because it went without saying that England needed all their leading batsmen available if they were to maximise their chances of winning at the Oval.

Knight, a former England international, was the star of the Warwickshire innings, making 118 before becoming one of Andy Bichel's three victims. Warwickshire now needed 40 runs for the last three wickets. Shane Watson effectively stopped that, claiming the wickets of Dougie Brown and Ashley Giles in quick succession, leaving them needing 20 off the last over. This proved too much for Makhaya Ntini, who was bowled by Chris Tremlett with the second ball of the last over, and Hampshire won by 18 runs.

Kevin was delighted with the result, and was especially pleased for Rod Bransgrove, who had worked so hard behind the scenes to get everything right at the club, from having the pitch in great condition to having proper services to cater for the players' welfare. However, he had been little more than a bit-part player in the match, and this was a personal disappointment for him. If he had put in a decent score with the bat, the Hampshire victory would have been a much bigger one, and he would've liked to have done more to repay their loyalty to him, in a summer where appearances for his county were few and far between.

With the Cheltenham and Gloucester final out of the way, all Kevin's energies were now firmly back on the Ashes and that vital final Test. In the days leading up to the match, much of the press attention was centred on him. The fact that he had a dyed streak of either red, blonde or blue in his hair obviously made him stand out from the crowd and inevitably drew attention to him, but other aspects of his lifestyle brought some quite negative comments from certain quarters.

Kevin had received sponsorship from a London jeweller and as part of the deal they had pledged to give him a neck chain with '100' made out of diamonds on it if he made a century. He was also presented with a pair of earrings worth £50,000 to wear during the game. This sort of thing caused both Geoffrey Boycott and Mike Gatting to launch some strong criticism of Kevin's lifestyle and his willingness to get involved in such things. He was infuriated by these comments; these were both men who had achieved plenty in the game and as far as he was concerned, they should know better than most that wearing a pair of earrings will not make his batting any better or worse. He didn't see any contradiction between being a good Test cricketer and leading a modern lifestyle, and felt that these comments were completely unnecessary and didn't amount to constructive criticism. Cricket was fashionable for the first time in as long as anyone could care to remember, and Kevin was at the forefront of this. Provided these peripheral matters didn't interfere with the cricket itself, he couldn't fathom why anyone would have a problem with it.

On the day before the match Kevin tried to remain as relaxed as possible, spending much of the day with Shane Warne, partly at a charity event. Some people might have viewed it as unusual for two opponents to spend time together on the eve of a big game, but Kevin thought it civilised and commendable that they could do something for charity, with the outcome of the Ashes just about to be determined. Shane tried to score a couple of psychological points in some television interviews, but Kevin knew him well enough to know that it was all good-natured stuff, and it didn't bother him at all.

They were raising publicity for a company called BGC, an American firm that was particularly badly affected by the September 11 attacks in 2001. Their two floors in one of the World Trade Center towers were directly struck by one of the hijacked planes, and they lost a large number of staff, so every year on September 11 they donate all their takings on the trading floor to the families of the victims.

Kevin and Shane were recruited to raise awareness, as September 11 fell during the Oval Test. The chief executive gave them $50,000 each to donate to their favourite charities. Shane donated his to the Shane Warne Foundation, which assists seriously ill and underprivileged children, while Kevin's went to Barnardo's, since he loved children and wanted to do something to help those who hadn't been given the sort of good start in life he had.

BGC went a stage further when, on the eve of the final day's play at the Oval, they rang Kevin's agent, Adam Wheatley, pledging to donate $500 to Barnardo's for each run he scored on the final day's play. He obviously didn't need any incentive to try and bat as well as he could in a deciding match in an Ashes series, but this extra little incentive made it even more important that he, personally, had a good game. The night before the game Michael

Vaughan had called his team together for a pep talk. He told them, 'This is what we have prepared for. This is what we have waited for. Enjoy it.'

There was good and bad news on the injury front. It became clear long before the big day that Simon Jones would be playing no part in the final Test, or in any other cricket match for the foreseeable future. On a brighter note, the cramps Ian Bell experienced during the Cheltenham and Gloucester Trophy final proved to be nothing more serious, and he was declared fit to play. Paul Collingwood was preferred to Jimmy Anderson to take Simon's place in the team. As for Australia, the big news was that Glenn McGrath was back, which would've come as a massive boost to their morale.

Despite his captain trying to keep things as normal as possible, Kevin found it hard to treat this as just another game. Goodwill messages came in from Prime Minister Tony Blair, David Beckham, and many other well-known public figures. On the morning of the match the mood was fairly subdued as the players tucked into their breakfast, each person retreating into his own private thoughts.

The papers were encouraging the public to send good vibes to the players by joining in the singing of 'Jerusalem', which was played on the public address system at the Oval prior to the start of the match. As normally as Kevin or any other England player tried to treat the occasion, the fact was this was far from 'just another match'.

It was definitely a batsman's pitch and the captain who won the toss would undoubtedly give their team a significant advantage. Once again luck was on Michael Vaughan's side and he made the obvious decision to bat first. Marcus Trescothick and Andrew Strauss got England off to a great start as Glenn McGrath struggled to break them down. The first hour went well, and both England openers looked set to make big scores. Then, with the ball still relatively new, Ricky Ponting called Shane Warne on to bowl. The great man was, not for the first time in the series, in deadly form. From being 82 without loss, England were quickly reduced to 104 for three, with Shane taking each of the wickets, including Ian Bell for a duck. Then it was Kevin's turn to face his great friend and rival.

The innings began well; Kevin knew from the early part of the series that he could get runs from Shane, but he had to bat smartly and only take calculated risks. Kevin appeared to be settling in well, when, on 14, he tried to hit a ball to mid-wicket, but instead heard the ball hitting his stumps. Once again he had made a good start and failed to put in a big score. After such a promising start to his Test career, it had now been a long time since he made a really decent number of runs. He also knew he hadn't really 'landed' in Test cricket until he'd made his first century.

England's team spirit had been strong all summer, and there was always someone who could step up to the mark when something really big was needed. This time it was Strauss and Flintoff who produced the goods, adding 143, with Strauss making his seventh Test century in his 19th Test. There was a target for Kevin to try and beat!

By the end of the first day they had slipped to 319 for

seven, with Shane taking five wickets in an innings for the 31st time in his career, and the ninth time in England. Four hundred was generally regarded as the total England should aim for in their first innings, but they fell slightly short when they were all out for 373 on the second day. Nonetheless, this wasn't a disaster by any means and there was still everything to play for.

Justin Langer and Matthew Hayden got Australia off to their best start of the series. They made batting look easy as they made it to 112 without loss when the umpires offered them the light. For some reason known only to themselves, they accepted it, which was baffling, considering they needed to win the match – a draw wouldn't be good enough. Another unusual occurrence followed when the England supporters started cheering the players off the field. People who've paid a lot to watch Test cricket normally want their money's worth, but on this occasion, getting victory beyond Australia's reach was their priority, even if that meant their day out was slightly shortened as a result.

The start of the third day's play was delayed due to rain, but when the covers came off, Langer soon got his century and Australia seemed to be in cruise control, with the England bowlers rarely threatening their wickets. Hayden later passed his century, at a time when he was fighting for his place in the team. At the end of Saturday's play Australia were 277 for two, 96 behind England, and with plenty of good batsmen still to come in.

The first three days of the match had resembled traditional Test cricket, developing slowly and gradually, as opposed to the edge-of-your-seat drama that had captivated the nation all summer. This changed on the penultimate day when normal service was resumed. Not for the first time in the series, Freddie was the hero. After some promising bowling on the Saturday night he really hit to form on Sunday, when in 18 overs he took the wickets of Hayden, Martyn, Clarke and Warne. Along with Matthew Hoggard, he dramatically changed the course of the game; Australia had gone from being 323 for three to 367 all out, giving England an unexpected first innings lead. Now came the really hard part. They had a day-and-a-half to make sure they got a draw out of this game, and this meant batting for as long as possible, whilst making a decent number of runs along the way just in case Australia were given the opportunity to bat again.

This is what the summer had come down to. All that hard work was in the past; the only thing that mattered now was this innings. Kevin, along with eight other members of the team, was powerless for the time being. They just had to sit in the dressing room and hope Marcus Trescothick and Andrew Strauss stayed in, preferably while making a few runs at the same time. The mood in the dressing room was that of an eerie stillness. The England pavilion was normally a hub of activity, with the coach and captain dispensing advice and the physiotherapist treating the various ailments that inevitably come with a long session in the field. Not this time. There was no nervous chewing of wristbands, Kevin's habit at Trent Bridge. Instead, all the players felt a sense of inner calm as they waited to see how things panned out.

A NATIONAL HERO

Being stuck in the pavilion meant they had no control over the situation.

With just two runs on the board, England suffered their first major blow when Shane took Andrew Strauss's wicket with the aid of a fine catch by Michael Katich. The next man in was their captain, Michael Vaughan. There was still no cause for panic. Andrew obviously hadn't done it on purpose. Besides, he had made plenty of big contributions in the series, including 129 in the first innings. It was a disappointing way to end a successful summer's cricket for him, personally, but he could walk back to the pavilion with his head held high, knowing he had done more than most to try and win the Ashes for his country.

Trescothick and Vaughan batted steadily, and they soon got the England innings back on track. With the score on 67 for one, Vaughan made a rare mistake when he pushed at McGrath, which produced a spectacular catch from Gilchrist.

There was still a long way to go, but this wasn't a terrible situation by any means. It was time for Kevin to get padded up. He calmly put on his first pad, assuming he'd be in the pavilion for a while yet. Out in the middle, Ian Bell was dismissed first ball when he was caught by Shane at slip from Glenn McGrath's bowling. Kevin had to rush to get his second pad on and get himself out to the middle as quickly as possible. The time had come for him to rescue the innings. He knew full well that whatever happened next would be career-defining, and an innings he would never be allowed to forget. Fortunately, he didn't have time to dwell on that fact.

The time had come; the nation expected big things from

him, and he expected big things from himself. His mother had flown in from South Africa, and they joined his brother, Bryan in the stand. His father was unfortunately unable to make it, due to business commitments in South Africa, but they all understood full well the enormity of the situation. Somehow, the slight butterflies Kevin was feeling in his stomach had eased by the time he got to the middle, and he felt totally focused as he prepared to face the hat-trick ball from Glenn McGrath. The delivery was lethal, hitting Kevin on the shoulder as he attempted to take evasive action, too close for comfort to his bat and glove. The ball travelled on to slip and the Aussies all leaped up to launch a loud appeal. They knew that if this appeal was successful the Ashes would more than likely be theirs.

Umpire Billy Bowden didn't raise his famous hooked finger. Instead, he just said 'not out' in a very calm but firm voice. Kevin allowed himself a slight smile at Glenn, but he knew that for now, he just had to stay calm and focused. Then it was time for Kevin's final tussle of the summer with Shane. These little battles had lived up to expectation in virtually every innings, but, on balance, Shane just about held the upper hand. His first ball was typical of the excellence he had produced all through the series; Kevin edged the ball, it took a slight deflection off Gilchrist's glove before Matt Hayden at slip dropped it. Kevin had been very, very lucky.

Kevin knew that concentration was the key, but his nerves returned in a major way when Trescothick survived a close lbw appeal. He tried to recompose himself and kept focusing on the fact that this innings would probably make or break his Test career, and indeed England's summer. With eight overs to go before lunch, another pivotal moment in the match came along. Kevin was on 15 and was facing Brett Lee's bowling when he tried to smash the ball, only for it to fall to slip at neck height. The ball went into Shane's hands – and straight back out again. He was having some incredible good fortune out there, but considering the main task was to protect his wicket and stay in for as long as possible, he was taking far too many risks for some people's tastes.

It was clear that Kevin was running out of chances and he couldn't carry on playing like this. A few nights before the game he had spoken to his friend Greg Matthews, the former Australian international, who had given him some advice following his indifferent form all summer. Greg told Kevin that he hadn't been playing his natural game, and it was time to go out there, be positive, be confident, be arrogant and stop messing about. Good advice under normal circumstances, but was this really what Kevin needed to hear when the task in hand was simply not to get bowled out?

There were plenty of people who would've preferred Kevin to have thought more about one of Clive Rice's golden rules, which is to protect your wicket at all costs, because you are not much use to anyone if you're sitting in the pavilion. But Kevin had made up his mind, and he was going to follow Greg's advice. He decided not to try and bat out 70 overs by being negative, but to do it being positive. He walked up to Marcus and said, 'I'm just going to whack it now.' This was high-risk stuff.

Kevin's strategy seemed to work at first when he hit Shane for two sixes. He had no particular plans for individual bowlers, but just reminded himself to watch the ball. It sounded very simple, but it was an extremely easy thing to forget when out in the middle. It was a case of so far, so good, but England suffered a massive setback when Shane got Marcus out lbw. This was Shane's 168th wicket against England, beating Dennis Lillee's record. At 35, Shane had proved that he was still as good and dangerous as ever, and, if he chose to, he could be around for a long while yet.

The next man in was Freddie, and when he and Kevin spoke on his arrival at the crease they agreed that they should both just play their normal games, despite this being anything but a normal situation. Just four overs later and with lunch approaching, Freddie was caught and bowled by Shane. The plan hadn't worked; England had lost another vital wicket and the match had now swung very firmly in Australia's favour. Paul Collingwood, a batsman with a style very different to Kevin's, made his way out. Paul was a man who knew how to make runs, but was good at protecting his wicket when the situation demanded it.

Kevin was hit in the ribs by a lightning fast ball from Brett Lee and called the physio, Kirk Russell, for treatment. He needed to get off the field as soon as possible to get some proper treatment; he didn't feel he was up to facing another over from Shane. All he wanted was to sort out his injury, get back into the dressing room and regroup.

England reached lunch in the precarious position of 127 for five, only 135 ahead. Michael Vaughan showed once more why he was one of the most respected captains in the game, telling Kevin and Paul that the most important thing to do was to protect their wickets. He knew that if they could get through until tea, England would be okay. Kevin got his ribs taped up and spent most of the rest of the lunch break receiving treatment for the back injury that had plagued him all summer. There was no time for food, which was probably just as well. Instead, Kevin tried to keep himself relaxed and not to get too preoccupied with the importance of the next few hours, which were undoubtedly the most vital he had experienced as a cricketer. The fact remained that if either he or Paul were out early on, England would be in real trouble.

Despite the match being on a knife-edge, Kevin didn't think that the session after lunch was a time for pushing and prodding. Instead, the thought that with such short boundaries, if he could get a bat on the short balls there was a good chance they would go for six. What he experienced immediately after lunch was a sustained period of extremely fast bowling from Brett Lee. He was fast under normal circumstances, but this was some of the most intense bowling Kevin had ever faced. Australia really didn't want to lose the Ashes, and they were going to make England fight in every minute of play that remained.

Kevin managed to hit Brett for two sixes. His plan was working, but so fast was Brett's bowling that he managed to hit Kevin on the body three times. Obviously, he was still somewhat sensitive from his earlier whack on the ribs, but he was relying on adrenaline kicking in to ease the pain.

There was no way he was going to retire injured unless he absolutely had to. He hit another high ball that went too close to Shaun Tait for comfort, but the fielder never stood a realistic chance of catching it. Kevin had got away with a lot, but the fact remained that he was still in, and was certainly piling on the runs.

It wasn't long before Kevin played the shot that would become the defining image of this innings. Once again Brett bowled very fast, just outside off-stump. It wasn't quite short enough to pull, but somehow Kevin hit it flat-bat straight past the bowler for a blink-and-you-miss-it boundary. This shot was pure instinct – it wasn't the sort of thing he could practise and certainly wasn't something that can be taught from a textbook. By now Kevin was in 'the zone', meaning he was experiencing an intense sense of focus and concentration. He was pumped up and raring to go. Speaking to Paul at the other end in between overs didn't really interest him, so he kept the chitchat down to a minimum.

When Shane returned to bowl, Kevin felt he had won a psychological battle with his pal. Shane was going to bowl around the wicket, which is a negative tactic in itself. Here was the greatest spin bowler in the world, and indeed of all time, bowling on a favourable pitch on day five of a vital Test match, resorting to negative bowling. Kevin didn't think that Shane could bowl him around his legs. Yes, Shane had got people out that way before, but Kevin knew that it would take a monumental error on his part to fall into this trap. Yet this is exactly what so very nearly happened soon afterwards.

A NATIONAL HERO

Kevin crossed the line between playing positively and being overconfident, executing a reckless sweep shot that hit straight onto his boot before flying up and being easily caught. Umpire Rudi Koertzen walked over to his colleague Billy Bowden at square leg. Kevin knew that if this was referred to the third umpire he might well be out. Shane said to Kevin, 'Let's get it referred and get the right decision.' Kevin told him to do what he wanted, portraying a confident facade when inside he was feeling anything but.

Umpire Bowden felt certain that the ball had hit the ground rather than his boot, so Kevin was given not out without the third umpire being called. Kevin had no idea how umpire Bowden could be so sure – after all, he didn't exactly have the best view from square leg – but he certainly wasn't complaining. This really was his lucky day. He gave himself a minor telling off for playing such a stupid shot before recomposing himself. He knew he shouldn't ruin it from here onwards, but sooner or later he was going to run out of luck if he kept on trying to be too clever. Paul became Shane's next victim when England were on 186 in the 51st over. He had only managed to make 10 runs, but more importantly it was another wicket gone and England were six down. Five overs later Geraint Jones was bowled by Shaun Tait.

With tea approaching, Kevin's great friend Ashley Giles joined him in the middle. The intense focus of earlier on had eased somewhat for Kevin. He was now in a more jovial mode and decided to nickname Ashley 'George' after the actor George Clooney. Actually, it was Ashley who invited the nickname. He started the George Clooney thing in the dressing room. He noticed more and more grey in his hair but announced to everybody, 'I'm not going to colour it. I'm going to go natural and have a new look, the Clooney look.' He left himself open to banter and Kevin made the most of it. The nickname stuck. The match had, by now, swung firmly in England's favour. But there were still more than 50 overs to go, and England were seven men down. Nothing was certain.

By now, Kevin wanted to chat with Ashley after every single ball. This was the most important partnership either player had ever been in. Kevin shouted, 'Shot, George!' every time Ashley defied the Australian bowlers. Kevin knew that he was in a position to get the total way beyond Australia's reach. Shaun Tait had pace, but he was bowling some bad balls and Kevin took advantage to hit them for four. Despite the enormity of the situation he preferred being out there batting than being stuck in the pavilion. If he were to be out and waiting and watching he would've been a nervous wreck, completely unable to change the situation. At least when he was on the pitch batting he was in a position to do something about it.

Kevin made good progress, making his way through the nineties as he made the most of Tait's bad balls. Then the big moment arrived. He hit a cover drive off Tait for four to reach his first Test century. This was the moment he had waited all summer for, and it had arrived at the most important time. Kevin felt an array of emotions, but the biggest one of all was relief. Despite making some credible scores, particularly in the early part of the summer, there were plenty of critics who felt his style was not compatible with Test cricket. He had been furious with himself on several occasions for not making a much bigger score after such good starts. Now he had finally made it. He pointed his bat first to the dressing room and then to his mother and Bryan who were sitting on the families' balcony. The crowd rose to give Kevin an enormous cheer and a round of applause. They knew that the game was edging towards an England victory.

Kevin walked over to Ashley who gave him a huge embrace, before shouting in his ear, 'The job isn't done! The job isn't done!' He knew his friend was spot-on, and Ashley was quite right to stop him getting too carried away. Both men were now counting down every over; the match was theirs to lose, and it was up to them to protect their wickets. They were great friends but had contrasting personalities out there in the middle. Kevin was prone to playing flamboyant, attacking shots, while Ashley was more of a calming influence.

This was turning into one of the best days of Kevin's life. He was playing the sport he loved, and was batting extremely well. There were millions of people watching, and he was playing on the biggest possible stage. This was exactly the sort of thing he had been dreaming about since childhood. All of those tough decisions and sacrifices had been for days like this. It was now up to him to make the most of it.

Shane returned to the attack and Kevin edged a couple of balls short to third man, so he brought in a second slip.

Kevin knew he had to get Shane out of the way so he played some attacking shots in the hope that the Australian captain would bring him off. With 35 overs remaining, Kevin knew that England were nearly there. Shane was very tired by now, and there was little left in the tank. Kevin reached his 150 and signalled to his mother and Bryan again. For the first time he allowed himself to believe that the match was safe.

Australia decided to take the new ball, and Glenn McGrath bowled Kevin a great ball which hit his stumps. Kevin was out for 158, and he just smiled at Glenn and said, 'Good ball'. As he started his walk back to the pavilion, Shane ran up to him and told him to savour this moment. Kevin took this as a wonderful gesture from his friend that summed up the spirit in which the series had been played.

The crowd erupted and gave Kevin an enormous cheer as he headed back to the dressing room. They knew he had done enough, and had been the star in England's innings that would win them the Ashes. Kevin struggled to take it all in. For those few minutes he was in a daze and the whole thing just felt incredible. After everything that had happened out there he began to feel drained, but also incredibly proud of what he had just achieved.

Kevin had faced 187 balls for his 158, hitting more than a century in boundaries, with seven sixes and 15 fours. By the time he was out, he was on his third Woodworm Torch bat, having broken the other two in the process of the innings. Yet Kevin didn't consider it a perfect innings. He had given the Aussies at least three good chances to get him out, but when he was positive against Shane and Brett Lee he had been very, very good. Even after such a famous innings he thought there was room for improvement.

The whole team wanted to kiss and hug Kevin by the time he got back to the dressing room. However, his priority was to get changed as quickly as possible so he could be on the balcony for when Ashley reached his 50. He had remembered all the unfair criticism Ashley had gone through earlier in the summer, and had admired the way he had fought back to become one of the real stars of the England team in the later Tests. In a strange sort of way, Kevin was happier for Ashley than he was for himself when the moment finally arrived, and when he was out he received a massive hug from Kevin.

England were 335 all out, and there was barely any time left. Kevin made a point of clapping his great friend Shane off the field. He had just gone through one of his greatest ever series, and this would almost certainly be the last time he played Test cricket in England. What's more, he had been a source of support and encouragement ever since they'd first got to know each other at Hampshire. Despite the fact they were now playing on opposite sides, Shane had remained a true friend throughout the series and Kevin wanted to show his appreciation as he left the field for the last time against England. He later won the Australian Man of the Series award and few would argue that it was thoroughly deserved.

Michael Vaughan told his men to wear their England caps and enjoy every second of the short time they'd be out there to field. Steve Harmison managed only four balls before they were called off for bad light. The England boys knew it was all over, but the umpires wanted to do things by the book and waited quite a while before they ceremonially removed the bails. When that moment finally arrived, the party well and truly began in the England dressing room.

There were massive hugs all round, and champagne, cigars and beer. Everyone grabbed their Ashes winners' cap and T-shirt, which they'd dared not wear until the job was definitely done. These were mad celebrations, like nothing ever seen in an England dressing room before, or at least not for many, many years.

For Kevin, this victory had made everything seem worthwhile. All the years of hard work and heart-wrenching sacrifices had paid off, and this was a moment to be enjoyed. What's more, he was named Man of the Match, which was an added bonus. As glad as he was to win the award, he felt that this was a victory for the whole team and that there were several other very worthy candidates for the award in the side.

The players came out to receive the Ashes to the sound of wild applause and loud cheering from the crowd, and then began their walk around the boundary to show their appreciation for the great support they'd received all summer. Doing this was important to Kevin, because he knew how difficult the series would've been to watch at times, with plenty of scary moments and narrow escapes.

Kevin clearly doesn't like viewing tight matches from the pavilion, because at least when he's out in the middle, he can do something about it. If he's forced to sit and watch, he becomes nervous, or starts pacing up and down the dressing room. For this reason, he appreciated more than most players what the thousands in the ground and millions watching on their television sets around the country were going through, because he probably couldn't do it himself.

It was now nearly six o'clock and the evening news was starting on BBC One. The Ashes victory, that had been confirmed just minutes before, was the lead story. After showing brief clips from Kevin's monumental innings, presenter Sophie Raworth began an interview with Fred Trueman from outside his home in Leeds. Fred, who died in 2006 aged 75, was a likeable man with many good qualities, but revelled in his reputation as a curmudgeonly character, and was notoriously critical of the modern game. However, on this day he showed uncharacteristic cheeriness and couldn't hide his delight at what the England team of 2005 had just achieved. His mood reflected that of the nation. English cricket was enjoying its highest profile in living memory, and this was certainly the most important series win for many decades, arguably of all time. All this was happening with Kevin Pietersen at the forefront of the action: he, and Man of the Series Freddie Flintoff, were the most high profile members of the team and got the most media attention that night.

Back at the Oval, the players returned to the changing room where the celebrations went on for quite some time. According to *The Sun* they ordered a total of 10 cases of lager, three cases of white wine, two cases of red wine, two cases of champagne and one bottle of brandy. Kevin popped into the Australian room to have a quick chat with his friends Shane and Stuey MacGill. The atmosphere there was predictably downbeat but they treated Kevin courteously. Kevin felt especially sorry for Stuey, who had no part to play in the series, having been kept out of the side by Shane, despite being a superb spin bowler in his own right. He decided not to stay in the Australian room for too long because it might seem as though he was gloating, and he was still feeling on a massive high at what had just been achieved.

That night, it was a chance for everyone to let off some steam. However much the players wanted to play in the series, it was undoubtedly stressful, not only for them but for their families as well. Now, it had all been lifted and it was time to be truly relaxed for the first time in many months. Kevin went to a club called Kabaret with Simon Jones and a few of the others, and returned to their hotel near Tower Bridge at around 2.30am. Other members of the team were more hardcore and partied through the night, like Freddie Flintoff, who was still at the hotel bar when Kevin got in.

Kevin managed around three hours' sleep before getting up again for a busy day of high-profile celebrations. The players were asked to wear their suits for the day, which began with a breakfast reception at the hotel. This was the first time Kevin had drunk alcohol for breakfast. It tasted disgusting but it was a time for employing the hair-of-the-dog to cure his hangover.

After the reception Kevin staggered onto the open-top bus for the parade with a full jug of beer for the journey. He rarely drinks beer, but protocol had already been broken once that day and he was already too drunk to make a fuss. He was glad that his mother could be there with him for this special occasion. She had made plenty of sacrifices of her own in relation to Kevin's future, and he felt it only right that she should share in the rewards. The only slightly sad element was that his father, Jannie, could not be there with him.

On reflection, it may have been better all round if this aspect of the celebrations had taken place the following weekend. The England and Wales Cricket Board had put the plans in place long before the Oval Test, and there were those who felt they were tempting fate by arranging something like this before the Ashes had been won.

Holding it at the weekend would have given the players the chance to do plenty of partying of their own without having to worry about having to get up and be on their best behaviour the following morning. It would also have staved off criticism of players like Freddie, and to a lesser extent Kevin, who were visibly tipsy and bleary-eyed throughout the parade. They were obviously perfectly entitled to celebrate in style, but they received some press criticism for appearing in public view in such a state. There was also the added fact that the parade was taking place on an ordinary workday, whereas if it was being held at the weekend an even bigger crowd, especially children, would've been able to attend.

Kevin cannot remember very much about the parade itself, and he doesn't think this is because of his alcohol intake alone. The lack of sleep, the adrenaline, and the release of pressure all took its toll. One thing he does remember, however, is asking for the bus to stop because he was bursting to go to the toilet. He dashed into Starbucks, where the staff kindly cleared a path for him to reach the gents.

Despite it being a weekday, there were still many thousands of people lining the streets to greet their heroes. Everyone wanted a good vantage point, and some people resorted to hanging from dangerous positions on buildings to see the bus. This was at least as big a celebration as the England rugby union team winning the World Cup two years earlier, and a day nobody in attendance would ever forget. When they arrived at Trafalgar Square, the team, along with the thousands in the crowd, joined in as the loudspeakers pumped out patriotic songs.

Later on, the team went on to 10 Downing Street for a reception with Prime Minister Tony Blair and his wife Cherie. Kevin openly admits that politics isn't his strong point and there was always potential for embarrassment at this reception, especially considering the amount of alcohol he had consumed by this time. He got chatting to a lady and when she moved on he asked Ashley Giles who she was. He quickly filled him in; the lady was Cherie Blair. It appears no harm was done.

The players were a bit disappointed when all that was on offer to drink in Downing Street was water and orange juice. They grumbled a bit, and it wasn't long before the situation was rectified and some cases of wine appeared. One person Kevin did recognise was the Prime Minister himself. He has never disclosed what Mr Blair said to him, choosing to keep it private, but insists that it was a pleasant chat, and that he was delighted with what the team had achieved.

After Downing Street it was time to move on to Lord's for yet another reception. The following day the papers carried some excellent pictures of the team, especially Kevin and Freddie, looking worse for wear. Yes, there was some criticism from certain quarters who believed they should have been better turned out in public, but the vast majority of people were quite prepared to put up with that after everything the team had been through during the summer.

Kevin had made a massive contribution towards giving English cricket its proudest day in living memory. It was an innings that had come about as a culmination of years of hard work and tough sacrifices, and the partying and the drinking continued for at least a week after the open-top bus tour. When the celebrations eventually stopped and Kevin returned to normality after his monumental high, he knew one thing for certain: he wanted more.

10

BACK DOWN
TO EARTH

By the autumn of 2005, Kevin Pietersen was as much a household name in Britain as other leading sports stars such as David Beckham and Jonny Wilkinson. His exciting style of play, along with his flamboyant nature and willingness to stand out from the crowd, made him a marketing man's dream. The now-famous jewellery endorsements were just one example of how advertisers wanted Kevin to be associated with their products, and in the weeks that followed the Ashes victory he was inundated with offers to put his name to all sorts of brands.

The commercial opportunities for Kevin came thick and fast during days that followed the Ashes victory. Volkswagen lent him a £70,000 limousine and Burrells, the jewellers, gave him a £55,000 diamond pendant. He even had a sausage named after him by a butcher in Somerset. His face appeared on stamps and children have been suspended from school for having their hair cut like his.

BACK DOWN TO EARTH

Inevitably, the papers were going to take an interest in all aspects of his lifestyle – they wanted to know what girls he was seeing, where and when he went clubbing, and which restaurants he ate out in. Kevin was hurt by the comments made by Mike Gatting and Geoffrey Boycott prior to the Oval Test, as he never felt that any of his social activities or advertising endorsements ever affected his performance on the pitch. Certainly, his dedication to training and his desire to be a world-class Test cricketer were never in any question from members of the England coaching staff.

In his playing days Geoffrey had been critical of some of his England team-mates for drinking in the middle of Test matches, or not being in bed by 11pm. Those who shared a hotel room with him soon learned that it was in their interests to be in bed well before the curfew – he never took kindly to people waking him up after he had gone to sleep. Yet there had never been any question of Kevin drinking in the middle of Tests. His weight was exactly right and his physique was good. The press quite often exaggerated the extent of his socialising during the series, and the truth was that Kevin never crossed the boundary between work and play.

In the gaps between Tests, Kevin would allow himself nights out, and it soon became apparent that he couldn't go anywhere or be seen with anyone without the press making a big deal of it. He led a modern lifestyle and did all the things many men in their mid-20s do. Yes, he did things and went to places not normally associated with cricket's traditional image, but he didn't see it as a problem, provided it didn't affect his dedication to cricket. Chelsea and England footballer Frank Lampard became a close personal friend and he was seen partying with numerous other showbiz names throughout the summer.

Kevin's relationship with Australian art director Cate Pugh, his girlfriend of three years, came to an end in the early part of the summer. Shortly before the Ashes series began he had a fling with blonde saleswoman Gemma Hayley, who spilled the beans about his bedroom behaviour to the press. She told the *Daily Mirror* that during sex, Kevin would demand that she remain absolutely silent, but towards the end would ask her to shout his full name very loudly. Kevin was infuriated that this sort of thing was being reported about him in the tabloid newspapers, though he has never taken legal action against them.

Prior to the start of the Ashes, Kevin took a break by spending a day watching tennis at Wimbledon, where he met former Big Brother contestant Vanessa Nimmo, who had shot to fame the previous summer with her snogging antics during her stay in the house. Once again, their short relationship resulted in Kevin becoming the subject of tabloid gossip. Vanessa told *The People* that during their one-month relationship it was quite normal for Kevin to text her 20 times and call her 10 times every day. She went on to say that he was a man obsessed with shopping, and even suggested they could become the new Posh and Becks. Vanessa claimed that on the day of the one-dayer at the Oval in July, Kevin began texting her as soon as he got back to the pavilion. He texted her about 15 times, even from the toilet, and told her that someone had asked what was wrong with his bladder as he kept going to the toilet so much. Vanessa claims that on the evening after the Oval one-dayer, she joined Kevin, along with the rest of the England team and Shane Warne, for a night out.

It was her claims about what happened when they returned to the hotel that caused Kevin the most hurt and embarrassment. She told *The People*, 'Kevin was desperate for sex and kept pestering me all day. He sent one text that evening saying "Can't wait". But sex was really dull. He is definitely just a missionary man. I think he's used to girls doing things for him. His manhood is nothing to write home about. It was just about normal size, but I only ever saw it in the dark as he doesn't have sex with the lights on. After sex he turned over and fell asleep. I let that one go as I thought his mind may be on the cricket, but it wasn't a one-off. Throughout the relationship, he pestered me for sex, but he was just a flop. I certainly wasn't hit for six by his performance. He was a once-a-night flop. Kevin wanted to get it over as soon as possible and made me do all the legwork while he lay back and thought of England.'

Whatever the truth about Vanessa's claims, Kevin was certainly learning the hard way that he had to be careful who he trusted, and what sort of girls he got involved with. In his autobiography, he did say that a lot of things printed about him in the tabloids during this period were untrue. But the British press would, from now on, be interested in every aspect of one of the country's leading sporting stars, and this was something he'd just have to learn to live with.

Their relationship hit the rocks shortly after they were seen together at Michael Vaughan's testimonial dinner at the Dorchester Hotel. Vanessa claims that later that week, Kevin sent her a text saying, 'Good night miss clingy' and another, 'U need to realise u are a nobody trying to be a somebody'. Kevin and Vanessa's relationship came to an end when he was spotted leaving a nightclub with a mystery woman. Vanessa claimed that he sent her a text saying, 'You'll probably find out im cheatin on u now cos I was snapped leavin a club last night with someone'. Vanessa's parting shot to Kevin was to accuse him of being a man who believed in his own hype, and was someone who needed to concentrate more on his performance under the sheets than his batting.

At the V Music Festival in Chelmsford, Kevin was seen with a mystery brunette, and by the time of the Ashes victory in early September he was in a relationship with TV presenter Natalie Pinkham, the former girlfriend of Prince Harry and of rugby player Matt Dawson. Their relationship only lasted for a matter of weeks, but fortunately for Kevin he had found a girl in Natalie who wasn't interested in selling her story to the tabloids.

In early October, Kevin flew out to Los Angeles for a break, which drew many showbiz reporters to conclude that he really was looking to turn himself into the cricketing equivalent of David Beckham. Kevin was quick to quash such speculation, saying, 'No Hollywood contracts. I'm a sportsman, not a movie star.' Despite this, he was soon hobnobbing with celebrities and being romantically linked to Paris Hilton, the heiress, after Mickey Rourke got him into a party.

During his time in LA he began a short relationship with the supermodel Caprice Bourret, who was eight years his senior. By this time he had clearly learned to expect press attention focusing on his private life. He told one interviewer that winning the Ashes had changed the lives of every member of the team, saying, 'The profile of each individual has lifted so much, you can't do anything without being noticed now.' Yet because of his sense of individuality and his high-profile partners, Kevin had attracted more publicity than any other member of the team. His brother, Bryan, put it rather more bluntly, saying, 'He might have them throwing themselves at him now, but that is only due to who he is – because he's not the best looking bloke, is he?'

When Kevin was selected for the one-day World XI to play Australia in the ICC's Super Series in Melbourne, Caprice accompanied him on the trip. The series saw many of the world's greatest players brought together to play in a series against Australia, who were eager to get back to winning ways as quickly as possible after losing the Ashes. Kevin found himself playing alongside Brian Lara, and the two of them hit it off from the start, realising they had a great deal in common as well as sharing a work-hard, play-hard attitude to life.

The trip was less successful from a cricketing point of view. The ICC had tried to get the world's greatest players into one team, and while Kevin tried to take the series seriously, the reality was that they felt a lot like benefit games. Most of the players agreed that it didn't feel as special or as important as playing for their countries, and it didn't come as a great shock when Australia had the better of both the one-day series and the Test that followed. Kevin rightly predicted that the format didn't have a long- term future as a serious fixture on the international cricket calendar, despite it being an enjoyable experience to be a part of.

One of the highlights of the trip for Kevin was the ICC's gala awards dinner. He believed he had a pretty good chance of success in the emerging Player of the Year category, but it came as a great surprise when he won the one-day Player of the Year title as well. This was, after all, only his first year in international cricket.

After the relatively short trip to Australia, Kevin's fling with Caprice soon came to an end. Once again he was the target of criticism from many traditionalists in the cricketing world for the way he conducted himself in his private life. In truth, Kevin wasn't any different to many 25-year-old men. He liked clubs, bars and women. There were plenty of members of the England cricket team who were behaving similarly, but they did not enjoy anything like the sort of high profile Kevin had, and they generally dated girls who weren't public figures in their own right. For these reasons, the tabloids weren't as interested in them, so they escaped the sort of criticism Kevin received.

The late, great football manager Brian Clough used to encourage his players to get married and settle down when they were still quite young, and not to leave it too long before having children. His reasons for saying this were that having a stable home life usually made them happier, more contented people. This, in return, made them more focused on their jobs and less inclined to want to indulge in life's excesses. It would be unfair to accuse Kevin of not being committed to his cricket. Even at the worst of times he was more committed than most in training, but it's true to say that finding contentment in his private life, and not having to worry about what dirt the papers would dig up next, would allow him to concentrate more on his cricket. He wouldn't have known it at the time, but Kevin's life was about to change forever.

Those close to Kevin say that he is the sort of person who would know straight away when he'd met the right girl for him. One day he said to a friend, who was involved in music management, 'You must have some good-looking girls on your books, can you get me any numbers?' Kevin was joking, but his friend immediately suggested Jessica Taylor, a member of the group Liberty X. He knew who she was straight away, and told his friend to get it sorted. The man got in contact with Jess and gave her Kevin's number, and she agreed to give Kevin hers. They started texting one another, and got to know each other pretty well before they had even met. They went on a couple of dinner dates and Kevin very quickly realised that she was the girl for him.

Liberty X had emerged from the original series of *Popstars*, consisting of those who had narrowly missed out on being a part of HearSay, the band the programme had created. After cruelly being branded '*Flopstars*' by some media commentators, Liberty X had 10 consecutive UK top 20 singles, and were active for seven years, while 'winners' HearSay's success lasted for only a matter of months. There was already a cricketing connection for Liberty X, as they performed live at Edgbaston during the interval of the Twenty20 Cup final in 2004, with former England coach David Lloyd declaring he was a fan of the group while commentating on proceedings for Sky Sports.

Kevin liked everything about Jess. In particular he liked the fact that she was an independent and successful person, but was also very family-orientated and took her commitments seriously. He had never made any secret of the fact that he always wanted to have a similar sort of relationship to the one his parents enjoyed, and it meant a great deal to him that his parents took to Jess immediately when they eventually met.

Although it was still early days in their relationship, Kevin's life had changed. From this moment on, the womanising and wild partying would stop. Of course, he would still allow himself the occasional night out and knew he had to celebrate significant milestones with the England team in style, but Jess had brought him a sense of personal contentment he had not experienced before. Jess had added a new dimension to his life, and taught him a great deal about himself. He wanted to be with Jess all day, every day, and still finds it difficult to be separated from her for any length of time.

From the start, they were very supportive of one another's careers. Kevin has always been very interested in music and has made many friends in the industry. In those early days he enjoyed learning about her way of life and the process of putting songs together. He went to see Liberty X in concert and was very impressed by what he saw, and had really liked the other members of the band when he met them. This was very different to any other relationship he'd ever been in. In the past, he'd always been the one who made the money, but in Jess he had a girlfriend who was financially independent and was with him for the right reasons.

The old Kevin, the party animal whose private life had been splashed all over the tabloids, was gone forever. He had been mixing with people who would let him down, but those days were over. From now on, Kevin was a family man first and foremost, and without all the outside distractions of old, he could become even more dedicated to his cricket.

11

A CHALLENGING WINTER

The summer of 2005 had been, cricketing-wise at least, a fantastic time for Kevin. Winning the Ashes and being the star of the team in the final Test was an incredible achievement for a man whose international career had only just started. On the domestic front, he hadn't played too many games for Hampshire due to England commitments, but he was proud to play in the Cheltenham and Gloucester Trophy final, despite it being a disappointing game for him personally. With his private life settling down, Kevin could not have been happier by the time attentions turned to the winter tours. He did not have a single regret about his career to date, and wasn't bothered by the fact that his old county, Nottinghamshire, had won the County Championship without him. As far as he was concerned, this was largely due to them changing their captain. His old adversary, Jason Gallian, had been replaced by New Zealander Stephen

Fleming, who Kevin regarded as one of the greatest leaders in world cricket.

The time had come to focus on the next challenge, and the first tour of the winter to Pakistan. In a sense, the hard work had only just begun. England had proved they were the best Test team in the world by beating Australia, and the task now was to stay there. Every serious cricket-playing nation in the world would now raise their game when they played England, and Kevin knew he had to be up for the new challenges this attitude brought.

The last time England had toured Pakistan was in 2000, when they had emerged victorious. Michael Vaughan's England team was the first side to tour the country for quite some time, due to security concerns, and this was something they had to be aware of for the duration of the trip. Kevin was very impressed by the level of security provided to the team, and the facilities in the hotels were fine. However, the limitations to where the players could go and what they could do proved very frustrating for him. Night after night was spent playing on the Playstation or watching DVDs, which isn't really Kevin's cup of tea. He prefers to be out and about, but this was logistically difficult because of the heightened security risk.

The England team suffered a major blow when Michael Vaughan experienced a recurrence of some previous problems with his knees while batting in a warm-up match in Lahore. Vice-captain Marcus Trescothick took charge in his absence. He was a very capable deputy, but losing a skipper of Michael's calibre was a bitter disappointment.

Kevin's build-up to the first Test had seen him putting in some low scores, but he wasn't overly concerned by this, as he felt he was in good nick and could make the runs when it really mattered. A more pressing concern was the continuing injury to the ninth vertebra in his back, which had been troubling him all summer.

The first Test, at Multan, showed that playing on the subcontinent was very different to playing in England or Australia, and the team's inexperience of the conditions soon showed. Kevin only managed to make five and 19 respectively, but the biggest disappointment was for the team as a whole. They had dominated the first four days of play and were chasing 198 to win. They continued to play the sort of positive cricket that won them the Ashes, but they crossed the fine line and didn't adapt to the needs of the situation, falling 19 runs short. They should've won that match and Kevin knew it. Marcus Trescothick made 193 in the first innings and proved a good captain in Michael's absence. This was made all the more remarkable because he found out during the match that his father-in-law had sustained a serious head injury after falling from a ladder back home, something he concealed from the team at the time. He later admitted that this caused him enormous worry and he considered walking out at that point, but had taken advice from Duncan Fletcher and Michael Vaughan and decided to stay on.

England had failed to chase a target of under 200 for the first time since the fourth Test of the 1998-99 Ashes. This was a massive disappointment for a side that had gone to

Pakistan hoping to confirm their status as the greatest Test team in the world.

The second Test at Faisalabad was eventful to say the least. Pakistan made 462 in their first innings, and England were making steady progress in reply when Kevin came out to bat. He'd got off to a good start when there was an enormous explosion from one area of the stands. Security had obviously been an issue during the series but this was the only occasion when it was remotely threatened. For a moment nobody knew what was happening, and Kevin thought that the team might soon be on the first flight home.

Everyone's attention turned to the area where the bang came from. It turned out that it was caused by nothing more than a Pepsi-Cola gas cylinder exploding, which came as a huge relief to all. In the moments that followed the bang, everyone's attention was on trying to establish what had just happened. Everyone, that is, except Shahid Afridi.

The Pakistan all-rounder took the opportunity to try and scuff up the pitch when he thought nobody was looking. He did it to try and bring a bit of life back into the surface, but it was totally and utterly unacceptable. Kevin told Shahid in no uncertain terms that what he had done was out of order. Afterwards, the match referee called the Pakistan cricketer in and told him to look at the TV and explain what had happened. Shahid didn't need to look at it, and admitted his guilt and apologised for this disgusting piece of gamesmanship. He was subsequently suspended for the third Test and the first two one-day internationals.

Back on the pitch, Kevin went on to score the second

century of his career, but immediately after doing so he pulled Shoaib Akhtar and was caught by Mohammad Yousuf. Kevin had got to know Shoaib a little when they were both part of the ICC squad in Australia. It had been a disappointing trip for Shoaib, who didn't really make his presence felt and he knew he had to prove he was committed to the game in this series.

Shoaib treated the crowd to an unusual celebration when he claimed Kevin's wicket. He started flapping his arms about like they were chicken's wings, the significance of which would've been lost on most people. There was a bit of a story behind it. Back on the ICC tour, they were in Melbourne when the South African Makhaya Ntini said that he thought Kevin walked like a chicken, which gave the rest of the boys a good laugh. Kevin couldn't notice any resemblance himself, but Shoaib was just letting him know that he agreed with Makhaya's sentiments. The incident was all a bit of fun and there was no malice involved.

The match was high-scoring and England were set a target of 285 to win. Kevin made 45 in the second innings but England ended the game on 164 for six when time ran out. If there was another day's play ahead, Pakistan would definitely have been in the driving seat and a draw was a generous result from England's point of view.

England went into the third and final Test of the series in Lahore with a chance of still being able to square the series. What followed was the worst display from an England Test team for quite some time. Kevin managed to score a modest 34 on a very good batting wicket, helping England to a poor total of 288. To put this into perspective, Pakistan made 636 in reply. Kevin only got one run on the board in the second innings, and the side were all out for 248, as they crumbled to a dire defeat by an innings and 100 runs, losing the series 2-0.

When Kevin reflected on the three Tests against Pakistan, he felt that maybe the whole emotional experience of winning the Ashes had taken its toll. While he was ready for action in Pakistan, and didn't question the level of commitment from any one of his colleagues, it did take them all a very long time to come back down to earth after the Ashes euphoria. It was an experience that had changed all of their lives forever, and he thought that perhaps they were emotionally drained. After all, they had landed in Pakistan only a matter of weeks after that famous day at the Oval.

A week after that dreadful third Test, England had a chance to redeem themselves as a five-match, one-day series got underway in Lahore. By this time Kevin's back injury was becoming a very serious worry, and he had received a cortisone injection to try and help him get through to the end of the tour. In the first match of the series, in Lahore, he scored 56 to help the side to a 42-run victory under the floodlights. The next match, at the same venue, was more disappointing. England were bowled out for 230 and Kevin only made 28 before being bowled by Naved-ul-Hasan. It was an easy victory for Pakistan; they won by seven wickets with 36 balls remaining.

Kevin's back injury wasn't getting any better and it became clear that he couldn't carry on. With another big tour to India starting in February, it was decided that he should go home to rest and get some specialist treatment. He hated missing matches, and in his absence England slumped to a 3-2 series defeat, although they ended the tour on a high by winning the final one-dayer in Rawalpindi by six runs.

One advantage of going home early was that it gave him the chance support his old mate Darren Gough in the final of *Strictly Come Dancing*. Kevin received some criticism for being seen out so soon after coming home injured from an England tour, but he didn't see any problem with it. His back injury wasn't going to heal any more quickly by sitting at home moping, and it wasn't as though he was doing any strenuous exercise sitting in a chair in the studio.

Darren was himself criticised after he had ruled himself out of contention for the one-day series in Pakistan so he could spend more time with his family. Soon afterwards it was announced he had accepted an invitation to take part in the television programme. This decision effectively brought his international career to an end, but he had his reasons for doing it.

Duncan Fletcher's perspective on the whole episode was quite different. Before Kevin had left Pakistan, Duncan had asked him to keep a low profile when he returned to England. He told him he didn't want to hear stories of him living the high life in nightclubs while the rest of the team were playing in tough matches thousands of miles away. Kevin had not long returned when his column in the *News of the World* announced his support for Darren's inclusion in future one-day teams. When Duncan found out he was uncharacteristically angry. He got straight on the phone and gave Kevin an almighty bollocking. He was seething with rage as he told Kevin that he'd only been on the scene for two minutes and he had no right to tell the selectors how to do their jobs.

Kevin's defence was that he had not written the article, and blamed his ghost-writer. Duncan wasn't having any of it. Take the money, take the rap was his response. He asked Kevin how he could look the likes of Liam Plunkett in the eye, after effectively branding them useless. Seeing Kevin in the audience of *Strictly Come Dancing* was the last straw. Kevin told Duncan that Darren was a close mate, and he was entitled to support him. 'Haven't you got any mates out here?' was Duncan's response before slamming the phone down. Not for the first or the last time, Kevin had spoken out of turn and had rubbed a few people up the wrong way in the process.

On the dance floor, Darren was a massive hit. He was paired with British National Champion Lilia Kopylova and, with the support of Kevin and the thousands of people who phoned in to vote for him, he won the contest in memorable style. In one way, Darren's decision to accept the invitation to take part made sense. He was now 35 and his days playing for England were bound to be numbered, especially considering the knee injury that had plagued him for quite some time, and he had to plan for life after cricket. Darren has a fun and lively personality, and taking part in a programme such as *Strictly* gave him the opportunity to let it show, and thereby help provide him with future media opportunities. In the years since he has taken part in the *Strictly Come Dancing* live tour and has established himself as a popular national radio presenter, it's apparent that the gamble appears to have paid off. Certainly, Kevin did not begrudge Darren the opportunity. He had been a superb and loyal friend to him during that first tour to Zimbabwe and South Africa and he wasn't going to forget it.

As Kevin was convalescing, he thought that 2005 would end on a low point and the injury that had seen him leave the Pakistan tour early would be the final part of the story. However, shortly before the year's end he received the news that he was to be made a Member of the British Empire in the New Year's Honours List. Every member of the Ashes-winning side was recognised, which in most cases meant an MBE.

It became clear to Kevin that the time had come to put the Ashes victory behind them. It was in the past now, there was a very tough tour to India beginning in February and they needed to be completely focused on the present and the future if they were to reassert their status as the greatest Test team in the world. They would allow themselves one final day of celebrations for the Ashes victory in February, when, a few days before they left for India, there was a date at Buckingham Palace to collect their awards.

Kevin and his family wanted to make the most of this special occasion. His parents and brother Gregg had flown in from South Africa and his mother was especially excited by the prospect of meeting the Queen. Getting into the palace proved to be an experience in itself. Everyone, no matter how well known they were, had to go through several security checks before arriving in a large hall for a pre-event drink. There was only water and orange juice on the drinks trays, which was probably just as well considering the state many of the guys were in when they turned up at Downing Street after winning the Ashes.

The players were then shown a video explaining the correct protocol and the way in which things would happen. Those receiving MBEs were then split into groups of four, and Kevin was joined by Marcus Trescothick, Andrew Strauss and Simon Jones as they walked forward to receive their awards. The Queen had a few words for each of them, and she said to Kevin that cricket must be a fun game to play and watch. Kevin replied that it was certainly fun to play but he wasn't sure how much fun it was to watch the Ashes, considering it was so dramatic.

Next came the team photo with the Queen and the Duke of Edinburgh, which Kevin has come to treasure as a special souvenir. He especially liked the fact that the Duke was a bit of a cricketer himself in his younger days, so he had an appreciation of what the team had been through. Her Majesty then spent some time mingling with the players' families, and Kevin was impressed by how well informed she seemed to be and how elegant she looked. She spent about ten minutes talking to Kevin's family about Africa, which his mother especially enjoyed. The Queen then asked Gregg if he played cricket, and he came up with the witty response, 'No, but I taught Kevin everything he knows!' Her Majesty seemed to enjoy the joke. It had been a wonderful day and a perfect way to put their Ashes celebrations to bed.

Kevin was looking forward to travelling to India, although he was well aware that it was one of the toughest places for a cricketer to tour. He considered it an amazing country, similar to Pakistan but with more for the western visitor to do. However, it was a more frenetic place than Pakistan in which to work, and the playing conditions would inevitably bring with them new challenges.

England's build-up to the first Test was plagued with unforeseen problems. Kevin had to retire hurt with a rib injury after scoring 47 against a President's XI. It wasn't the most serious of injuries, but it meant he went into the first Test slightly under par. There were serious concerns with two of the spin bowlers in the squad. Ashley Giles had failed to make the trip after suffering from hip problems in Pakistan. Kevin's Hampshire team-mate, Shaun Udal, needed treatment in a Baroda hospital after his stomach reacted badly to some food. Michael Vaughan was still having problems with his knees and it became clear that they'd have to manage without him for this extremely tough tour. Then there was Simon Jones, who had gone through more than his share of serious injuries in the last few years. He was working very hard to regain his fitness in time for the first of three Tests, when he broke down in the nets with a knee problem. This was terribly bad luck, at a time when England needed to be at their strongest.

Then, out of the blue, came the Trescothick affair. Everything had seemed fine with Marcus when he was batting in Baroda in that last warm-up game. He had been an integral part of England's success in recent times and was someone Kevin had come to respect enormously as a batsman and vice-captain. The players were told that Marcus was having to leave the tour to deal with certain issues and they all had to respect his privacy and ask no further questions.

At the time, Marcus alluded to suffering from a virus or maybe burnout, which was a very real worry for many modern international cricketers with such a relentless and gruelling schedule. The truth was far more complex. Marcus was suffering from clinical depression and his decision to pull out of this tour was the first in a series of episodes that would lead to his eventual premature retirement from international cricket in 2008. He had been suffering from anxiety attacks since the age of ten, and had struggled during the tour of Pakistan. Essentially, he found it difficult being away from his family for any length of time. Whilst he was, and still is, happy playing for Somerset, he can do so knowing he is never more than three hours away from his family. This is obviously not possible when touring with England, but none of the boys knew of the real reasons for his departure at this stage.

Not one member of the squad questioned Marcus's right to leave the tour, and Kevin just sent him a text later that day asking if he was OK and offering his full support. Kevin sent him occasional texts throughout the tour but was careful not to pry. He wanted Marcus to know that they were all thinking of him and he was there if he wanted to talk.

Losing so many key players was a massive blow for England, but it provided the opportunity for three players in the A party, who were touring the West Indies, to come and join them in India. Alastair Cook, Owais Shah and Jimmy Anderson all flew over and it became clear that this series was going to test how much depth there really was in English cricket. The Ashes-winning side had to be broken up at some point, but these changes were happening far more quickly than anyone would have liked.

Three players made their debuts in that first Test in Nagpur: Alastair Cook, Ian Blackwell and Monty Panesar. When Alastair arrived at short notice from Antigua he had no time to feel nervous; it was a case of being thrown straight in at the deep end. Kevin didn't know him particularly well at the time but on his arrival, he knew he had something about him and seemed up for the challenge, despite having just flown through several different time zones.

Monty was another player Kevin barely knew before the trip. He soon learnt that he was a calm, gentle character who was very easy to like. Monty was a Sikh from Luton with Indian parents, yet the Indian people loved him and he got a hero's welcome wherever he went, which was quite a contrast with Kevin's experience when he toured South Africa with England the previous year. He had already proved that he was a very capable left-arm spinner, but there were some concerns about his batting and fielding. Kevin soon found out that Monty was prepared to work very hard indeed to brush up on his weaknesses, which impressed him greatly.

Freddie Flintoff became captain in the absence of Michael and Marcus, and it began well when he won the toss and put

A CHALLENGING WINTER

England in to bat. The side made a good score of 393, with Paul Collingwood being the star of the innings with 134 and Cook getting his Test career off to a great start with 60. Kevin, meanwhile, was bowled by Sreesanth for 15, but the main thing for him was that he was completely fit after his rib scare and hoped he could make amends in the second innings.

India were bowled out for 323, with Matthew Hoggard being the most impressive of the England bowlers, showing that there was far more to him than just being a conventional swing bowler, taking six wickets for 57. This was a special innings for Monty, too. He had gone on record as saying that his childhood hero was Sachin Tendulkar, one of the greatest batsmen the world has ever seen. Not only did he get to bowl to his hero, but he also trapped him on 16 to claim a very special first Test wicket. Monty went berserk, jumping around and running wildly; none of the guys could catch him to congratulate him on his very special achievement. He went on to add the wicket of Mohammad Kaif to his tally.

In England's second innings Alastair and Kevin put on a very special partnership of 124 to help England on to a large total. This was turning out to be a brilliant debut for Alastair, who made 104 to become the first England player to score a century on debut since Graham Thorpe in 1993. Kevin was batting at his best at the other end, making 87 from 100 balls, helped by a stroke of luck when he appeared to be caught and bowled in the 20s, only for the third umpire to rule that the ball had bounced off the pitch immediately after hitting the bat.

Kevin was out, caught Dravid, bowled Kumble, when he had reached 87. He felt that since he was in such good form, he probably should've gone on to make a century, but the priority was to make runs quickly, and he had to bat aggressively to put the interests of the team before his own averages, which is exactly how it should be. This was a classic Kevin Pietersen innings, which included a six and 14 fours. After an innings like that, he knew that Alastair would be a great guy to be batting with in future Tests and he had every confidence that the England side would be seeing plenty more from him in the years ahead.

With time being of the essence, Freddie had to pick the right moment to declare. It's a great luxury to have, and happens all too rarely in Tests, especially against the stronger sides, but it's also a fine balancing act between ensuring a big enough lead and having enough time to bowl out the opposition. Freddie eventually ordered the declaration with England on 297 for three, leaving India needing 368 to win.

India soon showed that they fancied their chances of reaching the target, with Jaffer and Dravid putting on a very strong partnership early on, but the match was eventually drawn with India on 260 for six. The England side were extremely happy to earn a draw, because they had proved in the match that there was a healthy competition for places in the side, with two of the three debutants having very good games indeed.

The squad moved on to Mohali for the second Test, which proved to be a happier time for Kevin off the field than on. Jess was able to fly out and join him during a break in her busy schedule with Liberty X, and his parents came over from South Africa to support their son. Kevin knew from observing others that cricketers were often in a better frame of mind when they had their loved ones around them. He soon found out that he, too, benefited from having his parents and Jess nearby. It made him a happier, more contented person and he found it easier to focus on his cricket.

Freddie once again won the toss and put England in to bat. The side failed to take advantage of a favourable pitch and were bowled out for 300. Kevin and Freddie were the best performing batsmen, making 64 and 70 respectively, but they both agreed that one of them should have gone on to make a big score. It didn't help that four of the specialist batsmen under-performed, but the innings proved that Anil Kumble was still a truly great spin bowler, taking five wickets for 76. He wasn't in Shane Warne's class, but had been a superb servant to Indian cricket and here he was, proving he was still at his peak at 35.

Freddie led by example when India began their reply, taking four for 96, including the key wicket of their captain, Rahul Dravid, on 95, to help England regain control of the match. India fared little better than England, being bowled out for 338. It was now up to the England batsmen to make the most of this opportunity.

Their response was, frankly, pathetic. One batsman after another gave his wicket away cheaply, often to straight-forward catches, including Kevin, who made just four runs when he was caught Dravid, bowled Harbhajan Singh. India made easy work of their target of 144, losing only one wicket in the process.

England had been a shambles in that second innings, and nobody was more disappointed than Kevin. The young team had shown so much promise in Nagpur, which went some way towards proving that the losses in Pakistan had been nothing more than a blip. Yet now, England hadn't even put up a proper fight in this Test, and Kevin was hurting. This Test was important to him, not only because he wanted to build on the achievements of Nagpur, but because he wanted to reward his parents and Jess's loyalty to him with a big score, and give them a good reason to remember the trip by.

The team were slated in the press for their collapse in the Test. The match flummoxed everyone, even the professional gambler who had infiltrated the press box and was removed shortly before the end. There was, however, a chance to square the series in the final Test in Mumbai, and they all knew that they had to get back to work and recompose themselves in time for the game.

England's problems with injuries and illness were to resurface, and once again they happened at very short notice. On the team bus going to the ground for the first day's play, it became clear that Alastair had gone down with food poisoning and would be in no fit state to play. This gave an opportunity for Owais Shah to come into the team. Here was a man who had only played one-day international cricket up until now, and it was a big ask for him to adapt to Test cricket at such short notice. He didn't have the luxury of allowing himself some time to adjust, or take a few innings to get his Test match technique spot-on. He needed to perform well in his first Test, because the fate of the series may well depend on a big score from him.

The match also saw the return of Jimmy Anderson, a bowler who made a strong impact upon his arrival on the international scene but had gone off the boil a bit in recent times. He was a hit with the ladies, and had pioneered the dyed streak in his hair long before Kevin came into prominence. Kevin warmed to Jimmy very quickly on meeting him. He liked him because he was a quiet lad who had worked hard to win another chance, and he knew he would seize his opportunity in this game.

The Indian captain, Rahul Dravid, had won the toss and taken the surprise decision to put England in to bat. There was to be no repeat of the last Test, as every England specialist batsman made at least double figures. Andrew Strauss was the big scorer with 128, while Owais Shah wasted no time in settling in, making 88 in his first innings in Test cricket. Kevin added a respectable 39, while Freddie was back to his old self with a half-century. When England were eventually all out for 400, it became clear that there were definitely plenty of players who could step into the team and perform if called upon, but there were clearly problems in getting the team to perform well on a consistent basis, especially on unfamiliar territory.

Jimmy lived up to Kevin's expectations when India began their response, taking four wickets as the home side were dismissed for 279. England didn't achieve their perceived results in the second innings, proving the theory that they had plenty of talent and depth, but lacked consistency. They were bowled out for just 191, with Kevin caught and bowled Kumble on seven. The only person who put in anything like a respectable score was Freddie, making a half century before being narrowly stumped. This was bitterly disappointing, but India were still having to reach a demanding target in 313, and they couldn't take victory for granted.

During a break in play Freddie decided that the team needed some unconventional inspiration. Matthew Hoggard's iPod had the Johnny Cash song 'Ring of Fire' on it, which happened to be one of Freddie's favourites. He played it through a speaker and as soon as it came on, all of the players, including Kevin, stopped whatever they were doing and started joining in. It became a loud sing-along and worked wonders for team morale. The guys took to the field with their heads held high and a spring in their step. India never stood a chance, and were bowled out for just 100. The series was drawn and England were back on a high.

When the team returned to the dressing room, they put on 'Ring of Fire' again to toast their success, and it became their touring anthem from then on. A member of the press asked Kevin whether 'Ring of Fire' was meant as some sort of comment on the food poisoning a few of the guys were suffering from, but he wasn't going to go down that particular route. Some of the boys in the England dressing room gave Monty some light-hearted stick after he made a comical mistake while fielding. He squandered an opportunity to catch the big-hitting Indian keeper Mahendra Dhoni when England were closing in on victory. Dhoni hit the ball high into the air, and it was travelling slowly in Monty's direction. Instead of claiming an easy catch, he looked at the ball, and watched it fall gently to the ground in front of him. It was a highly embarrassing miss that simply shouldn't happen in international cricket.

Everyone saw the funny side, including Kevin, who turned around to the England supporters sitting behind him and tried very hard not to burst out laughing. Fortunately, England were well on their way to victory by this stage and the incident was of little consequence to the match, and besides that, Monty had become a massive hit with the England team and the crowd during the tour, which was probably just as well.

Just two balls later, Monty had an opportunity to redeem himself. Dhoni played a very similar shot, and this time Monty took full advantage and caught him. Kevin knew he couldn't be too hard on poor Monty afterwards. After all, Kevin had made plenty of fielding mistakes of his own the previous summer, although not quite on this scale. The important point was Monty knew that fielding was an aspect of his game he needed to work on, and he'd shown plenty of will to improve in this area.

The result was an especially happy occasion for Freddie, who had just become a father for the second time and hadn't yet seen his new son. This was also an important victory for Duncan Fletcher, who had received criticism from sections of the press for some of the decisions he'd made. This important victory on foreign soil was ample proof that he was taking the team in broadly the right direction.

Kevin experienced a range of emotions when he reflected on the series. Of course, it had been wonderful to win that final Test in such commanding fashion, and he was as delighted as everyone to have drawn the series. Yet despite having a reasonably good average with the bat, he hadn't scored a century. Before the tour began he had decided that he would set himself the target of scoring at least one century in every three Test series he played in from then on, and it was a matter of personal disappointment that he hadn't achieved it this time around. However, the team was doing well, and he was pulling his weight, which was the main thing. It was important to remain positive and enjoy the victory for now.

The one-day series that followed was less satisfactory for England, as they slumped to a 5-1 defeat in the seven-match series, with one game rained off. However, from a personal point of view, it did have a few high points. During the series he became the quickest Englishman to reach 1,000 one-day international runs, and the joint quickest of all time, along with Viv Richards. To have his name mentioned in the same breath as the great Sir Viv was a tremendous honour for Kevin, and it was testament to the wonderful start he had made to his one-day international career.

The series also saw him claim his first international wicket. Bowling had slipped way down Kevin's list of priorities in the last 18 months or so, but he had been nagging for a bowl during the whole tour. He'd been practising in the nets and felt the time was right to give his off-spin a comeback. Freddie had been promising him a bowl all tour, but for one reason or another it hadn't happened. Kevin's opportunity came when Freddie was rested for the penultimate match, in Jamshedpur, and Andrew Strauss was made captain. The series was long since lost, and if there was ever a time to experiment with risky new ideas in international cricket, this was it.

Andrew shouted to Kevin, 'You're on next over.' Kevin thought his captain was joking, and maybe the excessive heat had got to him. However, Andrew was being serious, because he needed Kevin to bowl while he sorted out his allocation for the other bowlers. His first ball wasn't great, but his second bounced, turned and hit Harbhajan Singh's off and middle stumps. Poor Harbhajan couldn't believe what had just happened – he was expecting an easy ride from a man who had never bowled in international cricket before. For a moment, he refused to go anywhere. He just stood still while Kevin celebrated. In the end, Kevin shouted, 'Get off the field, you've been bowled.' For some reason, the umpires needed to confer. Harbhajan must've thought that wicketkeeper Matt Prior had knocked the bails off, but considering the off-stump was at an angle, this was unlikely. He just stood there mouthing expletives for quite a while, and Kevin said, 'There's no point swearing, you've been bowled.' Harbhajan eventually accepted his fate and walked off, but got his revenge on Kevin later by dismissing him and copying his celebration routine.

Kevin didn't mind Harbhajan mocking him like that. He

was just glad to have got his first international wicket under his belt and hoped that he'd be allowed to bowl occasionally in future. It was certainly one aspect of his game he'd be looking to practise more often when he got back to England.

The biggest low point of the one-day series for Kevin was a terrible bout of food poisoning which struck him in Goa. Jess had come out to see him once again, and they went out for a lovely meal of prawns and lobster. Kevin was feeling very ill indeed in the days that followed, and he felt sorry for Jess, who had come to India to relax and watch him play cricket, but was now forced to look after him. Fortunately, she didn't make any 'Ring of Fire' jokes and did a superb job as his nurse. The experience brought them even closer, and Kevin was now in no doubt that he wanted to be with her forever.

On balance, this had been a good tour for Kevin, but there were clearly areas for improvement. He had received some criticism for selling himself a little short with his shot selection at times, and his technique still needed some work. Certain respected pundits accused him, with some justification, of not going on to score big hundreds once he'd made promising starts in both Pakistan and India. Yet at the same time, it wouldn't be fair to praise Kevin for being positive yet criticise him when he got out, so it was important not to try and tone down his aggression too much. More importantly, after a blip, the England team had recovered and reasserted themselves as the kings of Test cricket.

12

BEING
THE BEST

Setting targets had become something that Kevin found useful in each stage of his cricketing career. It helped to sharpen his focus and to give him a clear sense of what he was trying to achieve every time he took to the field, for both himself and his team. Usually, he kept these targets to himself, or at most told those closest to him. But at the start of the summer of 2006 he openly declared in his *News of the World* column that he wanted to be the best batsman in the world. It was as simple as that.

The summer began with a three-Test series against Sri Lanka, which presented Kevin with what he considered to be one of the most daunting challenges a cricketer could face – the bowling of one Muttiah Muralitharan. Whenever Kevin had faced spin bowlers in the past, no matter how good, he worked on the principle that he should watch the ball right from the start of the run up, through the delivery, through the air until it reaches his bat. This approach worked fine with every bowler, including true greats like Shane Warne. In Murali, he had found someone with whom this rule didn't always work.

Here was a man who was almost double-jointed, and Kevin could watch the ball as much as he wanted but it was Murali's wrist that did everything. Murali's action was controversial for years. There were those who thought he was a 'chucker', but like it or not, his action had long before been declared legal and people had to accept and respect him for the great cricketer he was.

Kevin had decided that he could only pick Murali occasionally, but not nearly as often as with other spin bowlers. He thought he had to pick Murali through the air, as it would be impossible to do so just out of his hand. His strategy was to play a lot more for the ball that turned away, rather than the one that came back at him. He knew that if he picked it wrong and the ball moved into him, he would be able to react because of his leg-sided dominance. This way, if he missed, the ball would hit his pads and he would probably be OK. He thought that regularly playing for the ball that turns away from the right-hander, the doosra, gave him a very good chance of hitting every Murali delivery. However, if the ball then turned into him, as in conventional off-spin, his shape and posture meant that he would be in the right place to hit the ball anyway, even if he'd misread the delivery. To be clear on his approach to such an unusual but brilliant bowler was vital if he was going to put in big scores in the upcoming series.

BEING THE BEST

The one thing Kevin understood perfectly well was that facing Murali was not going to be a bit like facing Shane the previous summer. Yes, Shane was a wrist-spinner who bowled leg-spin, but there weren't nearly as many variations as there were with Murali. Shane had a googly, but it hadn't been seen too often in recent years due to a shoulder problem, whereas Murali could turn the ball in any number of directions whenever he wanted to. Another danger was that Murali bowled with a scrambled seam. Normally with off-spinners, Kevin could see the seam coming down at him, but this was impossible with Murali. This was going to be one hell of a challenge.

A week before the first Test, Kevin's mother and brother, Tony, visited him at his flat in Chelsea. Kevin always enjoyed seeing his family and was especially glad to welcome Tony to England and give him the chance to watch him play. Tony was a religious minister with his own church in Durban, which meant that he rarely had the time or the money to be away from home for long, and was the only one of the brothers who hadn't yet come to see Kevin play. On this occasion their father, Jannie, had paid Tony's travelling costs.

Kevin was very fond of Tony and had a huge respect for him and the life he led. When he first started to make his mark in cricket, it was Tony who would ring Kevin and ask him to do various things. However, as time passed he became more aware how stressful the life of an international cricketer could be, and told people Kevin was too busy when they wanted something from him.

In the days leading up to the first Test at Lord's the England boys were boosted by the return of Marcus Trescothick to their ranks. Marcus was looking far happier and more enthusiastic than he had been when Kevin had last seen him in Baroda. The lads were all keen to help Marcus put his past problems behind him and move forward with the important summer's cricket that lay ahead.

Kevin's ambitions for the series were clear, but Duncan Fletcher spelt out his aims in even blunter terms. He asked his batsmen, 'When was the last time any of you got a double hundred? It's about time you did. When you get a start, make sure you make the most of it.' These might have sounded like strong words, but Kevin was more than happy to hear them. Duncan was a man who shared a mind-set with Kevin and had similar ambitions for the team.

Freddie Flintoff continued as captain in Michael Vaughan's absence, and knowing that the Lord's wicket favoured the batsmen, he was delighted to win the toss and make the obvious decision to bat first. England got off to a great start, reaching 86 before Andrew Strauss became Murali's first victim of the summer. Marcus announced he was back to his best in emphatic style by scoring 106 before becoming Murali's second wicket. It was an important innings for Marcus because it silenced the critics who felt he had not earned a recall. To be fair, most of them did not know the real reasons for his withdrawal during the Indian tour.

David Graveney had asked Kevin to play it straight for 20 minutes when his turn came to bat. Kevin replied that he'd give it ten. As it happened, he played very conservatively for 45 minutes, grinding out every single run before resorting to his more natural game. He made steady progress, proving along the way that he was maturing as a cricketer. On reaching the fifties he was caught off a no-ball and was lucky to be reprieved. For a moment he was very angry with himself, thinking he had thrown it all away after he had made such a great start.

He decided that this was his chance to make three figures. Apart from the obvious talents from Murali, he didn't really feel threatened by the other Sir Lankan bowlers most of the time. He achieved his century on the second day and decided that he was going to take heed of Duncan's words and use this opportunity to try and make a double hundred.

It didn't happen but he'd got to 158 before being bowled lbw by Chaminda Vaas. This was the exact same figure he'd made at the Oval the previous summer, but he told the press that this was actually a better innings. People assumed this was a heat-of-the-moment statement, but Kevin stands by it. He believes that the famous innings at the Oval was played on adrenaline and emotion, and he was dropped two or three times. This time, with the exception of the catch off the no-ball, he had played a more sensible innings, making sure his concentration levels were perfect throughout. By the time he'd returned to the dressing room, he found that someone had already added his name and score to the famous Lord's honours board using a piece of sticking plaster. It was obviously only a temporary measure, and he would soon have his name inscribed properly, but it still meant a huge amount to him. Scoring a century in a Test at Lord's was an achievement nobody could ever take away from him, and his name would forever be on that board with so many of the greats of the game.

England eventually declared at tea on the second day, scoring 551 for six. Matthew Hoggard took two quick wickets to dismiss the Sri Lankan openers, both via lbws, leaving them at 21 for two. However, the third wicket partnership scored 50 runs in 87 balls to bring some respectability to their scoreline before the close of play.

On the third morning, Kevin took Tony out to the middle so he could inspect the wicket and gain some idea of his brother's perspective of the game. They then went to the England dressing room, where Tony took pictures of the sticking plaster with Kevin's name on it on the honours board – a great souvenir to show to his parents and his friends back home. Next they took the walk out of the dressing room in the Lord's pavilion, down the stairs, through the Long Room and out onto the pitch. It was important to Kevin to give Tony as full a perspective as possible, because he knew that he wouldn't have as many opportunities as some of the other siblings to see him play.

England forced Sri Lanka to follow on, but the match fizzled out into a draw, due largely to a number of dropped catches by the England fielders. This time Kevin wasn't one of the key culprits, but he was careful not to be too hard on his team-mates, because he knew only too well how easy it was to let opportunities literally slip through their fingers. There were no real explanations and could be no excuses. It was something they all had to work on during training and put right next time around.

Kevin moved on to the next Test at Edgbaston in a hungry mood. His series had got off to a great personal start and he wanted to put in some more big scores. The visitors won the toss and chose to bat first, but it was England bowlers who dominated the first day's play, with everyone chipping in to dismiss Sri Lanka for 141 by tea. Liam Plunkett was the star bowler, taking three wickets for 43.

England made 295 in reply, but this was largely down to Kevin's efforts, since he made 142 of those runs. He started with a textbook Test innings, playing positively without taking too many risks, and played Murali the way he had at Lord's. On reaching his century he decided it was time to enjoy himself and entertain the crowd a little. Soon afterwards, he played a shot that nobody who saw it would ever forget.

Kevin was gaining confidence against Murali and decided that, to a certain extent at least, he had sussed out the great man. What followed was quite extraordinary. In simple terms, he played a slog reverse sweep off Murali that he caught on the full and middled so well that it went for six. As the ball had left the bowler's hand, he had turned around and hit it left-handed into the crowd.

Incredibly, Kevin's priority in the moments after he hit that shot was to get a man who was moving in front of the sightscreen to sit down. He was so at ease with what he had just done and didn't think of it as anything out of the ordinary. Freddie was batting at the other end, and couldn't believe what he had just witnessed. He walked up to Kevin and asked, 'What was that?' There was more logic and reasoning to Kevin's choice of shot than immediately met the eye. He had just come down the wicket three times to Murali and hit him over mid-off for four, through mid-off for four and then cut the doosra for four. Murali responded to this by moving his mid-off and mid-on back and putting men deep at cow corner and deep square leg, thereby blocking all Kevin's options for big shots. Or so he thought. Kevin, on the other hand, felt the need to continue to hit big boundaries because he was so well established, and just decided in a split second to go for it. That said, even he was a little surprised by how far it travelled.

Murali certainly hadn't considered that Kevin would try anything like that when working out where to place his fielders, so much so that he told Kevin afterwards that if he ever tried anything like that against him again he'd beam or bounce him. Kevin admitted afterwards that the shot was a bit naughty, but it was not without precedent. He had played a similar shot once before in a match and had a net session in India the previous winter when he practised his reverse-sweep again and again, but never envisaged hitting it as far as this.

Murali got his revenge two balls later when he claimed Kevin's wicket lbw, which was in no way connected to any attempt at further extravagance. Once Kevin was back in the pavilion he soon received texts from his father and brother, Bryan, reminding him that he used to play that shot in the courtyard when he was a child, and now he was doing it in a Test match!

Good bowling figures from Matthew Hoggard and Liam Plunkett helped England bowl Sri Lanka for 231 in the second innings, which left them needing just 78 to win with well over a day to spare. A solid innings of 34 from Alastair Cook set England well on their way to the target, while Kevin fell lbw to Murali on 13. This was the second time in the match that Murali had claimed his wicket in this way, showing that he still had some way to go before he had sussed him out completely.

England won the match with six wickets to spare, and it had been a comprehensive and well-deserved victory. Kevin was given the Man of the Match award, which he had truly earned. This Test, more than any other since the Oval, had been won largely due to Kevin's efforts. In the first innings he had been the only England batsman who had performed to his potential, and without him the dynamics of the match, and quite possibly the result, could have been very different. The reverse-sweep was the icing on the cake, but the most important fact was that England got the right result, and it was the first time the side had won a Test when Kevin scored a century.

Four days later the final Test began at Trent Bridge. The pitch there normally favoured the batsmen but on this early June occasion it was hot and dry, which played straight into Murali's hands. England bowled Sri Lanka out for 231, with Jon Lewis and Freddie being the key bowlers with three wickets each. England replied with 229, of which Kevin made 41. Only Paul Collingwood managed to make more runs than him with 48. Murali had been Sri Lanka's best bowler in that first innings, but they had all pulled their weight with some tight and disciplined bowling to dismiss England with a low total.

A 66 from Sangakkara and a half-century from Kapugedera helped the visitors to a score of 322 in the second innings, leaving England needing 325 to win. There was plenty of time left, but it was becoming clearer that the pitch was developing in Murali's favour and it was going to be a tall order. When facing Kevin, it was apparent that Murali had done his homework. He bowled straight, didn't give Kevin any width, and put pressure on him to create his own freedom. This was going to be tough work. Kevin decided that the best way to play Murali was to watch him bowl at somebody else from the other end.

The plan didn't really work, as Murali soon took Kevin's wicket for just six. Everyone knew that the Sri Lankan would be deadly on a pitch like this, but nobody quite expected what happened next. One by one the England batsmen fell to him; this was his day, and he was going to make the most of it. None of the England batsmen had a clue how to play him on a pitch like this. They were bowled out for 190, with Murali taking eight for 70. A drawn series was a disappointment for all the England boys, but it was something they could learn from.

There was a week before the players had to regroup for the Twenty20 and one-day series that followed and it gave Kevin the chance to do something rather important. From the time he met Jess the previous autumn it hadn't taken him long to realise that she was the girl he wanted to spend the rest of his life with. She had looked after him when he was ill with food poisoning and had experienced many of the highs and lows of the last eight months or so with him. He didn't miss the partying or the womanising one bit, and loved nothing more than spending an evening at home with Jess, or going to a restaurant with her. But these weren't the only changes Jess had made to Kevin. Shortly after they met, Kevin had his hair shaved short. The multicoloured streaks were gone but many people thought they'd be back at some point. Jess made it known that she preferred his hair short, so it seems unlikely the varying looks of 2005 will be making a comeback.

As the months progressed they had got to know each other even better, and he had no doubt whatsoever that she was the girl for him, and that he wanted to marry her.

Kevin's traditional values meant that he thought it right to ask her parents' permission before going ahead and popping the question. They were delighted and gave him their blessing, which was very important to him. Shortly after the last Test against Sri Lanka he told Jess that they were going to a romantic castle (he has never disclosed exactly where it is, because he wants it to remain special) and they would be travelling by helicopter.

He had a diamond and platinum ring made specially, and felt certain she would say yes. Even so, he had a very nervous time about two minutes beforehand, which was under-standable. Then, during the meal, he went down on one knee and popped the question. Jess burst into tears of joy and said yes over and over again. It was a wonderful moment and the ring fitted perfectly. Kevin's parents were thrilled to hear the news, and so were all the other people who really mattered in his life. They didn't dare set a date for the wedding at this stage – it all depended on when their professional commitments would allow them a few days to themselves. For now, Kevin was relieved, and ecstatically happy, that he and Jess would be together forever.

13

OLDER AND WISER

There was no doubt that the cricketing summer of 2006 didn't capture the public's imagination to anything like the extent of the previous year. The touring opposition of Sri Lanka and Pakistan didn't provide the same high level of prestige that the Ashes brought, and this showed in the size of the crowds that attended the Tests. It didn't help that the best Pakistan paceman, Shoaib Akhtar, would be missing for the entire series, and their next best, Mohammad Asif, would only be ready for the final Test.

Another important factor was that live television coverage of domestic Tests had moved from Channel Four to Sky Sports, which meant that viewers needed to pay a subscription to watch the games. Inevitably, this meant that only a fraction of those who watched the previous summer's Ashes triumph were able to follow the side this time around. That said, the ECB were faced with an impossible dilemma.

The money on offer from terrestrial broadcasters was not sufficient to cover the cost of central contracts, which most observers and players agreed would have been an enormous step backwards.

However, Kevin knew only too well that both he and the team needed to maintain good form in the upcoming one-dayers and the Test series against Pakistan if they were to carry the momentum through to the winter series in Australia.

In the event, the one-dayers were a massive disappointment for both Kevin and the team: he failed to make a century in any of the three matches in which he took part before being laid off through injury. His highest score was 73 at the Oval, with low scores in the other two matches, falling well below the level of standards he was now setting himself. The team went on to lose the series 5-0, and this emphatic defeat was a major worry for all concerned, with the World Cup less than a year away.

In the second half of the summer, the Test series against Pakistan was a success both for Kevin and for the England team, as they won the four-Test series 2-0. It started slowly for him at the first Test at Lord's, scoring 21 and 41, but he would remember that match for taking his first Test wicket – that of Kamran Akmal, who got a thin edge through to Geraint Jones.

England's first victory came in the second Test at Old Trafford, winning by an innings and 120 runs, but Kevin didn't play as great a part in the proceedings as he would've liked, making just 38. He did, however, make one important contribution in the field during the Pakistan first innings, taking a great catch to dismiss Inzamam-ul-Haq, who had made two half-centuries in the previous Test. This was an important moment for Kevin, not only because he had claimed the wicket of the veteran Pakistani captain, but because it laid to rest the ghosts of the previous summer when he dropped a series of potentially important catches. He had been working relentlessly hard in training to improve his fielding, and had proved, at long last, that he was a safe pair of hands who could be relied on to take good catches at important times.

It was a significant moment in Kevin's development as a player, given his aspiration had always been to be the best cricketer he could possibly be – and he knew that a vital attribute of a truly great cricketer was being reliable in the field. The real stars in this Test were Steve Harmison and Monty Panesar, who completely dominated the bowling, taking 19 wickets between them, the other being a run out. Geraint Jones aided with five catches despite suffering from a fractured finger.

Monty had taken his second five-wicket haul in three months, which led to some post-match praise from the Pakistan coach Bob Woolmer (who died in Jamaica during the 2007 World Cup), who had played alongside Derek Underwood, arguably the greatest England spin bowler of all time. Woolmer said, 'He's a fine bowler and is going to be a great bowler. He's a really good find for England. He beats people on both sides of the bat without a doosra, he's got a very good arm ball and bowls at a very good pace so people find it difficult to come down the pitch to him.' He added that Monty had got the better of Mohammad Yousuf, which was something none of the England bowlers had done for some time, and that he'd need to sit down with him to work out a way to play Monty. Kevin was delighted to see Monty making such a big impact after such a short time in Test cricket. He knew this was a man who would give the Australian batsmen a few things to worry about in the upcoming winter series and would be a regular fixture in the England team for many years to come.

By the time of the third Test at Headingley, Kevin knew that a really big score was long overdue, and this would be an ideal wicket on which to make it. Andrew Strauss won the toss and batted first. Kevin came in to bat with England on 110 for three; this wasn't a disastrous position to be in by any means but they needed one of the remaining batting specialists to put in a big score to give them a decent total.

Kevin knew this was a time for playing his natural game, but he now had a better understanding of where the fine line between playing positively and being reckless lay, having been playing Test cricket for more than a year. The innings that followed was one that summed up all that was good about Kevin's style of play. Any serious cricket fan either at Headingley or watching at home wouldn't have dared to leave their seats while Kevin was facing the bowling. He selected his shots in a smarter way than in the past, though when he had the opportunity he really made the most of it. He reached his century from just 123 balls before retiring hurt on 104 with cramp. When he returned to the crease the next day he pushed his score up to 135 before being caught by Shahid Nazir off the bowling of Mohammad Sami. This had been a breathtaking innings, with 20 fours and two sixes. After an indifferent start to the series Kevin had played an innings that showed he had matured and nurtured his ability, while still providing plenty of brutal and compelling moments.

A further century from Ian Bell, another from Andrew Strauss in the second innings, and some more brilliant bowling from Monty helped England to a 167-run victory, which won them both the match and the series. At last the England team had restored some of the damage done to their reputation the previous winter, and Kevin had been at the forefront of the victory with an innings that nobody who witnessed it would ever forget. There was one final Test to be played at the Oval, but the side more-or-less picked itself for the Ashes series ahead. Even if there were injuries, this summer's Test cricket had shown that there was enough depth in the squad to cope. Kevin couldn't have been happier with his own form, or the state of the side at this point.

The final Test of the summer at the Oval was one that will be remembered for all time as an occasion that did enormous damage to cricket's reputation. It started normally enough; Pakistan won the toss and put England in to bat. Inzamam-ul-Haq's decision to field first turned out to be the right one, as the England batsmen fell one by one, with Kevin falling to a golden duck off the bowling of Mohammad Asif. They were ultimately all out for 173, and Kevin's primary concerns at this stage were with England's lack of consistency. Although the series was won, he was keen to maintain momentum in the lead up to the Ashes and knew that they couldn't afford lapses of concentration like this while batting in Australia, no matter what the state of the match or indeed the series.

In response, the Pakistan batsmen took advantage of some indifferent England bowling, making 504, with Mohammad Yousuf top scoring with 128. The England batsmen regained their composure in the second innings, with Andrew Strauss and Alastair Cook both putting in respectable scores. Kevin continued the good batting and looked set for another century before falling just short after a rapid 96. It was frustrating for him because he played a shot he should have let go by, allowing wicketkeeper Kamran Akmal a relatively straightforward catch. This was a reminder that, although he had matured as a cricketer in the last 12 months, there was still a very long way to go before he was the finished article. Indeed, his mentality was such that he never considered himself to be a fully-rounded cricketer, and there was always room for improvement no matter how good he was. His priority now was to learn to keep his composure and concentration when he was batting well and making good progress. There was still an element to him that sometimes failed to seize opportunities to make big scores when he appeared to be batting well.

However, Kevin's innings would not be remembered for its brilliant stroke play or even the clumsy manner of his dismissal, but for an incident that occurred which would tarnish cricket's reputation for years to come.

The controversy arose when the umpires, Darrell Hair

and Billy Doctrove, ruled that the Pakistani team had been involved in ball tampering. They awarded five penalty runs to England and a replacement ball was selected by Kevin and Paul Collingwood, who were batting at the time. This was a serious allegation in itself but play continued as normal until the tea interval. It appeared as though the incident had been put to bed, at least until after the match. After the tea break, the Pakistani team, having mutually confirmed that no ball tampering had taken place and given consideration to the severity of the implication, refused to take the field. The umpires then left the field, gave a warning to the Pakistani players, and returned 15 minutes later.

After waiting two more minutes, the umpires removed the bails and declared England winners by forfeiture. The relationship between the two sets of players and respective boards remained cordial, and a deal was brokered between the cricket boards of England and Pakistan to allow the match to continue. The Pakistan team returned to the field 55 minutes after the umpires first took to the pitch for the resumption of play. Umpires Hair and Doctrove however declined to continue the game, maintaining their decision that Pakistan had forfeited the match by refusing to play.

The impasse continued until late into the evening, and Pakistan captain Inzamam-ul-Haq claimed Darrell Hair failed to inform him or the rest of his side of the reasons why the ball was replaced, and that Hair had implied that Pakistan were cheating. It was finally confirmed at a mid-evening press conference that the Test had been called off. The ECB statement said that England were awarded the match by the umpires as Pakistan refused to take the field after being warned that under law 21.3 failure to do so would result in them forfeiting the game.

This was a farcical situation, and was the only time in history that a Test had been decided in this way. The game of cricket itself was the biggest loser in the scandal. The Oval was traditionally the venue of the final Test of the summer and had produced many memorable occasions where a series had gone down to the wire, none more dramatic than the Ashes series of the previous summer. Now, it had become the scene of a ridiculous stalemate, which caused an embarrassing situation for the players, the respective boards, and the sponsors. This was the last thing the England players or the ECB needed, with an Ashes series around the corner, and when they were looking for sponsors and the general public to get behind the team in a major way, as they had done the previous summer.

As a result of Pakistan's forfeiting of the game, Inzamam was charged and found guilty of 'bringing the game into disrepute', though he was cleared of the charges relating to 'changing the condition of the ball'.

In January 2008 Pakistan's cricket board asked the ICC to change the official result to 'match abandoned' or 'match drawn' on the basis of having been subsequently cleared of ball-tampering by an ICC tribunal. In July 2008 the ICC changed the result of the match to a draw, though in October 2008 the Marylebone Cricket Club (MCC) said in a statement: 'The ICC has no power under the laws of cricket to decide that results should be altered, whether it feels it's "inappropriate" or otherwise.' The decision also angered former players, including Michael Holding who at the time was a member of the ICC cricket committee. Holding felt that Pakistan's refusal to play should not go unpunished, even though they were not guilty of ball-tampering. While commentating on a domestic match in England for Sky Sports, Holding said, 'I have just written my letter of resignation to the ICC cricket committee because I cannot agree with what they've done. That game should never, ever be a draw. When you take certain actions, you must be quite happy to suffer the consequences.'

After several years of wrangling, on 1 February 2009 the ICC reversed their earlier decision and changed the match result back to a win for England. It was an unfortunate end to what had been an enjoyable and ultimately successful summer of Test cricket, and it was a great shame that this little farce would be the one thing the world remembered from the series, rather than Kevin's innings at Headingley, Ian Bell's three consecutive centuries, or the rapid rise of Monty.

There had been a few blips, and consistency was still an issue, but it had been a largely successful summer's Test cricket for Kevin. He had scored 707 runs at 58.92 in the seven Tests, including three centuries, two of which had gone a long way towards giving England victory. His one-day form was much more of a worry, having failed to make a 50 in the end-of-summer one-day series, although he was on 42 not out when England won at Trent Bridge. The balance in the one-day side wasn't quite right, but the fact they had drawn the series 2-2 showed that there were promising signs with the World Cup around the corner.

The 12 months since the famous Ashes victory had flown by. So much cricket had been played and the squad had experienced an enormous number of highs and lows. Kevin had grown up as a cricketer and as a human being; he had contentment in his private life that hadn't been there a year before, and this in turn had taken an already ultra-professional attitude to cricket onto another level. In a sense, the Ashes victory felt like a million years ago, but in another it felt like yesterday, because he barely had time to reflect upon everything that had happened, so relentless was the schedule. The time had come once again to face the old enemy, but this time on their turf.

14
THROWING IT ALL AWAY

Nobody involved with the England setup doubted for a second that the upcoming tour of Australia would be tough. After all, England had the Ashes and the Aussies were bound to make them work twice as hard to retain them.

As far as England were concerned the purpose of the ICC Champions Trophy that took place in October and November was to get themselves in tip-top shape for the tour of Australia that followed. After losing their first match against India, England lost the second against the Aussies by six wickets. This was hardly what they needed and Kevin knew that the Australian press would give that particular match more credence than it merited. He scored 90 in England's final Main Round match against the West Indies, which came as a relief after his poor form in the previous one-day series against Pakistan just a few weeks previously.

When the boys arrived in Australia it quickly became

clear that this Ashes series would be played in a very different spirit to the last one. The papers were full of how this was the biggest and most important Ashes series of all time, and how the Aussie boys were more eager than ever to win back the famous urn. The Australian public are renowned for the level of support they give their team, but it seemed to elevate to a level not seen since the days of Kerry Packer's World Series as the days ticked down to the start of the first Test.

Respected cricket pundits in Australia had criticised Ricky Ponting and his men for their approach to the last Ashes series. They argued that the players had been too friendly with the England boys, and this was epitomised in the friendship that existed between Kevin and Shane Warne, although it's fair to say that this didn't affect the brilliance of Shane's bowling, which was as deadly as ever. This time, things would be different. The Australian players would keep a distance from the England men. There would be no socialising between Tests, and jokes and friendly gestures on the field would be kept to a minimum. Kevin's friendship with Shane was well documented but he genuinely liked mixing with Australians because they tended to share his mind-set and in-your-face attitude, so this change of approach was always likely to affect him more than most.

The England team experienced some setbacks even before a ball was bowled. Michael Vaughan, who had captained so brilliantly the previous summer, would miss the series through injury, as would Simon Jones who had proven himself as a serious threat to the great Australian batsmen.

Then, just over a week before the first Test, Marcus Trescothick left the squad due to a recurrence of his depression. The ECB and all of the players respected his decision, knowing, to a certain extent at least, the inner turmoil which he was going through. It was now very clear that he was suffering from a serious mental illness, and although he was still a reliable run-scorer back home, he found it very hard indeed to be away from his family and his familiar surroundings for any length of time. Kevin's main concern was for Marcus's welfare but there was no doubt that his departure also signalled a massive blow to England's batting line-up, as this was a man who, under normal circumstances, could play the best bowlers in the world as well as anyone.

Kevin's preparations for the first Test at The Gabba ground in Brisbane suffered an unwelcome distraction after some comments he made to *GQ* magazine caused an enormous controversy. He had professed his admiration for the late Hansie Cronje, who was banned for life after a match-fixing hearing, and claimed that Cronje had been a scapegoat for other players who were not punished. This was controversial in itself but it was his comments regarding Ashwell Prince's appointment as South Africa captain while Graeme Smith recovered from injury that really created a storm. Kevin denied he was a racist but questioned the motives behind Ashwell's appointment as captain. He said, 'I just thought it was further evidence that things were going downhill. It's got nothing to do with the colour of his skin. It's just that better players are being left out for political reasons and until that system changes, South African sport will continue to go downhill. I've got some mates who are now on the fringes of playing domestic cricket in South Africa who are better than three or four of those players in the South African side. I've got a very good mate who is actually a better player than me, who is now working for SA Breweries, because he can't get into the side for political reasons, and that's wrong.'

South Africa had asked for the ICC to take disciplinary action against Kevin for his comments, but he thought it was complete nonsense. He had received messages from a number of people he knew in South Africa telling him they were happy that at least one person was speaking out and telling it as it really was in the country. He might have had to face the serious charge of bringing the game into disrepute, which covers inappropriate public comment. It carries penalties ranging from a ban of two to four Tests or four to eight one-day matches. In the end, nothing came of it, but there were repercussions for his comments about Cronje further down the line. For the time being he was happy to brush off the fuss and focus on his preparations for the upcoming first Test, but it wasn't pleasant to have the word 'racism' associated with his name.

Preparations were going well for Kevin on a personal level. He scored a century in a warm-up game against an attack that contained four Australian pacemen. He lived the wickets in Australia more than the critics thought. There were those who believed they would be too quick for him, but he was really enjoying the experience. Of course he was slightly nervous, but he didn't consider this to be a problem because he needed to be nervous to get the best out of himself. The team preparation wasn't perfect, but Freddie Flintoff led his men out believing they had what it took to retain the Ashes.

On the morning of the Test at The Gabba, Ricky Ponting won the toss and elected to bat first. Steve Harmison was charged with the task of opening the bowling and his first ball became something that neither he nor anyone else who saw it would ever forget – but for all the wrong reasons. Back home, more than a million people had stayed up late to watch the opening exchanges, really believing their side could achieve something even greater than in the summer of 2005 by winning the Ashes on Australian soil. Their hopes suffered a comical blow immediately as Steve's first ball went incredibly wide to second slip. Kevin saw the funny side at the time and didn't read too much into it. In the days that followed Steve got a huge amount of stick for it, which Kevin considered to be grossly unfair. Yes, it was a dreadful first ball and would've looked more suitable coming from a quarterback in American football than from one of the world's leading fast bowlers. But Kevin felt that if a batsmen plays and misses, as he had done many times, it is quickly forgotten, but when a bowler bowls and misses, he gets a lot more stick from so-called 'experts'.

However, Steve's poor start was an omen for the rest of the innings, as the Australian batsmen made the massive total of 602 for nine before declaring, with England responding with a pathetic 157 all out, which included 17 from Kevin before he was bowled lbw by Glenn McGrath, who was returning to Test cricket after taking time out for personal reasons. Australia chose not to enforce the follow on, and continued their domination by reaching 202 for one before declaring, leaving England chasing a massive 648 to win.

When Kevin came out to bat England were on 244 for four, and he knew that his task was just to play for time, which was a tall order in itself, considering there was still more than a day's play to go. He made 92 before falling to an easy Damien Martyn catch off the bowling of Brett Lee, once again causing critics to say that he doesn't make the most of opportunities to make three-figure scores after good starts, but considering that Paul Collingwood was the only other England batsman to put in a decent score with 96, on this occasion he wasn't the main target of criticism.

While batting in the second innings, Kevin began to appreciate the extent to which the Australian's attitude had changed from the previous summer. They had adopted the nickname 'FIGJAM' for him, an acronym standing for 'F*** I'm Good, Just Ask Me'. This nickname had a slightly nasty edge to it, implying that he was somehow too big for his own boots and needed cutting down to size. Certainly, he knew he was good and rated his own ability, but, to his credit, he backed this up by playing flamboyant and match-winning innings at important times. There is a difference between being arrogant and bigheaded, and he felt that his confidence in his own ability was completely justified. Actually, the 'FIGJAM' nickname wasn't original

– it had been used for the American golfer Phil Mickelson long before.

Kevin often enjoyed sledging, provided it was done in the right way and didn't become too personal. This time, he noticed a nasty edge to it that wasn't there when the two sides met last. That said, he had been known to go a bit too far himself on occasions. During the one-day series in 2005 he responded to some harmless sledging by Shane Watson by saying, 'You're just upset because no-one loves you anymore.' This was especially harsh because Watson had recently been humiliated in the Australian newspapers after his high-profile girlfriend Kyn Johnson had left him for her dancing partner while she was competing in the Australian version of *Strictly Come Dancing*. It was an isolated incident, but it goes to show that Kevin was not always without blame in these matters.

This time, though, some of the remarks were a bit too personal and there was a coldness between the two teams that wasn't there the previous year. This was especially characterised with a marked change in his relationship with Shane Warne. The two had been close since Kevin signed for Hampshire and they shared a cricketing philosophy and a similar outlook on life. It was clear long before the Test that the warmth between the two men would have to be put to one side during the Ashes, but what happened when Kevin was batting during that second innings was something that would test their friendship to the limit.

Kevin knew that something more profound than on-the-field rivalry was taking place when Shane started to call

Kevin by his Christian name. Until now he had always been 'KP' or 'PK', but by addressing him in a more formal way it was clear that Shane wanted so send him some kind of message that the days of niceties between the two were over, at least until the end of the series. Shane then threw the ball at Kevin during the second innings as a warning not to step out of his crease. Kevin chose not to read too much into that particular incident.

Later, during a tense period of play, Kevin pushed one of Shane's deliveries to mid-off and stayed in his crease. Shane responded by hurling the ball straight at Kevin's head. This was going too far and was hugely unsporting on Shane's part. Kevin responded by calling Shane a 'f***wit'. He was absolutely livid at what a so-called 'friend' had just done. No matter how intense the rivalry between the two sides was, he should've known better than to throw a ball at a mate. It was clear that things would be different from now on.

Inevitably, the match was lost and the two men spoke afterwards to try and patch things up. Things were pretty much OK after the talk, and there was no more barracking for the rest of the series, although there was still a bit of an atmosphere between them and the friendship of old was gone. Although Kevin knew full well that Shane had received orders from on high to change his approach, it hurt him to lose a much-valued and close friend due to a cricketing rivalry. Duncan Fletcher was outraged at the extent to which the Australians had taken sledging in the first Test, describing it as, 'So foul-mouthed as to be a disgrace to the game.' However, the squad agreed that they would not allow the over-enthusiastic sledging from the Australians to distract them from the business of trying to retain the Ashes.

The second Test at Adelaide started brilliantly for England, with Kevin and Paul Collingwood leading the side to 551 for six declared. Paul had shown what a brilliant, if somewhat more conventional cricketer he was in his own right by scoring a double hundred, while Kevin scored 158 for the third time in his career, before being run out by Ricky Ponting. When Australia began their reply, Freddie and Matthew Hoggard seemed to be bowling brilliantly to dismiss the two openers cheaply. The match looked completely under England's control. Then, somehow, everything went horribly wrong. It started when Ashley Giles dropped Ricky Ponting and went downhill rapidly from there. Kevin felt really sorry for his good friend Ashley, who was normally such a safe pair of hands in the field. He knew only too well how Ashley was feeling, having done the same thing more than once in the last Ashes series.

Australia eventually reached 513, and England were 59 for one at the close of play on day four. All they had to do to secure a draw was bat through, or at least hold out for the vast majority of the day so the Aussies had no chance of being able to chase the required target in time. Things really started to go wrong when Shane dismissed Kevin for just two, to leave England on 73 for four. It was a dreadful dismissal, one of the cheapest ways Kevin had ever given away his wicket. Shane just bowled around Kevin's legs, while all he could respond with was an ill-timed sweep shot. Nothing went right from that point onwards, and they were bowled out for 129. After tea the Australians surged to 168 for four from just 32.5 overs.

The defeat hit Kevin hard, and after the match he reflected on what a bad shot that was. He expected far better from himself and felt he'd let the side down. To throw away a Test after making such a strong start was disgraceful and Kevin knew he had to accept a large chunk of the blame for that, even though the batsmen both before and after him had made some bad mistakes of their own. There was no denying the fact that with England now 2-0 down, and after the demoralising manner of the defeat, it would be very difficult to retain the Ashes.

In the days before the third Test at Perth, Kevin was interviewed by Alan Peacock of the ICC's Anti-Corruption and Security Unit, as part of a formal inquiry regarding those remarks in GQ magazine about Hansie Cronje being a scapegoat for other 'corrupt' players in South Africa. They were especially concerned by the following comments that were attributed to Kevin: 'At the end of the day (cheating) is wrong ... But I can see how it happens. Hansie copped a lot more than he should have. I think he took the brunt for the players. There are a lot of people who I think have done stuff that people don't know about and got away with it.' Kevin would have to wait several weeks before the findings of the meeting were published.

Meanwhile, there was talk in the papers of a heated disagreement between Kevin and Duncan Fletcher over his place in the batting order. The issue boiled down to whether it was right for Kevin to bat at number five. Kevin felt that this was his best position and the place from where he was of most use to the team. Duncan thought this meant that Kevin was batting with the tail too often, and wanted to move him up to number four. Kevin thought that by batting at five he would normally have enough time to build an innings. However, the way things had gone in recent matches, with wickets falling far too quickly, he often found himself facing the dilemma of whether to hit out, try to retain the strike, or bat normally far sooner than he was comfortable with.

This issue gained prominence during the second innings of the third Test, when England were chasing a massive 557 to win. If they didn't make the target, the Ashes were lost. It was as simple as that. When Kevin came out to bat, England were on 261 for four and the game seemed over. He took singles with the tail, thinking that he could put some faith in his team-mates and take runs when they were there. Then came instructions from the dressing room that he should wait a bit longer during each over before he took singles, to try and monopolise the strike a bit more.

Ricky Ponting saw what Kevin was doing and locked the field to stop him getting singles. The strategy worked and Kevin reached 60 before he ran out of partners and the game, and the Ashes were lost. Was this really the best use of England's most gifted batsman? In the end, Duncan let Kevin have his way and he stayed at number five, though it was certainly a controversial call on both their parts.

In truth, most people thought the Ashes were lost long before that final run-chase at Perth, and there was no real sense of shock or surprise at the end of this match as far as the travelling 'Barmy Army' were concerned. The consensus seemed to be that England blew it with the embarrassing manner in which they lost that second Test, and there was never really any comeback from there. Lots of things weren't right, and at a later date Duncan even criticised Freddie's leadership qualities.

The England players were hit hard by the reality that the Ashes were no longer theirs, and the mood in the dressing room was at an almighty low. Kevin felt that if the side, including himself, had played properly they would only be one down in the series. As it was they had been outplayed in three Tests, including the dreadful experience at Adelaide where they snatched defeat from the jaws of victory. The series, which had been built up as a huge clash of the titans, had turned out to be a one-sided farce dominated by Australia.

However bad England had been, and they were bad, all credit had to be given to Australia for the superb cricket they'd played. Their mind-set was that they not only wanted to beat England, they wanted to annihilate and humiliate them. They were like wounded animals after their experience in the last series and had regrouped, toughened up and worked hard to regain their status as the greatest Test side in the world. What's more, they had turned the most prestigious series in world cricket into a mismatch. The fact was, England's intensity levels weren't as strong as Australia's. There had been too many disruptions to their preparation, too many distractions and too many players under-performing or losing their concentration at vital times.

Back home, many supporters were outraged that Monty hadn't been included in the first two Tests. To many outsiders it appeared as though Duncan wanted to stick with the boys of 2005 as much as he possibly could, so he favoured keeping Ashley in the side for the time being. Yet Monty proved to be a real star when called upon in that third Test, taking five wickets in the first innings and three in the second.

However low Kevin and the rest of the England boys were feeling at the end of that third Test, it was all put into perspective by the terrible news they received midway through the match that Ashley Giles would be leaving the tour immediately because his wife, Stine, had been diagnosed with a brain tumour. It was a sharp reminder to Kevin that some things in life were far more important than cricket, and he offered Ashley, a close friend, all the support he could without wishing to pry into what was ultimately a private matter. The news soon leaked out and by the time Ashley's flight stopped off to refuel in Dubai it was being talked about on the TV news. It turned out that Stine's tumour was the size of a cricket ball and she required a major operation to remove it. Ashley received messages of support from all sorts of people in cricket, including a text from Shane Warne saying that his thoughts and prayers were with the Giles family. This really was a time for putting everything into perspective and keeping the Ashes in context. Fortunately Stine's operation, which she had just before Christmas, was a success and she has enjoyed good health ever since.

The Ashes victory also marked the end of an era for

Australian cricket. With the series won, Shane Warne announced he would be retiring from Test cricket once the remaining two matches were over. There soon followed similar announcements from Glenn McGrath and Justin Langer. All three were legends of the game in their own right, and would be a very hard act to follow. On Boxing Day morning, which saw the start of the fourth Test in Melbourne, Kevin accepted an invitation from Shane to be present at the breakfast for the Shane Warne Foundation. Despite their rather strained relationship in recent times, Kevin was struck by just how excited Shane still was about playing for Australia, despite everything he had achieved. This Test was to be his last at his home ground, the MCG, and a crowd of nearly 90,000 gathered in the rebuilt stadium to show their appreciation for one of the game's greatest ever players.

Prior to the match Kevin had another meeting with management about where he should bat. He reaffirmed his belief that he was most comfortable at number five, and they reluctantly agreed that any changes should only be made when he was mentally attuned for a switch.

Freddie won the toss and elected to bat, but the first two sessions were curtailed by rain delays. They were in the fairly neutral position of 101 for three, when, at 3.18pm, Shane bowled Andrew Strauss to become the first bowler to claim 700 Test wickets. Shane's celebration was over the top, even by his standards, but he had thoroughly deserved it. Kevin hugged his friend afterwards and said, 'Well done.' Shane clearly appreciated the gesture and said, 'Thanks for that.'

From that moment onwards their friendship was well and truly back on track. Kevin couldn't have been happier for Shane and knew that he was lucky to have played alongside and learned from one of the greatest players the game had ever seen.

England were all out for 159, due entirely to what was arguably Shane's greatest ever bowling performance, taking five for 39, including Kevin, who fell victim to the great man after managing 21 runs. Australia responded with a massive 419 as England's humiliation continued, thanks largely to 153 from Matt Hayden and 156 from Andrew Symonds, proving there was a lot more to him than just his fielding. The last time Australia were in England, Kevin had been involved in some humorous sledging at Andrew's expense. The Australian papers had claimed that Andrew had only been called into the side because of his fielding ability. During one match when Kevin was batting, he shouted 'Fetch!' every time he hit the ball in Andrew's direction, just to try and wind him up a bit. Now, after an 18-month wait, Andrew had well and truly got his revenge on Kevin by putting in a big score.

At the end of the first innings Kevin felt the time was now right to move up to number four. If there was ever a time for cutting your losses and experimenting for the future during a Test series, this was it. He was eager to make sure that Paul Collingwood was content with his wish, because he was the man who would have to move down the order to accommodate him. Kevin had further meetings with management and he was given the green light. The plan didn't get off to the best of starts, as Kevin was dismissed for just one run when he was bowled by Stuart Clark, and Paul Collingwood fell to Brett Lee on 16. England were once again bowled by Australia for a pathetically low score. They made just 161 runs, giving Australia victory by an innings and 99.

In the days that followed the Melbourne Test, statements were made by the Australian camp that made it clear that they were very hungry for the 5-0 series whitewash. Even Australian coach John Buchanan joined in the mind games, accusing Kevin of not being a team player. Buchanan offered little in the way of evidence to support his theory, but just added, 'Pietersen certainly talks of himself as a team player. I personally don't see any evidence of that, but that's from a distance. I don't reside in the England dressing room, but I do look at him on the field and he does seem to distance himself quite a bit from the team in where he fields. England may want him to field out on the boundary. But he's a good fieldsman and good in the ring. It surprises me that he always seems distanced from the rest of the group.'

Kevin chose not to fall for the mind games, insisting that his working relationship with his England team-mates was fine. He responded to the comments by saying, 'From what I could gather – so, from an outsider's point of view – the Australian team don't tend to listen much to John Buchanan anyway.' The fact was that Kevin regularly offered anyone in the England team advice on batting, which Monty in particular had greatly appreciated. As for the remarks about his fielding, it was pretty much up to the captain and the coaches where he should go, and that was all there was to it.

Before the start of the final Test at Sydney, a team meeting was held at which they agreed to draw a line under the 2006-07 series and start planning for 2009 in England. Even though this had been a truly dreadful series, they still had some pride to play for and it would've been fun to deny Australia the 5-0 scoreline they so badly craved. The Test really was the end of an era for Australian cricket, as this would be the last time that Shane Warne, Glenn McGrath and Justin Langer would be playing Test cricket for their country. It seemed pretty clear that they'd have some rebuilding of their own to do at the end of the series. In Shane they had a player who had surely guaranteed his place in the greatest XI of all time. There was a strong argument for including Glenn McGrath in such a side, with the West Indies attack of the 1980s his only serious rivals as the greatest fast bowler of all time. In Justin Langer they had a man with a batting average of 45.27, and someone who had proven himself to be a reliable run scorer in his 105 Tests over a 14-year period.

However much he admired and respected all three men, Kevin would've enjoyed nothing more than to spoil their farewell party. For once, England managed something resembling a respectable total, with 291 on the board, which included 41 from Kevin and 89 from Freddie. Even so, the fact remained that the momentum was very much with Australia, and this was a very difficult thing to fight against. They managed a total of 393, so going into the second innings the match was still competitive. It came as a surprise to very few people that England crumbled in the second innings: there seemed to be an inevitability about it. Andrew Strauss was unlucky to be given out lbw on 24, which wasn't the first time in the series that a close decision had gone against him. Kevin became one of McGrath's three wickets when he was caught by Gilchrist on 24, and the side was eventually all out for 147, leaving the Aussies needing just 46 to win. They managed it without losing a wicket in 10.5 overs, to complete the 5-0 scoreline for only the second time in Ashes history.

However inevitable it had seemed by the time of the Sydney Test, it had been a truly miserable experience for all the England boys, and Kevin knew he had to accept his share of the blame. He thought back to his dreadful mistake against Shane Warne in the second Test in Adelaide, after which the whole side collapsed and the Ashes began rapidly to slip away from England. All the hopes, the expectations and the excitement back home had ended with his humiliating damp squib. The travelling Barmy Army, who do so much to get behind the England boys at great financial and personal expense, had very few positives to remember this series by.

Kevin didn't spend too long in the Australian dressing room at the end of the final Test, and neither did any of the other England players. This was no place for them to be. None of the players thought at the start of the series that they could lose 5-0. Kevin felt totally drained, both mentally and physically. This was easily the worst low of his international career to date.

A few days after the final Test, Kevin received the

welcome news that the ICC's Anti-Corruption and Security Unit had accepted his assurances that he didn't have any specific knowledge of bribery or corruption in South African cricket. ECB chief executive David Collier confirmed that Kevin had been told to cease commenting on cricket in South Africa, though few who knew him expected him to stay silent for too long. Part of Kevin's character has always been his willingness to speak his mind, even if it lands him in trouble. In this instance he was forced into an embarrassing climb-down, as he was unable to back up his accusations with hard facts, but this was always unlikely to be enough to prevent him from speaking out in future.

England had the opportunity to salvage at least some credibility from the tour with the triangular one-day series that included matches against New Zealand. First, though, came a one-off Twenty20 match, which England lost by 77 runs. Kevin's luck wasn't changing, as he was run out by Shane Harwood on 11. Nonetheless, he felt that the upcoming one-day series was important both for him and the side, not only because it was an opportunity to salvage some pride, but because the World Cup was now only a few months away.

The first match against Australia seemed to be going well for Kevin. He was more like the Kevin Pietersen of old as he played some aggressive, attacking and flamboyant shots, making 82 from 91 balls that included four fours and three sixes. Just when it seemed as though his bad luck was coming to an end, he was hit on the ribs by a ball from Glenn McGrath. Coming down the wicket to McGrath was an attitude Kevin had adopted successfully during the 2005 Ashes and he felt no reason to change it. Glenn didn't like it, probably because not many people had done it to him over the years, and he didn't really seem to know how to cope with it. Kevin often succeeded in getting Glenn off his line and length by playing him this way. Yet this time, Glenn saw Kevin coming, and dropped it short, hitting him hard and fracturing his seventh rib in the process. Being hit in the ribs was always painful but this time it was especially so. Kevin's worst fears were confirmed when he was told shortly afterwards that he wouldn't be fit for the rest of the one-day series. He was not allowed to fly for a few days, but on the day he finally left Australia, England registered their first win of the tour by beating New Zealand in Hobart. He was both delighted and relieved for the team, but also bitterly disappointed that he hadn't been able to be part of a winning side.

Kevin's decision to leave the country so soon didn't go down well with a lot of people. He was heavily criticised after he was seen drinking in a Melbourne nightclub only hours after sustaining the injury. A few weeks later the former Australian captain Allan Border, speaking on Fox Sports' *Inside Cricket* show, criticised Kevin's decision to leave the tour early. He said, 'I've got to say he was on the plane before the X-ray came back. If he's got a broken rib, fair enough, but it wasn't displaced broken, it was just cracked, and given two weeks' break he could be playing. With England having a chance to scrape into the finals and he [would have been] a key man. Too quick on to the plane for my liking.'

Kevin considered Border's comments a massive insult. He firmly believed he would have had no further part to play in the series and his priority now was to be ready for the World Cup. He was furious that anyone should ever question his integrity, passion and commitment for the England cause. It came as even more of a disappointment to him when Graham Thorpe, the man Kevin had replaced in the England team, effectively endorsed Border's comments by saying, 'He was out of Australia pretty quick.'

On the other hand, Kevin had been far from gracious in some of the remarks he made on his return to England. He said it was a 'massive relief' to be out of Australia and added, 'It is a huge burden off my shoulders knowing I don't have to deal with all the abuse as soon as I wake in the morning. Mentally, the boys will come back tougher because it is an extremely hard tour, but I was glad to get away.'

In Kevin's absence England won the Commonwealth Bank one-day series with a convincing 2-0 finals victory over Australia, which was a considerable consolation prize. He was delighted that the lads managed this, which he considered a tribute to their character and determination to end such a disappointing tour on a hugely positive note. At the same time it was a massive personal disappointment for him that he wasn't there with them to share in their victory.

By winning the one-day series, England had sown seeds of doubt in the minds of the Australians, who went on to lose a one-day series against New Zealand 3-0. This was a great sign for England, and indeed all the other cricketing nations, with the World Cup now just around the corner. Kevin considered the win a huge tribute to the efforts of Duncan Fletcher and the captaincy of Freddie Flintoff. Yet for all the positives they could take from the one-day series, the winter of 2006-07 will forever be remembered as probably the most disastrous in English cricketing history.

15
MOVING ON

Although there were still more than two years to go before Australia would be returning to England, Kevin knew that preparations for the next Ashes series had to begin immediately. When he allowed himself a period of reflection after returning home, he realised that both he and every other member of the squad had to remember how bitterly disappointed, hurt and angry they felt with the way that the winter had gone, and make sure that it never, ever happened again. The Ashes tour had been a disaster but Kevin knew that England had not become a bad side overnight, and he was incredibly determined to come back.

Duncan Fletcher's position was a matter for immediate concern. He had been heavily criticised for several key decisions he made during the tour, especially his preference for Ashley Giles over Monty Panesar, which angered many fans and critics alike. The ECB announced after the tour that his position was 'under review', although he was given a reprieve for the time being. The general consensus was that if England's one-day form at the end of the tour hadn't been so good, Duncan would have been a goner.

The 2007 World Cup in the Caribbean was a massive disappointment for English cricket, and a low-point in the reputation of the sport itself. There was so much wrong with the tournament at every level: ordinary fans, especially the local population, were priced out of matches, and there were lots of empty seats in the various stadia used, particularly during the early stages. The tournament was too long, there were far too many mismatches, and too many games of no consequence took place. The suspicious circumstances of the death of Pakistan coach and former England player Bob Woolmer in March cast a dark cloud over the entire tournament. Two years later, the real cause of his death is still not certain, nor is it ever likely to be.

For the England team, 2007 was a tournament to forget. It will forever be remembered for the 'Fredalo' scandal when Freddie Flintoff got drunk after their match against New Zealand in St Lucia and had to be rescued from the sea after stupidly taking to a pedalo. However, one fact that is often overlooked is that six members of the squad were caught drinking into the early hours after their loss to New Zealand. They hadn't all acted quite as foolishly as Freddie, but was this really the sort of behaviour that was called for with further important matches just around the corner? Kevin knew that if he hadn't settled down with Jess by that stage, the person on the pedalo could easily have been him.

Michael Vaughan, who had returned as captain, believes the incident was largely responsible for England's dismal performances from the rest of the tournament. He said, 'We arrived at the World Cup in a positive frame of mind, but unfortunately incidents happened which affected the team. You have to be honest, the "Fredalo" incident did affect the team. It did affect morale. Suddenly you've got players who have no freedom left. I like to see players enjoy themselves but no-one would dare go out after that incident – and you can't create any spirit then. That incident changed the whole atmosphere in the camp.

'We went into the New Zealand game with a really good attitude but we didn't play well and after "Fredalo" we just started taking it all too seriously. That might sound silly but everyone was too tense and desperate. There was no escape – and even on the field you have to be pretty free, especially in one-day cricket. I was more tense than I've ever been as a captain. Duncan Fletcher was more tense than he'd ever been as a coach. And sometimes the captain and coach have to look at the way they're acting because the team follows. I didn't captain as well as I should've done because of the pressure I put myself under. I'd admit that. But I couldn't switch off because away from the field there was so much going on – with Bob Woolmer and "Fredalo".'

Among all the chaos the one man who could leave the World Cup knowing he had performed to the best of his ability was Kevin. He managed to block out all the unwelcome distractions and stick to what he does best, scoring 444 runs in nine innings with an average of 55.50.

In the games where it really mattered, he showed professionalism and dedication, making 104 against Australia and 100 against the West Indies, as well as two fifties against Sri Lanka and New Zealand. By the end of the tournament he was officially the world's best one-day batsman. Only two other England batsmen, Marcus Trescothick in 2005 and Allan Lamb in 1989, had ever achieved this feat.

A week before England's final game of the World Cup, the ECB announced that Duncan Fletcher's tenure as coach would finish at the end of the team's involvement in the tournament. He was quickly replaced by Peter Moores, the man who had coached Sussex to the County Championship title in 2003 and had more recently been involved with coaching the England academy. Kevin was immediately unimpressed. He didn't think Peter was suitably qualified for the job, having had a very ordinary career as a player. He'd led Sussex to victory in the County Championship but in his book this wasn't sufficient proof of Peter's ability. He believed there was far too much mediocrity in county cricket for this achievement to prove anything meaningful. He would have much preferred the ECB to show more ambition and approach a coach with known world-class credentials, such as his old mentor Clive Rice, or Mickey Arthur.

As they prepared for the upcoming Test series against the West Indies in the summer of 2007, Kevin soon found out that things would be working very differently under the new coach, and he didn't like it one bit. With Duncan Fletcher, the approach to coaching had always been calm and thoughtful. Whatever differences Kevin may have had with Duncan, he always respected him and acknowledged he was a man with ability. Peter's approach was, from the very start, much more in-your-face. There were certain little rituals for players who came last in drills and there was far less taking into account of the views of the captain. Senior players, who had earned their place in the England side and proved reliable and decent men over a long period of time, needed to be managed carefully, but Peter stuck to his egalitarian principles and treated them in the same way as he treated his county players at Sussex. His methods in training had quite a lot in common with the stereotype of the secondary school PE teacher, shouting and blowing his whistle.

Despite Kevin's reservations, and some general unrest in the direction of the coaching from a few of the more established players in the England side, the series against the West Indies was a great success, with a comfortable 3-0 win from the four Tests. The West Indies attack was relatively inexperienced and certainly didn't bring with it the sort of intense bowling that they had received from the likes of Glenn McGrath and Shane Warne the previous winter.

Kevin knew that the inexperience of the bowlers gave him the opportunity to make big runs. In the first Test at Lord's he scored a century that would surely have paved the way for an England victory on the last day if there had been better weather. He followed this in the next Test at Headingley with his first double hundred, scoring 226 off 262 balls, including 24 fours and two sixes. This was the highest score from an England player since Graham Gooch's 333 at Lord's in 1990.

By the end of the four Test series, Kevin had scored 466 runs. He now had 25 Tests under his belt and despite the inconsistencies, and the sometimes sloppy way in which he threw away his wicket, he had proven himself to be a brilliant run-scorer. Only Don Bradman had made more runs by his 25th Test. Kevin's tally of 2,448 runs at 54.40, including eight centuries, put him ahead of Everton Weekes and Viv Richards. On winning the Man of the Match award, Kevin said, 'I believe the recipe for success is hard work. I've been criticised for throwing my wicket away, and I tried to make it count here.'

Once again Kevin had shown that he was still an incredibly hard-working cricketer, who was constantly trying to improve himself as a player. While the team was doing well and he was performing to such a high standard, it was relatively easy to block out the problems he was having with Peter Moores.

The second half of the summer saw England take on India in a three-Test series, which turned out to be an evenly-matched and entertaining short series to watch. Kevin found some form in the first Test at Lord's with a knock of 134 in the second innings to set up a potential England victory. He described this century as technically his most complete innings to date, although it wasn't enough to win the match, as rain halted an England victory on the final day. In the second Test at Trent Bridge he didn't make an impression with the bat, but will be remembered for a bizarre incident on the Sunday when the Indian tail-end were batting. Kevin had played his part in the considerable amount of sledging that went on between the two sides, which included calling Sreesanth 'Harry Potter' because he wore glasses, but things soon went a step too far for Zaheer Khan's liking.

Jelly beans have long been a favourite among cricketers who use them as an energy boost, and also help to turn saliva sugary, which makes it easier to polish the ball. Kevin got into the habit of eating them at Hampshire thanks to Shane Warne, although Shane blames the sweets for his considerable weight gain in the late 90s. A jelly bean was placed at short leg, which caused Zaheer to lose his temper, so he walked up to Kevin at gully and brandished his bat menacingly. Zaheer thought it was put there as a reference to his weight, which had been a talking point for some time. Kevin seemed bemused and told anyone who would listen that Zaheer had got the wrong man. Alastair Cook was the most likely culprit, since he was the man fielding closest to the bean. Zaheer noticed another one behind his wicket, and then found when he turned around a few moments later that someone had thrown some more in his direction. The umpires ordered all sides to calm down and the remainder of the Test, which India eventually won, was played in something of a sour spirit. After the match, Zaheer remained adamant that the jelly beans were a bizarre piece of sledging, and was clearly insulted by the gesture. A charitable explanation for the jelly bean was that it was left to mark the short-leg fielding position for Ian Bell, but this didn't explain why so many were found behind Zaheer.

Kevin scored his tenth Test century in the third and final game at the Oval, helping England to draw the game with 101 and keeping the series deficit down to 1-0. On a personal level it had been another terrific summer for him in Test cricket, scoring 811 runs in 13 innings, which included four centuries and an average of 62.38. However, his one-day form was becoming more of a concern after the World Cup, but he recovered to end the season on a high. He scored 53, his first 50-over half-century in nine matches, and 71 not out as England won a thrilling series against India 4-3, giving new one-day captain Paul Collingwood a good start to his tenure.

England travelled to South Africa in early autumn to take part in the inaugural World Twenty20. In England's first game against Zimbabwe on 13 September, Kevin hit 79 runs off 37 balls, his highest Twenty20 score, including four sixes and seven fours in an English total of 188-9. England won the match by 50 runs. However, this was to be his largest contribution in the competition, as he only scored another 99 runs over four more matches, ending the series with an average of 35.60. England beat a poor Zimbabwe in the group stage, but then lost heavily against Australia. When they progressed to the Super 8s stage they lost all three of their matches against South Africa, New Zealand and India.

The winter schedule was busier and more complicated than normal, with the one-day squad arriving in Sri Lanka in late September, before everyone returned home on 15 October. Then, those taking part in the Test series would return to Sri Lanka on 15 November before coming home shortly before Christmas. This was followed by a tour of New Zealand in February and March.

The lifestyle of a modern international cricketer requires them to keep to a relentless schedule that has led many critics to say that this will, over time, cause a surge in instances of burnout and psychological problems. They are also often away at Christmas, missing out on special moments, like seeing their children unwrapping their presents. Fortunately, in this particular year, they would arrive home just before Christmas and would get to spend a good few weeks with their loved ones in January before preparing for the trip to New Zealand. Kevin decided to take advantage of this opportunity by arranging his wedding for late 2007, on 29 December.

During the one-day series in Sri Lanka it took Kevin until the fourth match to find his form, scoring 63 to help the side to a series victory. His form was still fluctuating in the warm-up matches for the Test series, scoring 4, 1 and 59 against the Sri Lankan Cricket XI. This run continued in the Test matches, the only highlight being 45 not out to secure a draw in the second Test.

In the first innings Kevin's dismissal was to be the source of much controversy. He edged his fifth ball to Chamara Silva at slip, who flicked the ball up for wicketkeeper Kumar Sangakkara to complete the catch. The two on-field umpires conferred over the validity of the catch, as it was unclear whether the ball had touched the ground prior to Silva flicking the ball up. Daryl Harper, standing at the bowler's end, gave the decision that the wicket had been taken, but while walking off the field, Kevin saw a replay on the big screen and questioned the validity of the decision. This led for calls for similar catches to be referred to the third (TV) umpire, but this can only take place if the on-field umpires have not made a decision. Kevin passed 3,000 Test runs during the series, becoming the fastest player (by time) to do so, but only averaged 25.20 and failed to score a half century in a series for the first time.

This was a poor series by his standards and was disappointing for the side as a whole, as they slumped to a 1-0 series defeat. Mahaela Jayawardene claimed that England's approach had been too negative, which certainly seemed true in the first innings of the final Test when they were bowled for 81. Bob Willis, speaking on Sky Sports, described England's batting performance as an 'absolute disgrace'. In truth, they were probably only spared defeat in that final Test due to some considerable assistance from the weather during the last two days.

When the team had been playing well, Kevin found it easy to put his problems with Peter Moores to one side. Now that things had started to go very badly wrong it wasn't quite so straightforward. Kevin would've appreciated some guidance on how to return to form from a coach he looked up to, and there was a very strong argument for changing the team line-up substantially. Many of the changes Peter had made evidently hadn't worked. Monty had also gone through a terrible series, after making a brilliant impression during most of his first year in international cricket. Every player goes through a bad spell at some point, and it is a test of character as to how they come through it. Right now what Kevin, Monty, and possibly a few others, needed was help from a coach who knew how to get the best from them, and that person didn't appear to be Peter.

Kevin received a welcome break from all the nonsense when he arrived home just before Christmas, as it was now only a matter of days before he was due to get married. By this stage, everybody could see that Jess was the girl for Kevin. He had known from very early on in their relationship that she was the one for him, and nothing that had happened in the two years since had changed his mind one bit.

The partying and the excesses people associated with Kevin when he first came on the England scene were now well and truly in the distant past. By now, on the odd occasions he still went to nightclubs, it was with her, but the couple were more likely to be spotted in posh restaurants, with Brinkley's in Chelsea being a particular favourite. Jess had made Kevin a calmer, more contented person. In the past he was sometimes a bit short with people who asked him for an autograph or picture, but Jess had reminded him that he could really make someone's day by doing this simple act that only took a few seconds of his time. He knew she was right, because he remembered how happy he was to get autographs from famous people when he was a kid. Nowadays, when people want an autograph or picture from him, he tries to accommodate them whenever he can.

Jess had helped turn Kevin into a well-rounded person. He did enjoy some of the trappings of fame, but not the excesses. He had developed friendships with Frank Lampard, Piers Morgan and Lewis Hamilton, but didn't feel the need to show his face at the opening of every fridge door. Most nights, he was usually happy to cuddle up with Jess on a sofa. In removing all of the excesses and nonsense from his life she had allowed him to concentrate on what really motivated him professionally, which was being successful. Yes, it was nice to have money and to be involved with so many product endorsements. He was making around £450,000 a year from his central England contract and international appearances, but made at least double that from his sponsorship deals. It certainly helped that he was being looked after extremely well by Mission Sports Management, which had Sir Ian Botham as Chairman. The arrangement began when Kevin was playing grade cricket in Sydney. Sir Ian and the company's Managing Director, Adam Wheatley, were out there filming a commercial and had heard on the grapevine about Kevin. He visited them on the set and they just took it from there. His wild partying days behind him, Kevin's was a name plenty of big brands wanted to associate themselves with, and Sir Ian's management group had made him a fortune in the last few years, thanks to lucrative deals with the likes of Citizen Watches and Adidas.

Yet being successful was the main thing that really motivated Kevin, and the fact that he had plenty of money coming in was a consequence of that. One person he admitted to hugely admiring was Simon Cowell, because of what he achieved and represented. He liked the way Simon handled himself and fought back to be bigger than ever after losing everything when he suffered a setback in the early 1990s. He knew that the real Simon Cowell was a million miles removed from his reputation as 'Mr Nasty' and that away from the cameras he was a courteous man who made time for people who wanted to speak to him. In Simon, Kevin had found a suitable role model in terms of being successful yet managing to keep his feet on the ground.

Another man Kevin had grown to admire was Cristiano Ronaldo. Despite not being a massive football fan he had a soft spot for Manchester United and once went to see them play Chelsea at Stamford Bridge. He made sure he arrived at the ground a good half hour before kickoff so he could watch Ronaldo warming up and observe how he went about his preparations for the game.

In many ways, Jess was a similar person to him. She shared his outlook on life, was very competitive in her desire to make it in her profession and worked hard at everything she did, yet beneath all the fame and glamour her success had brought, she remained very family-orientated and down-to-earth. Everybody who saw them together knew they were right for each other, and those who know Kevin all agree he is a much happier person when she is around.

Kevin's stag do, which saw him travel to Edinburgh for a few days with some close friends, was a relatively restrained affair. Darren Gough, Paul Collingwood and Michael Vaughan were all invited but couldn't attend due to prior commitments, so the only cricketer who could make it was Simon Jones. His brother, Bryan, ever the party animal, would be joining them, as would Adam Wheatley, who, as an ex-army man and close friend of Sir Ian Botham, was always likely to be up for a good drinking session. They took the train up from London and, as expected, Bryan and Adam were leading the way. Simon was the one who couldn't really handle his drink. They played golf the next day, but Simon was too hung-over to join them. Kevin wasn't much of a one for heavy drinking sessions since meeting Jess, but showed that he could handle his drink well and was in surprisingly good shape for the golf.

Kevin had spent the night before the wedding enjoying a quiet meal with his family and best man Darren Gough, in a private room at the £300-a-night, five-star Manor House Hotel, in Castle Combe, Wiltshire, which dates back to the 14th century. Some of his England team-mates enjoyed a moderate drinking session in a separate room in the hotel complex. The following morning his parents helped him fine-tune his speech. Everything felt right, and he wasn't experiencing any nerves about getting married. He knew that marrying Jess was definitely what he wanted, more than anything else in life, and was certain that she felt the same way.

The wedding took place at St Andrew's Church in Castle Combe and was attended by many of Kevin's England team-mates, both past and present. Jess's dress was a backless ivory silk chiffon design, tightly ruched at the front with sparkling beads hanging like icicles down the pleats. After the 45-minute ceremony, which included the carol 'Silent Night', the bridal party and 200 guests walked back to the

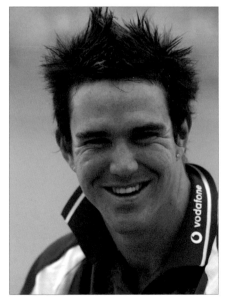

bove: Kevin Pietersen aged 17 in a school photo from Maritzburg College,
outh Africa, in 1997.

elow left: KP sports his trademark daring hairdo in 2005.

elow right: Preparing for the 2005 Ashes at Old Trafford.

England's Ashes-winning Test series in 2005. England clinched a historic 2-1 series victory after the fifth and final test was drawn at Lord's.

Above: The Ashes-winning team celebrate with a parade through London on 13 September 2005.

Below: The team pictured with the Queen and the Duke of Edinburgh on 9 February 2006, having been honoured for their performance in the Ashes.

Above left: In December 2005, Kevin Pietersen was awarded an MBE.

Above right and below left: KP with his wife, former Liberty X singer Jessica Taylor. The pair married in 2007.

Below right: KP is out for a duck against Pakistan at the Oval in 2006.

KP celebrates
reaching his double
century in the second
Test of the 2010
Ashes in Adelaide.

Above: Stepping up against Sri Lanka at Lord's in 2011.

Below: Playing for the Delhi Daredevils in the Indian Premier League in 2012

...actising in the nets ahead of the first ODI match against New Zealand in ...ay 2013.

KP turns out for a 'Cricket for Kids' charity match at Cirencester Cricket Club in June 2013.

hotel where all 48 rooms had been booked for the wedding. Many homeowners with cottages backing on to the hotel grounds had agreed to the couple's request for white sparkling lights to be hung from windows lining the route, in keeping with the winter wonderland theme of the day. The couple had been offered a six-figure sum to sell pictures of their wedding to *OK!* magazine, but had turned it down, instead choosing to keep it a special day for their family, friends and the people of the tiny village where the wedding took place.

Everything had gone so well and it had been a truly magical day for the happy couple. Despite everything that he had achieved in cricket, this had been by far the most important and happiest day of Kevin's life.

16

THE CONTROVERSIAL CAPTAIN

The next Ashes series was now less than 18 months away, and although there was still plenty of cricket to be played in the meantime, Kevin wanted all his efforts, and that of the team, to be geared towards the summer of 2009. As an established member of both the Test and one-day squads for three years, his role in the dressing room was now changing. In particular, he was the man the one-day captain Paul Collingwood turned to for advice more than any other, even though he had made quite a bad mistake in the World Twenty20 when he miscalculated Freddie's bowling allocation. He also became something of a mentor to the new members of the squad, in the same way Ashley Giles and Darren Gough had been to him when he first came on the scene.

Having been England's best batsman for most of the last three years, Kevin felt he was entitled to express an opinion with regard to the direction in which Peter Moores was taking the team. It was fairly obvious that England's form, particularly in Test matches, had declined sharply in the time since Duncan Fletcher's departure, and Kevin was still far from impressed with the way Peter went about doing things.

The first action of 2008 saw England travel to New Zealand, which would be quickly followed by a return visit in the early part of the English summer. On England's tour of New Zealand, Kevin averaged 33.00 in the one-day series, with one score of 50 in the tied fourth match. This was a series England were expected to win and Kevin's discontent at the way things were going increased further as they lost the series 3-1. He also made a top score of 43 in the first of two comfortable Twenty20 wins. He had a quiet first two Test matches, making little impression with the bat. However, in the first innings of the Napier Test, he rescued England from a disastrous start of three for four, guiding them towards 259 with 129 – his 11th Test century.

New Zealand then came to tour England and Kevin again struggled in the first two Test matches, scoring in the single figures in the first match. In the second, he scored 26 in the first innings, then ran himself out on 42 having looked well set. He struck a century in the third Test, forming a valuable partnership with Tim Ambrose and making a crucial 115. Kevin continued his return to form by hitting a winning 42 not out in the Twenty20 match.

The first match of the one-day series in Durham saw Kevin do something truly extraordinary. He was batting well and seemed in a confident mood when he faced the medium-paced bowling of Scott Styris. What happened next eclipsed his reverse sweep against Murali two years earlier. This time he turned his body around and switched hands, effectively batting as a left-hander, hitting two sixes over cover and long off en route to 110. Nobody, but nobody had ever seen anything quite like it.

Several noted commentators called for the shot to be outlawed straight away. Ian Healy said, 'If you want to hit to one side of the field, you've got to do it in a cross fashion, and not swap the way you're facing or your grip. Otherwise you are going to start to allow the bowlers to go round the wicket, over the wicket, and keep swapping during their run-ups.' Michael Holding suggested that if Kevin's shots were acceptable, then bowlers should not be made to inform the umpire if they intended to change their delivery. Another argument for outlawing the shot was that it effectively removes the possibility of the batsman being out lbw. Jonathan Agnew suggested that a right-handed batsman could take his stance as a left-hander, and then switch stance as the bowler runs in, thus being able to kick away any balls that land outside his now off-stump.

Speaking afterwards, Kevin didn't mince his words when he slammed his critics, saying, 'That's ridiculous, absolutely stupid. The reverse-sweep has been part of the game for however long. I am just fortunate that I am able to hit it a bit further. Everybody wants brand new ideas, new inventions and new shots. That is a new shot played today and people should be saying it's a new way to go. There are new things happening for cricket at the moment and people shouldn't be criticising it all the time.' The MCC ultimately ruled that the shot was legal and Kevin is free to attempt it again in future. For the record, England went on to win the match by 114 runs.

Kevin's first shot at the England captaincy came about by accident when the ICC banned Paul Collingwood for four one-day international matches due to England's slow over-rate in the fourth match of the series, with England having bowled only 47 overs in the required time. They also fined the rest of the English team 15% of their match fee.

By his own admission, Kevin had no real experience of captaincy at any level, even as a schoolboy. The only record of him captaining any side came in a single 50-over Second XI game for Nottinghamshire in 2002, when he scored 113 to lead them to victory. He knew he had to make a big impression from the start, and he rang the one coach he respected above any other, Clive Rice, for advice. Clive told Kevin that he'd better be asking lots of questions, and of all the answers he got, pick the best idea. If that doesn't work, pick the next best one, then the next. He told him he had to do that to create the right impression, and reminded Kevin that this could be the one and only time he ever got to captain England, and he had to make the most of it.

Kevin needed to lead England to victory to level the series at two-all, but he only managed to score six from 23 balls, as the side slumped to a 51-run defeat. He seemed to command the respect of the team, but there was a clear gulf between the ethos of him and Peter Moores.

The main Test series of the summer saw England take on

South Africa. Even after all this time, Kevin took particular delight in showing his country of birth what they had missed out on in letting him go. On the first day of the first Test at Lord's, Kevin hit an exhilarating 152 off 181 balls. He looked as though he was enjoying every second of it and when he was eventually out, the Lord's crowd gave him a huge standing ovation, which he described as the most emotional two minutes of his career. At the press conference later on he declared that he'd never felt so English.

The first Test was drawn and England suffered a heavy defeat in the second at Headingley. In the third Test at Edgbaston, England were fighting their way back into the game in the second innings as they looked to set their opponents an un-reachable target. Kevin looked at his most confident and brash as he raced his way to 94, before crossing the line between aggression and recklessness, hitting Paul Harris's off-spin straight into the hands of AB de Villiers, who was fielding near the boundary.

With the series lost, many people were questioning Michael Vaughan's role. Few argued that he had lost his ability as captain, but he hadn't been performing as a batsman for quite some time, and the likes of Geoffrey Boycott were saying that on his form, he didn't deserve to play. The following day Michael resigned in tears, the mental anguish of the situation having clearly taken its toll. He also decided to make himself unavailable for the final Test at the Oval, saying that he would return to play for Yorkshire and try to concentrate on his batting. Paul Collingwood, who still had three one-day matches of his ban to serve, followed suit half an hour later and resigned his captaincy of the one-day side.

The ECB had three realistic choices when seeking a new captain, and they didn't have time to hang about, because the Oval Test started just five days later. Until quite recently Paul Collingwood had generally been considered Michael Vaughan's heir apparent. Yet his reign as one-day skipper had been mixed and he had lost three series England should really have won. He also led England to a poor performance in the World Twenty20, and had been caught visiting a lap-dancing club by *The Sun* the night before the game against South Africa, something that Paul later called 'unacceptable' and 'a mistake'. His ongoing ban for slow play was probably enough to rule him out of the Test captaincy. Andrew Strauss was the conservative option and was generally regarded as a safe pair of hands, but he hadn't been part of the one-day side for the last two years and the ECB seemed pretty set on the idea of having one captain for all forms of the game. This left Kevin as the one remaining option left, but he was the unconventional maverick, and the men in suits knew that this was a man who would want things done his own way. He was unafraid of taking on obstacles, and his pursuit of success was total. If he had to upset a few people to achieve this end, so be it. At the same time, there were similarities between him and Ricky Ponting, in that he would be strong, assertive and demand the best from his players.

His relationship with Peter Moores was, to put it mildly, already strained, so the two men had clear-the-air talks at a Northampton hotel before Kevin formally accepted the post.

Kevin told Peter that he would drag England upwards kicking and screaming. He also asked Peter to take more of a back seat, so that he could be more involved in the running of things.

Kevin left the meeting thinking that he and Peter had reached an understanding, and was delighted and humbled to accept the greatest honour to bestow any cricketer – to captain his country. He spoke to the media and paid a warm tribute to both Michael Vaughan and Paul Collingwood, but insisted that he would be doing things his way from now on. He didn't have long to dwell on the swiftness of his appointment or sit back and appreciate just how far he had come in the last few years because he was quickly faced with his first challenge, which was to pick the side for the upcoming Test, something the selectors had allowed him to do on this occasion. He opted to replace Vaughan with a bowler in the shape of Steve Harmison, when many people would've expected him to go for another batsman in Ravi Bopara.

It rapidly became clear that the characteristic boldness that had defined Kevin as a batsman would be reflected in the style of his captaincy when he entrusted the first over to Steve Harmison, something no other captain had dared to do since that double-wide in Brisbane. Kevin had sympathised with Steve at the time, and this was his way of telling him that he had every confidence in his ability as a world-class bowler. Some observers wondered whether having the burden of the captaincy would force Kevin to change his approach to batting. They were quickly silenced when, with England on 51 for two, he came out and entertained the crowd with a century, which ultimately helped the side to a six-wicket victory and helped wipe the smile off Graeme Smith's face.

Kevin's methods were clearly having some kind of impact. The players took to the field in that final Test, and in the one-day series that followed, with their heads held high and a spring in their step. His positive 'can do' attitude and work ethic rubbed off on the rest of the boys as they thrashed South Africa 4-0 in the one-day series. He could be persuasive as well, and successfully urged Steve Harmison out of one-day international retirement, although getting Marcus Trescothick to agree to an England comeback proved illusive, since he was still recovering from his illness.

With the Ashes now less than a year away Kevin felt that at long last the side were all pulling in the same direction and they were playing like a team that could at the very least give the Aussies a run for their money. That said, he felt this was happening largely in spite of Peter Moores rather than because of him. With the rift between captain and coach being patched up rather than healed it was only a matter of time before the team fell from grace.

October saw Kevin's men travel to the Caribbean to take part in the Stanford Super Series, which was a series of Twenty20 games backed by the now-disgraced Texan billionaire Sir Allen Stanford. The main match would see England take on the Stanford Superstars in a match worth $20 million to the winning side. The short trip turned into farce as peripheral issues dominated the build-up to the big game, including problems with player illness, the floodlights, the pitch and even the conduct of Stanford himself, who was seen behaving inappropriately with some of the England players' wives and girlfriends. Kevin would go on to describe him as 'a sleazebag'.

Halfway through the week, Kevin said that he couldn't wait for the match to be over, which was hardly the sort of approach needed when he and his team could be about to make more money for three hours' work than they would normally make in a year. On the other hand, he did warn his players not to behave like clowns if they went on to win the match, because he knew full well that Britain was at the start of what looked to be a long and deep recession, and the last thing the fans back home would want to see would be the players gloating after winning all that money. He needn't have worried. England slumped to an embarrassing 10-wicket defeat against a team that had only been playing together for a week.

The rift between Kevin and Peter Moores was the last thing the squad needed as they embarked on a gruelling tour of India shortly after the Stanford match. Their abysmal one-day form continued as they slumped to a 5-0 defeat. Kevin had performed reasonably well with respectable scores of 63, 33 and 111 not out. Some of the other batsmen had pulled their weight but the bowlers had, with the exception of Freddie Flintoff, been appalling, and Kevin felt exposed.

He outlined to the ECB Managing Director Hugh Morris his worries about the lack of guidance being offered by Peter. He said, 'There is a lot of mediocrity that people settle for in England in terms of county cricket and the comfort zones of international cricket. But I am not settling for mediocrity, that is far from my thoughts.' It was now becoming obvious that his opinion of Peter hadn't changed and he didn't think the new coach had grown into the job.

The one-day series was curtailed after the fifth match following the terrorist atrocities in Mumbai in which at least 173 people were killed. Hugh Morris made the decision for the players to catch a flight to London at the earliest opportunity so they could be with their families for a few days while the situation was assessed by security experts. Kevin said that he wouldn't force any player to return against their will, but his instinct was to complete the tour for some unfinished business. Some of his colleagues with young families didn't share his enthusiasm. Flintoff, Harmison, Collingwood and Strauss all had misgivings, while Jimmy Anderson was understandably anxious because his wife was due to give birth to their first child in a month's time.

Hugh Morris and Sean Morris of the Professional Cricketers' Association spoke to the players regularly on their return home to update them on the situation. An announcement was made that the squad would train in Abu Dhabi for a few days while ECB security adviser Reg Dickason ensured that sufficient security requirements were made for the Tests at Chennai and Mohali, which replaced Ahmedabad and Mumbai as the venues for the two Test matches.

In truth, the risk level for the players was relatively low, as westerners weren't regarded as specific targets by the terrorists. However, they were understandably traumatised by the pictures of the attacks that were shown on Indian TV, which were far more graphic than those broadcast back home. During this period, even Kevin's harshest critics expressed admiration for the way in which he went about his business. After Dickason's report gave thorough assurances about security, several meetings were held at Abu Dhabi to gauge the mood of the squad. Kevin succeeded in persuading every single member of the squad to return to India to continue the tour. He arrived back in India a stronger leader with his authority enhanced, as well as being something of a national hero. The people of India greatly appreciated his hard work in persuading the team to return, while his sincere and heartfelt words brought comfort to many in what was a very difficult and tense period.

Among all the upheaval, Kevin's working relationship with Peter had not improved a great deal, and now the stress of everything was beginning to affect him. In the first Test he recorded two single-figure scores for the first time in his career, scoring four and one respectively. As India chased their target of 387, Kevin felt as though he had no control over the field placings, which seemed to have been pre-determined by Peter. The likes of Sachin Tendulkar managed to snatch singles from the England bowling with ease as they helped their side win the match comfortably. Kevin knew the situation was heading for a showdown. In the first innings of the second Test, Kevin entertained the crowd with a thrilling 144, showing he had the maturity to protect his wicket yet still have the confidence to play big shots. His innings played a large part in running down the clock to give England the draw.

The players were to return home for Christmas before playing a series in the West Indies in January. Kevin knew that what he regarded as a farcical situation couldn't continue when the side regrouped after the break. He was fed up with Peter's coaching, his methods and his unwillingness to embrace computer technology, something Kevin had firmly believed in ever since his time at Loughborough. Kevin also strongly believed that Michael Vaughan should be included in the squad for the Caribbean, but the selectors and Peter were thought to hold the view that England should move on from his era.

Kevin left for a safari holiday with Jess just after Christmas believing that he had won the selectors over and Vaughan would be included in the squad, only for him to discover a few days later that Peter had succeeded in changing their minds. This was the final straw as far as Kevin was concerned. He wanted urgent talks with Giles Clarke, the ECB Chairman, as soon as possible once he returned from holiday, but made it clear that he wasn't willing to return early. Senior people at the ECB suggested an email dialogue, but Kevin didn't feel in the mood for diplomacy.

On New Year's Day the press finally found out about the deep rift that had been stewing for months, although exactly who leaked the information to them is not clear, but we now know it wasn't Kevin himself. When questioned, Kevin said there was an 'unhealthy situation' in the camp that needed to be resolved. On 7 January, Peter Moores was removed as England coach by the ECB, while Kevin resigned as captain. All attempts at dialogue had failed as it became clear that the rift was too deep to be healed, and a working relationship between the two men for the greater good of English cricket would be impossible. In an interview several days after his resignation, Kevin revealed that he had not intended to resign as captain, but was told by ECB officials that he was resigning.

It was clear that this wasn't going to be the end of the matter.

17
THE AFTERMATH

A lot was said and written in the days and weeks following Kevin's 'resignation', much of it with no basis in fact. There is a strong argument for saying that Kevin's biggest problem was his lack of political prowess. If he had been more tactful and subtle he could have sown the seeds of doubt into the minds of those that mattered in the ECB, and indeed among his team-mates over a period of time. Not everyone in the England dressing room shared his opinion of Peter Moores. Steve Harmison was widely considered to be an ally of the coach, as was Freddie Flintoff, but the tour of India was his first under Moores, due to injury. Meanwhile, the younger players who had been brought in under Pietersen seemed to have a great respect for their captain. Yet this is not to say that Freddie and Steve were necessarily enemies of Kevin as a consequence.

The main topic that was covered in the column inches was

the extent to which Kevin had overstepped the mark in this whole affair. The one issue that was never really considered was the possibility that Kevin may have been right after all to force out Peter Moores. Yes, he hadn't exactly been a skilled and subtle diplomat in the way he went about it, but was the intention really such a bad thing? Under Moores, England had won eight of their 22 Tests, seven of which came against New Zealand and a pretty weak West Indies bowling attack. Surely if the ECB had confidence in Moores's ability they could just as easily have sacked Kevin as captain and told him to get on with the business of scoring runs under their wonderful coach?

The ECB knew that Kevin was a tough character who wanted things done professionally and brought out the best in people. This was exemplified in the manner of the 4-0 win over South Africa in the one-dayers when he first took over the captaincy. Yet as soon as he challenged the establishment, they found they didn't really want an uncompromising, no-nonsense, forward-thinking man leading the team after all.

England travelled to the West Indies under the captaincy of Andrew Strauss, while Andy Flower was promoted to coach, initially on a temporary basis, although this was eventually made a permanent appointment. Kevin returned to the rank and file, and was free to concentrate on scoring runs. He is a more sensitive person than many people realise, but he is good at masking his emotions. He was genuinely hurt at some of the comments that were made about him by certain journalists who didn't really know him at all and blindly believed some of the rubbish they had been told. However, just 28 days after losing the captaincy, Kevin was glad to be returning to Test cricket and doing what he does best.

He wasted no time in reminding the world how good a batsman he was, scoring 97 in the first Test, but he and Stuart Broad, who took five wickets for 85, were the only stars as England crumbled to a defeat by an innings and 23 runs. The second Test was abandoned due to a dangerous outfield after only 10 balls had been bowled, and by his standards, Kevin disappointed in the third and fourth Tests, which were both draws. In the second innings of the fifth Test, Kevin scored 102 in 92 balls. The West Indies needed 240 to win, with time against them. They managed 114 for eight before time ran out. The series was one, which, on paper, England should have won comfortably but had ultimately ended in further humiliation. Kevin hadn't quite hit the heights that supporters had been used to in recent years, but he still managed 406 runs in four Tests.

As Strauss and Flower settled into their respective roles, there were signs that England were starting to turn the corner by the time of the one-day series, which they eventually won 3-2, but it wasn't until the last match in St Lucia that Kevin produced the goods, scoring 48 as they won by 26 runs. This was hardly perfect preparation for the Ashes summer, though with Flower's appointment now permanent and Strauss quickly learning the ropes, there are signs that England may be back on track for a competitive fight in the Ashes if nothing else. One thing is for certain: Kevin can be relied upon to make runs in the series.

If Kevin had kept a relatively low profile during the tour by keeping quiet and letting Andrew Strauss get on with his job, he let his guard down in an interview with the *Daily Mail* midway through the one-day series. In it he admitted that he was at the end of his tether and, if he was honest, he couldn't wait to get home. He and Jess hadn't spent so much time apart since they had been a couple, and he was finding it very difficult to cope. She had made a commitment to take part in the TV show *Dancing on Ice*, which meant that she couldn't possibly fly out to be with him. Kevin said he was ready to 'do a Robinho' and disappear home. What wasn't revealed in the article was that Kevin didn't join the rest of the touring party in the Hilton Hotel during the Barbados Test, instead staying at the Royal Westmoreland. It transpired that he had been denied a request to return to England for 48 hours to spend some time with Jess between the third and fourth Tests. The fact that he asked to travel such a long way for such a brief period suggests he was finding it very hard to cope out there.

In the same article he launched an unnecessary attack on West Indian batsman Shivnarine Chanderpaul, who Kevin accused of playing for himself and seldom fielding after making a big score. His comments were in particularly poor taste considering Chanderpaul had scored 147 not out in Barbados, and 299 in six innings. West Indies captain Chris Gayle demanded an apology, but none was forthcoming.

When Kevin finally did arrive home he barely had time to relax before jetting off to South Africa to take part in the Indian Premier League. The event had been moved from India to South Africa due to security concerns after a bus containing the Sri Lankan team and match officials was set upon by terrorists in neighbouring Pakistan. The Indian liquor baron, Vijay Mallya, brought Kevin to his Bangalore Royal Challengers side for $1.5 million, making him the highest paid IPL player alongside Freddie Flintoff. Due to the clash with the start of the Test series against the West Indies at home he would only be available for the first three weeks of the competition, but during that period he would be on a salary comparable to what his friend Frank Lampard received at Chelsea.

Vijay announced that during his three weeks with the side, Kevin would be captain, before being replaced by Anil Kumble when he had to leave. Unfortunately, Kevin struggled to adjust to the demands and intensity of the matches and was twice out for a duck in four innings. It goes without saying that Kevin and England's other leading players will want to be available for the entire IPL programme in future years and the cricketing authorities will have to adjust their calendars to accommodate this highly lucrative event.

Despite not impressing on this occasion, Kevin loved the IPL – the whole atmosphere and way in which it was packaged suited his style of play. It was charismatic, colourful and attacking. It gave him the opportunity to play alongside, and learn from, some of the very best players from right across the world. Things hadn't gone so well this time, but Kevin looked forward to returning to India each April for many years to come.

18

A FRUSTRATING YEAR

Following the disappointing IPL campaign in the spring of 2009, serious questions were being asked about Kevin's form, and about whether the events of the last six months had taken their toll on his confidence.

This was an Ashes summer, but there was a great deal of cricket to be played before then. First came a two-Test series against the West Indies, then a three-match one-day series, followed by the World Twenty20. All this was before they faced Australia in any form of the game. Even for the most physically and mentally prepared cricketer, this was a gruelling challenge.

Many people involved in cricket – players, coaches, journalists, and supporters, were unimpressed with the ICC's scheduling. There was just too much cricket being played, with a very short gap between winter tours ending and the summer beginning, especially if they were playing in the IPL as well. The ICC had never properly dealt with the growth of T20 and the scheduling international matches was often messy. England playing Tests against weaker nations at the start of the summer was nothing new, but a two-Test series against an established and popular cricketing side like the West Indies was regarded as something of an insult, even though their current crop of players wasn't a exactly a vintage.

It was therefore no surprise that reports of burnout and mental health problems were becoming increasingly frequent among cricketers. Where was the time to stop and analyse their game, and work with coaches to improve things, in an environment where the pressure was off? More importantly, when were they supposed to spend time with their wives and children? Kevin was enjoying married life and made no secret of his desire to start a family at some stage. Being a good father was important to him and he wanted to play a full and active role in the upbringing of any future children.

As he prepared for the first Test against the West Indies in early May, Kevin's confidence didn't improve. He wasn't in the right frame of mind as he came out to bat in the first Test at Lord's, and he was out first ball as he faced a full, swinging delivery from Fidel Edwards. However, a century from Ravi Bopara and some solid batting from, Alastair Cook, Matt Prior and Stuart Broad helped England reach 377. England's bowlers, Broad, Graham Onions and Graeme Swann, quickly sussed out their opponents and the West Indies were bowled out for 152, and the 256 they amassed on the follow-on was nowhere near enough to prevent England from recording a resounding ten wicket victory.

Kevin celebrated enthusiastically with his teammates on the famous Lord's balcony, and there were few signs that this was a man lacking confidence, or that this was a group of players who didn't get along.

In the second Test at Chester-le-Street, Kevin made a quick 49 before being caught by Lendl Simmons off the bowling of Sulieman Benn, while centuries from Cook and Bopara helped England's total reach 569 in the first innings, while the West Indies could only manage 310 followed by 176 on the follow-on, giving England victory by an innings and 83 runs. Jimmy Anderson, Stuart Broad and Graham Onions had been the main stars with the ball on this occasion, while Bopara's batting performances earned him the Man of the Series award.

Shortly after the second Test, Kevin suffered what appeared at the time to be a minor right Achilles injury, and was subsequently ruled out of the ODI series, which England won 2-0. Although Kevin was disappointed not to be taking part in the series, there were far bigger matches ahead later in the summer and he wanted to be in the best possible shape for those.

In early June, Kevin made the headlines following a rather unfortunate incident at Loughborough University. A 15-year-old schoolboy called Reece Topley, the son of former Essex and Surrey paceman Don Topley, had the opportunity to bowl to a number of England batsmen, including his favourite player, Kevin Pietersen, in the nets. Kevin drove a flat delivery to Reece, which struck him on the side of the head and knocked him out! He was taken to Leicester Royal Infirmary where he received stitches to his right ear and was kept in hospital overnight.

Following the incident, Kevin was concerned and sympathetic, and soon gave Reece a signed bat as compensation. Reece later claimed to have got a hand on the ball, which his father joked would've counted as a dropped catch in some people's eyes. Reece fully recovered from the incident, and has since signed for Essex, where he has made a promising start to his professional career, with Michael Vaughan describing him as a potential future Test star.

Just a few days later, and with England's first World T20 match against the Netherlands fast approaching, Kevin's Achilles problem flared up and he was forced to watch from the sidelines at Lord's as England suffered a humiliating four wicket defeat.

He returned for the second match against eventual champions Pakistan at the Oval and top scored with 58 off 38 balls, which included three sixes, one of which was measured at over 100 meters. Kevin's innings was vital in helping England to a 48 run victory.

In the Super Eights, Kevin managed just 19 in the seven wicket defeat against South Africa, while in the next match he made a vital 46 to help England to a narrow victory by three runs against India. In the rain-affected must-win match against the West Indies, Kevin managed a respectable 31, but this wasn't enough to prevent England from suffering a five wicket defeat that would send them out of the competition.

A FRUSTRATING YEAR

Despite missing the first match, Kevin ended the tournament as England's leading runscorer with 154 at an average of 38.50. He had silenced his critics, and it looked as though he would be playing a pivotal role in England's upcoming Ashes series, despite failing to surpass single-figure scores in the warm-up match against Warwickshire.

With the World T20 not long over, the build-up to the Ashes series was relatively short this time around. All the T20 games and ODIs against Australia would take place after the Ashes, and there wasn't the same level of intense media scrutiny and hype seen four years earlier. The fact that British live TV coverage was on the subscription-only Sky Sports, whereas in 2005 it was free-to-air on Channel 4, also didn't help when it came to building up a strong national mood of anticipation and excitement for cricket's most prestigious Test series.

The opening Test of the series was staged at the SWALEC Stadium, Cardiff, (formerly known as Sophia Gardens) which had recently undergone a massive expansion to bring it up to the standard required for such prestigious international matches. The stadium was one of the most unusual in world cricket. It was tucked away behind a row of Victorian buildings in an affluent inner-city area of the city. To get there, you had to turn down an unassuming side street, where you would be greeted by an ageing leisure centre and a small car park. Tucked away in the left hand corner was a large set of gates, behind which you could just about see the back of one of the stands.

However, once inside, you were in an impressive, if

somewhat compact ground that was more than suitable for a match of this stature. It's true to say that most of the picturesque views from before the redevelopment had been replaced by concrete and plastic seats, but it was nonetheless an opportunity to show that ECB stood for the England and *Wales* Cricket Board. Welsh cricketers, such as Tony Lewis, Robert Croft and Simon Jones had contributed hugely to England's success down the years, and this was seen as a chance for Wales to prove it was more than capable of becoming a regular home for England Tests.

A packed crowd in excess of 15,000 greeted both sets of players on that sunny opening morning. Prior to the start of play, the players were introduced to Wales's First Minister, Rhodri Morgan, who had a few words of encouragement for Kevin and each of the England players as he was presented to them by captain Andrew Strauss. Morgan was a keen cricket fan and was no stranger to this stadium. During the National Assembly's summer recess, he was frequently seen at Glamorgan matches, often wearing casual clothes and a cap so that he could camouflage into the crowd without drawing attention to himself. Now, though, he was wearing a suit and was, for a few moments, the centre of attention as he enthusiastically greeted the England players.

Soon, the pleasantries were over and it was down to the main business of the summer. England batted first, and Kevin helped England recover from 90/3 as he and his friend Paul Collingwood built up a 138 partnership to put the innings back on track. Kevin top scored with 69 before being caught by Simon Katich off the bowling of Nathan Hauritz, after what had been an entertaining but occasionally reckless performance. They were eventually all out for 435, but this was a real team effort, with the all-rounders and lower order all doing their bit to help the team recover from a poor start, while Panesar was the only batsmen not to reach at least double figures. However, England's bowlers struggled, as Australia made 674/6 before declaring in an attempt to push for a result in a rain-affected match.

The second innings was a different story. Kevin made just eight before being bowled by Ben Hilfenhaus, and with the notable exception of Paul Collingwood's 74, all of England's batsmen disappointed, with several giving their wickets away playing silly shots. There was a very real possibility England would be bowled out without making Australia bat again, but they eventually clung on to end on 252/9 before the match ran out of time. The lengthy rain delays on the third and fourth days had effectively saved the Test. This was hardly something to celebrate. The last man partnership of Anderson and Panesar gave England a slender lead, but as the match drew to a close, every dot ball was cheered by the crowd as the clock ticked down to 18:40 and a draw was declared. After the match, Australia captain Ricky Ponting accused England of time wasting, as twelfth man Bilal Shafayat came onto the field twice without good cause. Shafayat was a former teammate of Kevin's at Nottinghamshire, and they both burst onto the scene around the same time. Great things were expected of Shafayat as a youngster, with many pundits claiming he would be a permanent fixture in the England side within a few years but he never really got to grips with the psychological side of the game and he was, by this stage, a fringe county player at Notts. Unfortunately, this was as far as he is likely to get towards taking to the field for England.

Kevin's strong first innings performance had played its part in helping England secure a draw, but he was disappointed by his, and his teammates' performance in the second innings. There were clear problems with the top of the order batsmen as Strauss, Cook and Bopara all struggled with form. This was hardly what was needed with four gruelling Tests ahead, against an Australia side that, although radically different and not as powerful as four years ago, was still very much a force to be reckoned with.

There had been signs during the first Test that Kevin's Achilles problem was rearing its ugly head again, but in the intervening week between the first and second Tests, Kevin was confident that it was not problematic enough to prevent him from playing at Lord's.

Kevin had proved his fitness and was cautiously selected for the Lord's Test. England's batsmen got off to an impressive start and the score was at a healthy 222-2 when he came out to bat. This was a trademark innings from Kevin, and he was going well before being caught behind by wicketkeeper Brad Haddin off the bowling of Peter Siddle for 32. Even so, Strauss's 161 and 95 from Cook helped England to a total of 425 in the first innings, and some superb bowling from Anderson, Onions and Broad got the better of the Australian batsmen, and they were all out for 215.

With plenty of time left in the match, this was a real opportunity for England to go 1-0 up in the series, and although the openers hadn't scored as heavily as in the first innings, they had built up a lead of almost 300 by the time Kevin came out to bat alongside Ravi Bopara.

Kevin played some decent shots and this was a performance he could be proud of, but as the innings wore on, it became increasingly clear that his right Achilles was causing him considerable distress. Running between the wickets was turning into a major struggle, and he knew this was not a problem he could put to the back of his mind for much longer.

Despite being hampered with this injury, Kevin made 44 before once again being caught behind off Siddle. England left Australia chasing a whopping 522 to win the match, but there was enough time remaining for them to win, and Kevin knew this wasn't a time for sloppiness in the field. Yet as the hours passed by, his injury was showing no signs of getting better as he hobbled gingerly around the field. Australia's batsmen put up a decent fight, with Michael Clarke top scoring with 136, but they were eventually all out for 406 (which included a five wicket haul by Freddie Flintoff, which saw him achieve the rare feat of making both Lord's honours boards), giving England a 115-run victory.

Even though England's bowlers took their foot off the gas a bit during the second innings, this was an occasion worth celebrating, but for Kevin, this was the last thing on his mind. The Achilles injury required urgent attention, and after the match, it didn't take long for the medical team to conclude that an operation was required and Kevin's participation in the Ashes was over.

Kevin was understandably devastated. Despite all the innovations and money-making opportunities T20 had brought to the game, the Ashes was still very much the pinnacle of Kevin's cricketing ambitions. To have to leave a winning team with three Tests still to play was heartbreaking, but he had no choice. Yes, he had been happy with the treatment he had received earlier in the year, and he honestly believed that any further action could wait until the end of the summer, but it became increasingly clear as the Lord's Test progressed that this was something that couldn't be delayed.

Many pundits were surprised that Kevin was ruled out for the whole series. They expected him to miss one Test, but his complete withdrawal from the squad came as something of a shock. However, just two days after the conclusion of the second Test, Kevin underwent surgery, performed by the world's leading Achilles specialist, and it was clear he was in for a long lay-off, with no guarantees about his availability for the winter. Kevin's run of 54 consecutive Tests was at an end.

With Kevin out of action, Ian Bell was called into the squad for the remainder of the series. The third Test at Edgbaston was heavily affected by rain and ended with an inevitable draw. In the next Test at Headingley, England were all out for an embarrassing 102, which paved the way for Australia to win by an innings and 80 runs. It was a humiliating defeat, but it paved the way for a mouth-watering series decider at the Oval.

A FRUSTRATING YEAR

Following the batting disaster at Headingley, the decision was made to drop Bopara and give Jonathan Trott his Test debut. England batted first and made a respectable 332, with Kevin's replacement Ian Bell top scoring with 72. Australia were bowled out for just 160, with Broad and Swann taking nine of the wickets. In the second innings, debutant Trott made 119, which was the key innings in helping England reach 373, which left Australia chasing a massive 546, although with two-and-a-half days still available, this was still a very gettable target.

Australia started strongly, and it looked as though they were going to put up a considerable fight before Simon Katich fell with his side on 86, and fellow opener Shane Watson went in the following over. Ricky Ponting and Michael Hussey's partnership took Australia to 217, before Flintoff, playing in his final Test and struggling with injury, threw a superb direct hit at the stumps to dismiss the Australian captain.

From then on, Australia relied heavily on Michael Hussey, but although he batted well and eventually reached 121, his partners fell at steady intervals before he became the 10th wicket, giving England a comfortable 197 run victory. England had retained the Ashes.

It's fair to say that this victory didn't capture the public's imagination to anything like the same extent as it did in 2005. There were a number of possible reasons for this. England's home Tests, had, by now, been broadcast on Sky Sports for four years, and this inevitably attracted a far smaller audience, with considerably fewer casual viewers tuning in, or indeed following the progress of the team in general. Secondly, this Australia side didn't have the same prestige as four years earlier, with Shane Warne and co now long retired. Thirdly, and more positively, the public's expectations of the England team were higher. They were the more experienced side coming into the series, and were arguably the strongest team in Test cricket. That said, they still had a lot to prove, and winning an Ashes series Down Under would go a long way towards them earning the status as a truly 'great' Test side.

For Kevin, this was a time of mixed emotions. Yes, he was delighted that England had won the Ashes at home yet again, but this had been a long wait on the sidelines for him, and a return to action was still some months away. He also became very aware that England were capable of success without him. Andrew Strauss had returned to form, and as captain appeared to have the support and respect of the entire England setup. Ian Bell had proven that he thoroughly deserved his recall to the side, while Jonathan Trott, although 28 by the time of his Test debut, showed that he had the potential to become a consistent run scorer at this level for the next decade. In other words, England's success in Test matches didn't depend on Kevin – he would have to earn his place in the team like everybody else, and a few poor performances could put a giant question mark over his selection.

That said, Kevin saw the positive in this situation. He had always believed in the pursuit of excellence, and expected high standards from himself and from his teammates. He knew it was quite right that he should be expected to play at his best consistently, as did ever other member of the side. Competition for places was a good thing: It kept everybody on their toes and meant that an injury to one player wasn't the end of the world so far as the team's chances went.

As the summer drew to a close, Kevin watched on as the two T20 matches against Australia were washed out, while England crashed to defeats in all but the last of the seven matches in the ODI series, often by heavy margins. With the next World Cup still two years away, it was very clear that a great deal of work was needed in this form of the game. It could easily be argued that Kevin's return was far more important to England's chances of success in ODIs than in Test matches at this time.

With the tour to South Africa still some months away, Kevin had enough time to recover, but there was little he could do in the meantime to prepare physically for another intense winter of cricket. This was a frustrating, unsettling time for Kevin. He was just starting to put the debacle surrounding the captaincy episode behind him. The team was moving on, and while not every player was exactly a close friend, these were a group of dedicated players, hungry for success, with whom he could build a long-term, constructive working relationship. In Andy Flower, they had a coach who was a firm, no-nonsense disciplinarian who knew how to bring out the best in the players. Kevin wanted to be a part of it, but for now, there was little he could do apart from follow the doctor's orders. Yet as summer turned to autumn, he received some good news that would change his life forever – Jess was expecting their first baby.

19
DISAPPOINTMENT IN SOUTH AFRICA

Kevin was now 29 years old, and while he could expect to play cricket at the highest level for another five years or more if he stayed free from injuries, he knew he couldn't hang about if he wanted to fulfil his remaining ambitions in the game.

In the year ahead, there was a Test series in South Africa, followed by home Tests against Bangladesh and Pakistan, before the really big one arrived – a chance to defend the Ashes in Australia. He knew that was the kind of series that could seal his legacy as an all-time great batsman.

Yes, the upcoming series against South Africa was a major one. They and India were England's biggest rivals for the status as the world's number one Test team. Yet Kevin didn't feel the same sense of hostility and antipathy towards South Africa as he had during the early years of his international career. England was very much his home now, and that was that. On a personal level, he liked many of the South African players.

Things weren't even that bad between Kevin and Graeme Smith these days. The intense dislike they had for one another some years earlier had developed into a relationship of grudging mutual respect. Journalists were often quick to remind them of their earlier feud, but the insults between them were now jokey and it was more of a pantomime rivalry than anything.

Before the series against South Africa, the country staged the ICC Champions Trophy, but Kevin was left out of the side as he had still not fully recovered from his Achilles injury. In his absence, England's one day side raised their game from the shambles of the late summer and reached the semi-finals, where they came up against Australia, where they suffered yet another heavy defeat, this time by seven wickets. They had been impressive against many of the world's leading sides en route to the semi-finals, but this still wasn't good enough and there was still a lot of work to do, particularly in the field, if they were to fulfil their potential in this form of the game.

Around this time, Kevin suffered a setback when his wound became infected, and Andy Flower suggested to the press that his participation in the upcoming tour was in doubt. This would be a major blow to Kevin, as if this happened, he would have been out of the Test side for around 10 months and a recall in the summer was far from guaranteed.

It was therefore a massive relief when Kevin was declared fit for the series. First up came two T20 matches, which, although good entertainment, were not top of England's priorities. Kevin sat out the first match at Wanderers, Johannesburg, which England won by one run under Duckworth Lewis, but he returned for the second match at Centurion and made 29 before being bowled by Roelof van der Merwe. It was a disappointing return, but most of the England batsmen were poor, with the exception of Trott, as South Africa recorded a comfortable 84 run victory.

Kevin had a disappointing ODI series. In the three matches played (the other two were rained off without a ball being bowled), Kevin made two single-figure scores and one moderately impressive 45, although for the side as a whole, things were looking up, as they won two matches by seven wicket margins, giving them a 2-1 series victory. Kevin knew that the pressure would be on him to perform to his best in the upcoming Test series, and that his critics in the media would be ready to pounce if he had a few bad innings.

In the first Test at Centurion, Kevin made 40 in the first innings before being bowled by Morne Morkel, and in the second he made 81 from 143 balls before being run out when going for a suicidal single, which he later described as his 'brain-freeze moment'. Kevin hated giving his wicket away cheaply, especially when he was feeling comfortable and batting well. He knew he should have gone on to make a century or more, and he was deeply frustrated with himself. After Kevin was gone, the wickets fell like dominoes and they were lucky to get a draw. Although the run out was reckless, he felt comfortable with the bat and he looked to be returning to something approaching his best.

As was so often the case with international cricketers, there was little time to relax and enjoy the Christmas period. The second Test started on Boxing Day in Durban, which, of course, was not far from where Kevin grew up. However, he was far more at peace with South Africa in general this time around. The battles and injustices of his youth were a long time ago and he could see that for him at least, things had worked out for the best.

His relationship with the South African crowds was a good one. Yes, there was some booing here and there, but there wasn't much of a nasty edge to it these days. When fielding, he enjoyed bantering with the crowds, and was happy to sign autographs when there was time. He found long periods in the field could be quite boring, so interaction with the crowd was a good way to keep going.

Yet a few days before the Boxing Day Test, Kevin made it known in an interview that he objected to the crowd swearing during the banter. Kevin had a very traditional, Christian upbringing and thought swearing in front of children was totally unacceptable. It wasn't a case of his impending fatherhood making him more sensitive to these things. He had always believed there was no excuse for swearing in front of children, and had, on occasions, asked stewards to deal with members of the crowd because of it. Apart from this issue, Kevin was enjoying a good relationship with the crowds.

In the second Test, South Africa batted first and were all out for 343. In response, Kevin made just 31 before he was out LBW to Paul Harris, but centuries from Cook and Bell gave England a total of 574-9 declared, and their bowlers were on fire as they bowled South Africa out for 133, giving them victory by an innings and 98 runs.

The final two Tests of the series were a disaster for Kevin. He recorded just one score in double figures (12) and gave his wicket away cheaply. He was far from the only player who underperformed, but he had to accept his share of the blame for the fact that the third Test was drawn and South Africa took the last to level the series at 1-1.

There were a number of theories as to why Kevin's game had deteriorated so badly following a promising start in the first Test. Geoffrey Boycott had rightly detected that Kevin was suffering a technical glitch of playing across the full ball. Others pointed to outside distractions. Some said Jess's pregnancy was a factor. Others suggested that the controversy surrounding his brief spell as captain had never really gone away. Nasser Hussain called for Andy Flower to have a heart-to-heart with Kevin, fearing that the rich pickings of the IPL could cause Kevin to conclude that Test cricket was more trouble than it was worth. Hussain's fears were unfounded. Despite all the controversy that surrounded Kevin, he was sincere in his commitment to English cricket and hadn't forgotten how the country had embraced him as an outsider all those years ago. Of course making money was important, but for Kevin, being part of a great England side was the absolute pinnacle of the game.

As he headed for the two-Test series in Bangladesh, Kevin knew his place in the side was under threat. However, an important first innings of 99 in the first Test and a series-clinching score of 74 not out in the second, during a stand of 167 not out with Cook, saw Kevin re-establish his reputation as a world-class batsman, an entertainer, and a man who could be counted on to make a big innings at crucial times. He ended the short series with a total of 250 runs and an average of 83.33.

Following the conclusion of the Bangladesh tour, Kevin joined up with the Royal Challengers Bangalore in the IPL, scoring 236 runs with a high score of 66 not out. His average of 59.00 was the highest in the IPL in 2010, and played no small part in helping RCB finish in third position, earning them a place in the Champions League Twenty20.

With the English summer about to begin, things were starting to look up for Kevin. His injury had healed, he had rediscovered his form, and, best of all, it was now just a matter of weeks before Jess was due to give birth to their baby boy.

20

PERSONAL HIGHS, CRICKETING LOWS

The international calendar was as relentless as ever, and there was barely time to take stock before Kevin headed off to the Caribbean as part of the 15 man England squad for the World Twenty20. This was going to be another gruelling summer. When they got back to England, there was a short Test series against Bangladesh, followed by an ODI series against Australia, then ODIs against Bangladesh, before further Tests against Pakistan, who they would then face in a ODI series to round off the summer.

Even by modern standards, this was ridiculous scheduling. Few people could see the point of an ODI series against Australia, when they had played plenty of matches in this format at the end of the previous summer, as well as at the Champions Trophy, and would meet again Down Under the following winter. The only possible explanation for this was that Australia would be playing two Tests against

Pakistan in England that summer, because security concerns meant that Pakistan couldn't host international matches at that time, and these ODIs against England would act as a lead-in to that. Yet not one ODI against Pakistan was scheduled as part of the tour, which seemed totally illogical. Nevertheless, Kevin and the rest of the boys had to go along with what the ICC had decreed, however baffling.

Kevin's time in the Caribbean got off to a bad start when he was dismissed for a duck in England's warm-up match against South Africa, and things got little better in their first tournament match against the host nation, where he scored 24 from 20 balls before being dismissed on the pull by Darren Sammy. The match was rain-affected and the West Indies only got to bat 5.5 overs, but the Duckworth Lewis method gave them a seven wicket victory.

In their last group match against Ireland, he made just nine before being caught by John Mooney off the bowling of Kevin O'Brien. The match was heavily affected by rain and no result was declared, but England had done enough to earn a place in the Super 8s.

Kevin's 72 not out was instrumental in giving England a six wicket victory over Pakistan in their first Super 8s match at the Kensington Oval. In their next match against South Africa at the same ground, he top scored again with an aggressive 53 from 33 balls as part of a 94 run partnership with Craig Kieswetter and a 39 run victory for England. The magnificent performance earned him the Man of the Match award.

Suddenly, everything was going right for Kevin. He had been the stand-out player of the tournament to date and had played a massive part in getting England to this stage of the tournament. Yet back home, something even more exciting was happening in his life. Jess was very close to giving birth, and with England already safely through to the semi-finals, he made the decision to skip the final Group E match against New Zealand and take a short visit back home to witness the birth of his son. Kevin had indicated to the England management prior to the tour that he would like to make a brief trip home for the birth, and it appears likely that he would have done so, even if victory against New Zealand was vital to England's progression in the tournament. Most people understood Kevin's decision, but Sir Ian Botham, during his punditry with Sky Sports, made a few grumpy comments about how it didn't happen in his day.

Following the 4,000 mile long flight, Kevin arrived at the hospital just in time for the birth. Baby Dylan was born without complications and Jess was doing brilliantly. Kevin couldn't have asked for more. During a brief chat to the press, Kevin described it as the most amazing experience of his life.

Dylan's birth caused Kevin's outlook on life to change rapidly and radically. He was now responsible for another human being and would have to behave accordingly. Meeting Jess had caused him to curtail most of his wild ways but now he was a father first and foremost, and everything else, such as partying, and even cricket, had to come second. This truly was the best and most important experience of his life.

Kevin and Jess had a few precious days together with their

new son before he had to fly back to the West Indies for the semi-final match against Sri Lanka. In Kevin's absence, England had beaten New Zealand by three wickets, Eoin Morgan top scoring with 40.

Sri Lanka won the toss and batted first, but some tight bowling, especially from Stuart Broad, made it hard for them to make runs, and they ended the innings on 128/6. Once again, Kevin's superbly-judged innings led England to victory, and he ended the match 42 not out, giving his country a seven wicket victory with four overs to spare. Throughout the match, Kevin had a relaxed demeanour and seemed in a jovial mood, which was undoubtedly down to his renewed confidence with the bat combined with joy at having just become a father for the first time.

This had been a magnificent tournament for England. Paul Collingwood had rightly been praised for his superb captaincy and some great catches he had taken in the field, although he had been disappointing with the bat. Craig Kieswetter, who only debuted earlier in the year against Bangladesh, had settled in nicely and was a great wicketkeeper batsman, and comparisons had been made between his batting style and Kevin's. At the age of just 22, there was every reason to believe he would be a regular fixture in the England side in the shorter formats for many years to come, and eventually, a Test star in his own right. Stuart Broad's tight bowling had played no small part in England's road to the final. However, it was Kevin's performances that were the stand-out factor in England's progress to the final.

The final saw England face the old enemy, Australia, yet

again. Kevin had never played in a match like this in his life. Yes, there had been T20 matches against Australia before or after Ashes series in the past, but they were largely treated as knockabout fun and they didn't grieve for too long if they lost. This was different – it was the climax of a major tournament and it was a chance to prove that England weren't just a great Test side, and could adapt to other forms of the game.

In the final, at the Kensington Oval, England won the toss and elected to field. The England bowlers contained the Aussies and some tight fielding kept the score down. Ryan Sidebottom was the star bowler with figures of 2/26, as Australia ended the innings on 147/6.

In response, Michael Lumb, playing in his first series for England at the age of 30, was soon out for two, but the dream partnership of Craig and Kevin was the key factor in giving England victory with three overs to spare, scoring 63 and 47 respectively.

This was a tremendous victory for England, giving them their first ever ICC trophy. For Kevin, this was a career highlight, made all the more special by having beaten the Aussies in the final.

When Kevin arrived home, he was still on cloud nine following the birth of his son. It soon became clear his new outlook on life had seen him become a radically changed man. By his own admission, he was now a far calmer person, and while he only had a night out every once in a while, the vast majority of evenings when he wasn't away on cricket duty, he would be at home relaxing with his family.

On the cricketing front, England would face home Test series against Bangladesh and Pakistan, along with those bizarrely-scheduled ODIs against Australia. With all due respect to the summer's Test opponents, Kevin's mind was already turning towards the defence of the Ashes Down Under in the coming winter, and this was never far from his thoughts as he prepared for the summer ahead.

First up came a two-Test series against Bangladesh. In the first Test at Lord's, Kevin made just 18 and 10 not out, but England dominated the match, with a double century from Trott and a total of nine wickets from Steven Finn saw England ultimately win by a very comfortable eight wickets, having earlier enforced the follow-on.

The second Test at Old Trafford saw another comfortable victory for England, this time by an innings and 80 runs, and Kevin made a reasonable contribution, making 64 before being stumped. Shortly after the series, attention was drawn to the fact that Kevin hadn't played a County Championship game for Hampshire at the Rose Bowl since 2005. The days of England cricketers playing Championship games for their counties in the weeks between Tests were long gone, but most would make an effort to turn out for them when the schedule allowed.

Kevin made one T20 appearance for Hampshire against Surrey after the Bangladesh series, his first appearance for his county in any form of the game for two years. Shortly afterwards, he announced to the media that he would be leaving Hampshire at the end of the season, saying: 'Geographically it just doesn't work. I live in Chelsea'. This statement didn't cut much ice with many people. The Rose Bowl was only around a 90-minute drive away. Plenty of people commuted from Southampton to London for work each day, and it wasn't as though he'd have to make the journey too often. This argument looked all the more absurd when one considered that travelled far greater distances around the country to play for England each summer.

Rod Bransgrove, the Hampshire chairman, was unimpressed to learn about Kevin's decision through the media. Rod was a decent, principled man who had taken Kevin under his wing when he came to the county from Nottinghamshire, and the two seemed to share a vision about how a county should be run in the modern era, and both were naturally ambitious people. After all he had invested in Kevin, picking him up from his lowest ebb after leaving Notts, he felt he deserved to be treated with more respect.

'It's been great to see him but it's not enough,' he said. 'He does play in all forms for England and supports us as best he can from where he is, but the [ECB's] policy for releasing players to play for their counties is quite opaque and I don't fully understand it.'

Kevin's attitude towards Hampshire was in stark contrast to that of his former mentor at Hampshire, Shane Warne. Despite being one of the biggest names in world cricket, Shane made an effort to learn the names of every single member of staff at the Rose Bowl, and following the conclusion of the 2005 Ashes, he rushed back to play for the county. On the other hand, following his single T20 appearance, Kevin was asked by a journalist what he thought of Chris Wood, a promising young left-arm seamer who had taken three wickets. Kevin had to check who Wood was.

Things got even worse the day before the first ODI against Australia, which was played at the Rose Bowl. Rod had set up a question and answer session for supporters the night before the match, and was miffed when the ECB wouldn't permit Kevin to take part. Rod was hardly an ally of ECB chairman, Giles Clarke, and went to considerable lengths to make his county as financially self-sufficient as possible, so that they didn't have to rely too heavily on ECB money. For example, they formed a powerful marketing alliance with IPL franchise the Rajasthan Royals. This decision by the ECB could've been motivated by personal animosity.

The situation at Hampshire was put to one side, for the time being at least, as England faced Australia in the ODI series. England won the series 3-2, but Kevin managed a highest score of just 33. Just when Kevin appeared to have tackled his demons following the difficulties of the previous summer, his confidence was once again at rock bottom.

Kevin was 'rested' for the three ODIs against Bangladesh (which England won 2-1), partly due to a thigh injury he picked up in the final ODI against Australia, but Andy Flower considered it important that Kevin played some competitive cricket before the first Test against Pakistan, and made it clear that he fully expected Hampshire to pick him for their 40 over game against Kent the Sunday before the first Test.

However, Rod Bransgrove had other ideas. Going into the game, Hampshire were already all but out of the CB40, a tin-pot competition, so it wasn't as though the county had a lot to play for, but Rod insisted that Michael Carberry, Jimmy Adams, Michael Lumb, Liam Dawson and James Vince all be retained in the side. He saw all of these players as potential England stars and felt a far greater sense of loyalty towards them than he did to Kevin, and wanted to give these batsmen every chance to impress. It was very clear that Kevin had no future at Hampshire.

Things got little better in the Test series against Pakistan. Kevin top scored with 80 in the first innings of the second Test, but this was the only time he passed 50 in the entire series and in the fourth and final Test (which was famously marred with proven instances of spot fixing by three Pakistan bowlers), Kevin ended the summer with a golden duck.

The problem was very much Kevin's, rather than England's, as despite his poor form, they won the series 3-1, with their victories coming by enormous margins. Prior to that final Test at Lord's, Kevin admitted that he was low on confidence, and this led to many in the media, including Geoffrey Boycott, to suggest that he could do with playing some county cricket before the winter Ashes series.

With Kevin's confidence at an all-time low, he was dropped from the England squad to face Pakistan in the ODI series, the final home action of the summer. The ECB brokered a loan move to Surrey, which would enable Kevin to try and find some form before the Ashes tour. Kevin announced his omission from the side on Twitter, describing it as a 'fuck up'. The tweet was quickly removed, and Kevin apologised soon afterwards. He said he had intended it to be a direct message to a friend, rather than a general tweet which the public could view. He made it clear, as he had in the past, that he disliked swearing, and that his relationship with the England set-up was fine. His poor choice of words was put down to frustration about his own lack of form.

In Kevin's absence, England's ODI side beat Pakistan 3-2, with the series going down to a final match, ironically held at the Rose Bowl, in which Eoin Morgan's 107 not out helped England to a 121 run victory. Other batsmen also had a good series, especially Andrew Strauss, and it was now clear that while an in-form Kevin Pietersen would be a welcome addition to the side, it wasn't the be-all-and-end-all by any means.

Kevin made his Surrey debut in a 40-over game against a weak Worcestershire attack at The Oval. Chasing Worcestershire's imposing 40-over total of 376-6, Kevin played second fiddle to Surrey captain Rory Hamilton-Brown, who smashed 80 off 41 deliveries. When he came out to bat, Kevin received warm applause from the nearly 8,000 spectators while hitting six fours, before being out for 38 when he fell to novice slow left-armer Shaaiq Choudhry. Earlier, Kevin had bowled a single over of off-spin but was smashed for 17 by Gareth Andrew and

Vikram Solanki. This was hardly the sort of start he was hoping for.

A few days later, Kevin played in Surrey's final CB40 match against Sussex at Hove, and sent a loud and clear message out to the England selectors, and to his critics in the media, that although his confidence was fragile, he had lost none of his ability, as he smashed six sixes on his way to 116 from just 105 balls. Coming in at the fall of the first wicket, Kevin put the Sussex attack to the sword until he was finally ninth man out, bowled by James Kirtley as Surrey reached 240 and tied the match.

Just two days afterwards, Kevin made his County Championship debut for Surrey against Glamorgan at The Oval. In his international career to date, he had fallen to left-arm spinners on 38 occasions, and he didn't seem comfortable as he prepared to face Dean Cosker, who was one of the most reliable in county cricket. Kevin pushed the first ball defensively and prodded forward indecisively at the second, and was hit on the front pad. Umpire Nick Cook (himself a former left-arm spinner), raised his finger after an almost theatrical delay.

The second innings fared little better, as Kevin scored just one run from 23 balls, before being given out LBW to young fast bowler James Harris.

That match ended a draw, and the final game of the season saw Surrey travel to Gloucestershire. This was an important match for Kevin's new county. They had been through a terrible season, and they came into the match with the possibility of them ending the season the lowest-ranked county in the country for the first time in their 165-year history.

Kevin came out to bat on a rain-affected first day and made 40 by the close of play, but early the following day, he was caught by Chris Dent off the bowling of newcomer, medium-pacer Gemaal Hussain.

Surrey declared on 180-3 in the second innings, because having enough time to bowl Gloucestershire out was vital, so Kevin wasn't required to bat. Gloucestershire were all out for 250, giving Surrey a tight 10 run victory, and they ended the season third from bottom, with Middlesex and Derbyshire below them.

Although Kevin was delighted to have played a part in helping his new county avoid the humiliation of finishing bottom of the pile, he hadn't made the kind of impact with the bat he'd hoped to. With the exception of that fabulous innings at Hove, this had been a disappointing time. He had given his wicket away cheaply on many occasions. Yes, Dean Cosker was a decent left-arm spinner at county level, and paceman James Harris was regarded as a possible future England star, but the rest of the bowlers who claimed his wicket, were, with all due respect, either inexperienced or were never likely to make it at international level.

Kevin knew he would be facing far more difficult bowlers in the coming Ashes series, and there was a great deal of work to be done before he was physically and mentally prepared to face them. This was probably the lowest point in his cricketing career to date. Yet at the same time, he loved being a dad and things couldn't have been better at home, so there was still plenty to be grateful for in his life.

21

MIXED FORTUNES DOWN UNDER

The upcoming Ashes series in Australia was inevitably going to be a career-defining tour for Kevin. He knew that his stature as an all-time great batsman would be elevated if he performed well during the series, especially if England went on to win the Ashes Down Under. However, he also knew that he was in completely the wrong frame of mind mentally following a largely disappointing few matches with Surrey, and that it was up to him to do everything he possible could to put that right before flying to Australia.

Kevin was much more at peace with South African cricket and indeed the country in general than he had been in the early years of his career. He found the last tour there with England a far more comfortable experience than previous visits, and the fact that he and Graeme Smith now had a cordial relationship was a measure of how much things had moved on in recent years. Things had improved so much that he signed up with Natal (by now known as Kwa-Zulu Natal or more often, the Dolphins), where he would play two four-day matches, without payment, in a bid to find some form before the Ashes. It was a measure of how much things had moved on that he was willing to play for free for the team that had dropped him to fulfil a quota system all those years earlier.

His first match against the Warriors took him even closer to home as it was played in his home town of Pietermaritzburg, the town where he was born and enjoyed a happy childhood. Kevin had a sedate start but seemed to settle in well as he hit six fours. Unfortunately, Kevin's problems with his technique continued as he was out for 36 from 48 deliveries during an 80-run partnership with captain Imran Khan, in what was to be his only innings of the match. This innings received considerable coverage in the British press, with some journalists quick to remind people that Kevin hadn't scored a century for England since March 2009.

His second and final first-class match against the Titans in Durban was even worse, when he was out for a duck, and he wasn't required to bat in the second innings as the Dolphins won by nine wickets with more than a day to spare. Kevin's return to the place where it all began was at an end, and he was forced to accept that he would be travelling to Australia with a massive question mark hanging over his head with regards to his form and whether he deserved his place in the England side.

Kevin understood the enormity of this series for the England side, and indeed in shaping his own legacy in the game. Despite the fact that this was an Australia side in transition following the retirement of the 'golden generation', the Ashes was still a series like no other. Yes, it was easy to argue that India and South Africa were both stronger sides at this time, but in terms of prestige, the Ashes was still the 'big one', the one the fans wanted more than any other, and the one that would be talked about years after Kevin retired. England hadn't won the Ashes in Australia since retaining them in 1986/87, and Phil Edmonds taking the last wicket in that series-clinching match in Melbourne was still etched in the memory of England fans. Kevin knew this was a tremendous opportunity to create a similar historic moment with the bat.

Kevin found some form as he made 58 in the opening warm-up game against Western Australia, but he only managed 35 and five in his other two pre-Ashes innings. A few days before the first Test at The Gabba, Brisbane, Surrey confirmed that Kevin had made his move to the county permanent by signing a one-year contract. Kevin made it known in a statement that he enjoyed his time there at the end of the previous season, and was looking forward to spending time at the club following the Ashes, while chief executive Paul Sheldon let it be known that he was in talks with the ECB that he was in talks for Kevin to be released for a Championship match after the World Cup, before the Test matches in May, and for a few T20 games.

The first Test had arrived, and Andrew Strauss won the

toss and elected to bat. In the first innings, Kevin made 43 before being caught by Ricky Ponting off the bowling of Peter Siddle, as England were all out for a disappointing 260. Centuries from Michael Hussey and Brad Haddin helped Australia to a total of 481. England's opening batsmen were superb in the second innings. Alastair Cook made his maiden Test double-century with 235 not out, which was also the highest Test score by a batsman at The Gabba, while Strauss and Trott both made centuries. Kevin wasn't required to bat again in this rain-affected match as England played out the draw. In a sense, the big scores from the opening three batsmen helped relieve some of the pressure on Kevin as some scaremongering journalists suggested that England stood no chance of winning the Ashes unless Kevin was back on top form. This second innings display showed that England weren't overly-reliant on Kevin when it came to batting, and that the other leading batsmen were more than capable of pulling their weight.

In the four days between Tests, Kevin continued to work hard in the nets to iron out the faults and bad habits he had picked up in recent times. He had worked hard in the run-up to the series, but following the strong batting display by his colleagues in the second innings of the opening Test, he felt the pressure to perform and make a big innings of his own.

Australia made two changes for the second Test at the Adelaide Oval. Out went Mitchell Johnson and Ben Hilfenhaus, and in came Doug Bollinger and Ryan Harris. Neither was exactly experienced at Test level, but it was clear changes needed to be made. The home side won the toss and batted first, but made the worst start to a Test match in 60 years, when they lost the opening three wickets for two runs, with Jimmy Anderson taking two and a run out thanks to Jonathan Trott. 93 from Michael Hussey helped Australia recover to a respectable, but still disappointing 245.

In response, England lost Strauss early on, but by the end of day two, Cook had reached 136 not out, which, combined with his score of 235 not out in the second innings of the first test, gave him the record for runs scored and minutes at the crease without being dismissed, with 371 runs in 1,022 minutes of play. Kevin was at the other end when Alastair reached this feat, and although he was delighted for his teammate, this increased the pressure on him to raise his game. That said, Kevin was feeling more comfortable out there than he had done for quite some time, and knew this was a golden opportunity to make a big score.

Early on the third morning, Kevin reached a century, his first since March 2009. Alastair was eventually out for 148, but Kevin had excellent support at the other end from his close friend Paul Collingwood, who added 42, followed by Ian Bell. Kevin kept batting positively and reached a double-century for the second time in his career. The Adelaide crowd of 32,000 took to their feet to applaud Kevin. He had silenced his critics and regained his old confidence in spectacular fashion. He eventually reached 227, his highest Test score, before being caught by Simon Katich from the bowling of Xavier Doherty.

MIXED FORTUNES DOWN UNDER

This was exactly the sort of innings Kevin was hoping for from the series. He played plenty of characteristic exciting shots, and it allowed him to finally put a hugely disappointing six months behind him. The confidence of many cricketers is notoriously fragile, and Kevin was by no means immune to this. The innings gave his self-esteem a huge boost, and even his harshest critics in the media had to concede this was an impressive return to his very best.

England eventually declared on 620/5, and this was the first time the England team had passed the 500 run mark in successive innings in the Ashes, and left Australia needing 375 to make England bat again. Kevin and Alastair had put England in a very strong position indeed. Kevin was given a rare chance to bowl, and took the wicket of Michael Hussey with the last ball of day four, who, with 80 runs, was the most impressive of the Australian batsman. A five-wicket haul from Graeme Swann helped bowl Australia out for 304, giving England victory by an innings and 71 runs, and a 1-0 series lead. Kevin's innings of 227 from 308 deliveries earned him the Man of the Match award. He couldn't have asked for a better match.

After such a convincing victory, it was always going to be a challenge for Kevin and the rest of the team to keep their feet on the ground in the nine days between Tests. There was plenty of celebrating on the night of the win, but after a few days' recuperation, Andy Flower was keen to get back down to work and iron out any remaining faults as they prepared for the Perth Test at the WACA.

Australia made some radical changes following the

disaster at Adelaide. Johnson and Hilfenhaus returned to replace Bollinger and Doherty, all-rounder Steve Smith replaced Marcus North, while opener Phillip Hughes replaced the injured Katich.

The star of the first day was Kevin's Chris Tremlett, who returned to the England side as a replacement for the injured Stuart Broad. Chris had played alongside Kevin at Hampshire, and had made the move to Surrey from the start of the 2010 season. In the first innings, Chris took three wickets to help reduce Australia to 69/5, however, the middle order rescued the side and they were finally bowled out for 268.

England started positively, reaching 78/0, before Johnson took the wickets of Cook and Trott, and added Kevin's for a duck after just three balls. Collingwood fell soon after to leave England on 98/5, before they were all out for 198. This was the worst possible scenario for Kevin. After performing so well in the last Test, he had come crashing back down to earth.

A century from Hussey helped Australia to 209 in the second innings, leaving England needing a gettable 391 to win. Strauss and Cook fell cheaply, while Kevin soon followed when he was caught by Shane Watson off the bowling of Harris for just three. England fell well short of the target and were bowled out for 123. The blame for England's batting collapse was not entirely Kevin's – all had fallen short of the standards they'd set themselves in the previous Test, but they had grossly underestimated the quality of the Australian attack, especially Harris and

Johnson. It was worth remembering that the latter was named the ICC's Cricketer of the Year award in 2009, and as a youngster had been described by Dennis Lillee as 'a-once-in-a-lifetime prospect'. One bad match at the start of the series didn't make him a bad player, and in this Test he had impressed with both bat and ball.

Christmas was now only a matter of days away. Being away from his wife and new son during his first Christmas was hard enough, but it was made harder still due to his poor performance in the last match. Kevin worked hard with England batting coach Graham Gooch to try and put things right in the six days before the Boxing Day Test. Graham was a man who had enjoyed a 24-year professional career and had experienced all of the highs, and all of the lows a cricketer could face, and if anyone could help put Kevin right, both in terms of mental preparation, and in tweaking his technique, he was the man to do it.

Graham saw his role as primarily one of building relationships, and understood that, as a coach, he couldn't just come in and try to change someone's game. He had to get to know the players, especially strong characters like Kevin, and find out what made them tick. He liked to call himself a coach of run-making rather than batting. Graham also tried to coach shots that he would never have advocated when he started coaching at county level a decade earlier, and had adapted to the more attacking era we now lived in, of which Kevin was at the forefront.

Meanwhile, Andy Flower had a great deal of work to do as he struck a balance between bollocking them for such a poor display in the last Test, and building them up for the two Tests that were still to come. Andy was a naturally calm character, but when he spoke, he had a certain aura about him that made people sit up and listen. He always referred to players by their surnames, and while it would probably be a step too far to say the players feared him, they knew he commanded respect. He was intelligent, thoughtful, and always acted with precision and purpose. He was the perfect man to get his players focussed on the next battle.

The Boxing Day Test was something of a national institution in Australia, so much so that Christmas Day was sometimes referred to as 'Test Match Eve'. The home team's confidence was sky high following their spectacular return to form in the previous Test, and they even looked like moulding into a side that could potentially match the standards of their predecessors in the 1990s and early-mid 2000s. Despite being England's leading wicket taker in the series to date, Steven Finn was rested and replaced by Tim Bresnan, while Anderson was cleared to play after suffering a slight side strain.

Andrew Strauss won the toss and elected to field. Chris Tremlett got 4/26 as Australia underwent an extraordinary batting collapse and were all out for 98 before tea, with all ten dismissals coming from catches in the slips. In response, England were all out for 513, with Trott top scoring on 168 not out, while Kevin managed 51 before falling LBW to Peter Siddle. Kevin had looked good either side of lunch on that second day, but Siddle knew he had got his man as soon as the ball struck the pad, and he had no cause for complaint. Kevin had fallen victim to some variable bounce and appreciable seam movement.

Bresnan justified his call-up by taking 4/50 as Australia were all out for 258 in the second innings, giving England victory by an innings and 157 runs. With England 2-1 in front with one to play, they had retained the Ashes. This was the first time in history that Australia had lost two matches in a home Test series by an innings. This was a truly magnificent achievement, and every single player who had represented England during the series had played their part in making this possible. Yes, Kevin would have preferred to have made more than 51 in this particular Test, but his double century was instrumental in giving England victory in the second Test.

The 'Barmy Army' made up just a fraction of the crowd, but they made all the noise as England closed in on victory. All those years of embarrassing, one-sided series defeats in Australia were over. England had prepared properly, and crucially, had been sharp in the field. It's true that this was very much an Australia side in transition, and they had problems with captain Ricky Ponting and vice-captain Michael Clarke being severely out of form, but that's not to say that this England side hadn't thoroughly deserved their win. There was plenty to build on, as with the exception of captain Andrew Strauss and Paul Collingwood, there was every reason to believe all the rest of the players would still be part of the England side that returned to Australia three years later.

Back home, the victory lifted the mood of the country,

during what was in many ways a difficult time. The nation had been through a tough time with the economy, and much of the country had been covered in snow and ice for the previous few weeks, which made travelling during the Christmas period extremely difficult in many areas. By late morning, Prime Minister David Cameron had given an interview outside his snow-covered constituency home in Witney. He described the victory as a 'great late Christmas present for the country', and spoke knowledgeably about the game as he revealed he had seen quite a lot of the match, and had taken his Blackberry to bed with him the night before so he could follow the action.

This was one of, if not *the* defining series of Kevin's career to date, but victory would taste even sweeter if he could help England win the remaining Test at the SCG. If Australia won this match, the series would end 2-2 and England would've *retained* the Ashes, but victory in the Test would see England *win* the Ashes outright.

There were a few days' rest to do some celebrating and see in the New Year, but Kevin and captain Andrew Strauss were keen to end the series on a high. A finger injury kept Australian captain Ricky Ponting out of the side, meaning Michael Clarke, widely regarded as Ponting's heir apparent, took charge. However, there were still signs that this was an Australian side in transition, as debutant Michael Beer became the 10th spinner to feature in the side since Shane Warne's retirement.

Australia batted first and made a modest 280, and were largely saved by Mitchell Johnson's knock of 53, proving he was a genuine all-rounder who could be relied upon to make runs at important times. England were magnificent in response, as Cook, Bell and Prior all made centuries. However, for Kevin, this was something of a disappointing innings, as following a solid start, he was out, caught by Beer at backward square leg off the bowling of Johnson for 36.

England's lower order all pulled their weight and they were eventually all out for a massive 644. Australia needed to make 364 just to force England to bat again, but three wickets each for Anderson and Tremlett helped bowl them out for 281, giving England victory by an innings and 83 runs. This was a massive victory for England, and they had won the Ashes outright. Astonishingly, they had won by an innings for the third time in the series, and in doing so became the first touring side that had won three Tests by an innings in a single series.

Alastair Cook, who had been made an MBE in the New Year Honours, was named Man of the Series after scoring 766 runs for England, and was also Man of the Match for his 189 runs in the first innings. This was also the end of an era as Kevin's close friend, Paul Collingwood, announced his retirement from Test cricket after being a magnificent servant for more than seven years.

The unusual circumstances of the series meant that Kevin was required to bat two innings just once during the five Tests, so he didn't have as many opportunities to put in big scores as he would've liked, but this was largely because the England side was doing so well.

Just five days later, the sides met again in the first of two

KP: BIOGRAPHY OF A REBEL

T20 internationals. The first match, a day/nighter at the Adelaide Oval, was preceded by a minute's silence for the victims of the recent flooding in Queensland. Precise figures were hard to come by at this time, but in the days that followed it was revealed there were 38 confirmed deaths and a further six people were missing. In total, around 200,000 people in 70 towns had been affected. This was a sharp reminder to Kevin, and indeed all the players in both teams, that this was only a game of cricket, and that there were far more important things going on in life. At the end of the day, win or lose, Kevin's family were healthy, safe and happy, and these terrible floods put cricket firmly into perspective. Both teams donated part of their match fees to the victims and around £18,000 was collected by spectators in the ground.

Australia batted first, and Kevin made a decent contribution in the field as he took a relatively easy catch to send Cameron White back to the pavilion for just six runs, giving Chris Woakes his first international wicket. The Aussies ultimately made 157/4, which, as the score suggests, meant England's bowlers had put in a disciplined performance, while the batsmen were often too conservative for this format of the game.

When Kevin came in to bat with England on 16/1, he made a strong start and played some ambitious shots successfully, but he became a tad too confident and played one stroke too many – David Hussey at mid-off timed his leap to perfection and took a brilliant catch to dismiss Kevin. England won the game on the last ball with nine wickets down. They had won, but only just. Kevin knew that his recklessness very nearly cost his side a win. Nevertheless, this was England's eighth consecutive T20 win, a new international record.

In the second and final T20 at the MCG, Kevin took at great catch on the boundary's edge to dismiss opener David Warner for 30, and Australia posted a total of 147/7. Kevin came into bat with England on a promising 60/1, thanks to a decent opening partnership between Bell and Steven Davies. However, Kevin lasted just two balls before he was out when Johnson bowled him a delivery that invited a massive drive. Unfortunately, Kevin's attempt picked out White at cover who held an excellent low catch. England managed 143/6, and lost by four runs. Their excellent run in T20 games was over, and Kevin knew that he had to accept a large portion of the blame by crossing the fine line between being attacking and irresponsible with the bat.

The ODI series that followed the Ashes had something of an 'after the Lord Mayor's show' feel to it, but with the World Cup just around the corner, this was a chance for England to find some form, and to build on their narrow series victory over Australia in this format of the game the previous summer.

In the first match of the series at the MCG, Kevin made 78 from 75 deliveries to help England post a competitive score of 294, however, England were defeated, largely due to Shane Watson's monumental 161 not out. Kevin followed this by a first ball duck in the second match, his fitness became an issue and he missed the next game with a groin strain. Kevin returned for the fourth match but made just 12, but three days later he announced to the media that England could make a miraculous comeback and win the series from 3-1 behind.

In the remaining matches of the series, Kevin made 40, 29 and 26 respectively, and Australia took the series 6-1. Furthermore, most of Australia's victories had been by substantial margins, and there were few causes of optimism with the World Cup now less than a fortnight away.

For Kevin, this was a somewhat unsettling end to the tour. All the evidence suggested that England were a superb Test and T20 side, but fell well short of the required standard in ODIs. A series of six defeats, mostly by heavy margins, could hardly be described as a blip. With regards to his personal game, consistency was a major issue. At his best, he could be absolutely superb, and was arguably the greatest batsman in the world, but all too often, he would give his wicket away, often playing crazy shots that defied any kind of logic or reason.

The Ashes series win now felt like a very long time ago. England would fly home to London a battered and bruised side, whose confidence was at rock bottom just days before they would fly out to the World Cup, which was to be hosted by Bangladesh, India and Sri Lanka. What Kevin needed right now was to spend some time with Jess and to catch up with his rapidly-growing baby boy, if only for a few days.

22

THE CRACKS BEGIN TO APPEAR

Soon after arriving home, it was revealed that Kevin was suffering from a hernia problem. At first, it was assumed that this was manageable and he would be operated on when there was a convenient window in the calendar, probably at some point in the early summer. However, he was expected to play a full part in the World Cup, and he was told that he would be opening the batting for England in the warm-up matches and throughout the tournament. Kevin had never opened the batting for England in ODIs before, and had done so just six times at lower levels throughout his career.

After a matter of just four days at home with Jess and Dylan, Kevin flew out with the 15-man squad to Bangladesh to prepare for the tournament. Shortly before they flew out, a report appeared in the Daily Mail suggesting that Kevin was going to quit ODIs following the tournament, as he was becoming increasingly irritated by the absurd scheduling of matches and wanted to spend more time with his family, but he quickly took to Twitter to categorically deny these reports. He had criticised the ICC's scheduling of matches in the past, but as they prepared for the tournament, Kevin slammed the drawn-out format of the World Cup, which was to last nearly two months, saying, 'How can the England team play once and then in six days' time play again, and then in six days' time play again? It's ridiculous but there's nothing we can do about the schedules. I wouldn't say we're going to be knackered because it's going to be the World Cup, and we all want to win this World Cup.'

Following the abysmal performances in the recent ODI series in Australia, it was imperative that England made the most of the warm-up matches, and for Kevin, he knew that getting some runs under his belt would do his confidence a world of good.

Things got off to a bad start for Kevin in his role as opening batsman. In the first warm-up match at Fatullah, he was bowled for just 24 as England just about managed to beat Canada by 16 runs. However, things went considerably better just two days later at the same venue as Kevin made a match-winning 66 from 78 balls as England beat Pakistan by 67 runs, although he had perhaps been a tad careless to get himself stumped.

In their first match of the tournament against the Netherlands in Nagpur, India, Kevin made a steady 39 as they chased a target of 293 with six wickets to spare. The next match saw England take on one of the hosts, India, at the M. Chinnaswamy Stadium, Bangalore, formerly Kevin's home ground in the IPL. India batted first and 120 from the great Sachin Tendulkar helped the hosts to a total of 338. The opening partnership of Kevin and captain Andrew Strauss was going well until Kevin was caught and bowled by Munaf Patel for 31 in what was a truly bizarre dismissal. Kevin played a full delivery back to Patel, who put his arms out, more to prevent the ball from smacking him in the face than anything. As Patel fell to the ground, the balled popped up off his palm and gravity caused it to fall back down. Patel, now sitting on the ground, put his left arm out to calmly take a comfortable catch. The crowd were going crazy and Kevin couldn't believe what had just happened, but he was out, and that was that.

Andrew went on to score an impressive 158 and the match was eventually tied on the last ball. It wasn't an ideal result but it was a thoroughly entertaining match between two of cricket's greatest sides, and the tie was probably a fair outcome.

The next match against Ireland at the same venue was a humiliating experience for England. Kevin was on 59 when he had faced two deliveries from Paul Stirling, neither of which he had played very well, before attempting a cute, reverse-dab, but he managed a top edge that looped up for Kevin O'Brien to catch behind the stumps. It was a ridiculous end to what had been a promising innings. Jonathan Trott's 92 helped England to 327/8 at the end of their innings, but with the exception of Graeme Swann,

England's bowlers were poor and Ireland won the match with five balls and three wickets to spare.

England's next match saw them take on a strong South Africa side in Chennai and it was another disappointing effort for Kevin, who became Robin Peterson's second victim in the first over when he handed first slip Jacques Kallis an easy catch after making just two runs. Once again Kevin had given away his wicket cheaply. England were all out for 171 with more than four overs to spare, but some superb bowling from England's attack saw South Africa all out for 165 after 47.4 overs, handing England a six run victory. Kevin had played his part with the ball too, having bowled eight overs, and while he didn't take any wickets, he conceded just 30 runs during his spell. Only Trott and Bopara had put up respectable scores with the bat, and it was England's bowlers who deserved most of the credit for this victory.

Kevin had complained of further soreness due to his hernia during his bowling spell, and spent time off the field, but it wasn't until after the match that the extent of the problem came to light. Within hours of the victory, Kevin announced that his World Cup was over and he would be flying home that evening. Furthermore, he confirmed that he wouldn't recover in time to play for his new team, the Deccan Chargers, in the IPL. Realistically, he was going to need six weeks to recover from his impending surgery.

However, every cloud had a silver lining, and Kevin was very much looking forward to spending time at home with his family and friends. He hadn't been at home properly since 29 October, and it was now early March. That was a long time to be away for anyone, let alone somebody with a baby son. Kevin let it be known that he couldn't wait to see Dylan.

It was at this time that the first cracks began to appear between Kevin and the England coaching staff. Andy Flower said that he thought Kevin could have made it through the tournament with careful management, and said that he might have tried to, in his words, 'bite the bullet'. His view was shared by the England medical staff. Flower was no fool, and always chose his words carefully when talking to the press. It was clear that there was a difference of views as to what course of action Kevin should take, and the divide between Kevin, the coaching staff and some of his teammates was to widen during the following year or so.

Just two days after arriving home, and after claiming to be in a great deal of pain, Kevin was spotted at a notorious new Soho nightclub, The Box, which featured shows involving live sex acts. Kevin was seen downing shots and partying well into the night in the company of his brother, Bryan, his agent Adam Wheatley, while celebrities were also in the vicinity, including Arsenal striker Nicklas Bendtner, just one night after his club was knocked out of the Champions League in Barcelona.

With England struggling to stay in the World Cup thousands of miles away, Kevin's antics so soon after arriving home, allegedly in a great deal of pain, undoubtedly did further damage to his relationship with the coaching staff and some of the players. In Kevin's absence, England scraped through to the quarter-finals of the World Cup where they suffered a humiliating 10 wicket defeat to Sri Lanka.

In early April, not long after undergoing surgery for the hernia problem, Kevin was once again spotted at The Box, this time with comedian James Corden, who had himself recently become a father just three weeks earlier. Kevin left the venue with Corden at 3:30am. Later that day, fellow partygoer Gabe Turner tweeted Kevin to ask whether he was suffering from a hangover, Kevin replied: 'Massive!!!! The Box is amazing hey?'

Kevin's antics divided opinion on two fronts. There were those who believed that, with another gruelling summer of cricket just a month away, Kevin should be doing everything he could to ensure his recovery happened as quickly as possible, so he could get some much-needed practice in to try and regain some form before the series against Sri Lanka. Others argued that while Kevin was entitled to enjoy a night out, his choice of venue was not appropriate for someone who was expected to set an example both as a role model and as a husband and father.

There was another tough summer of cricket ahead, but while many argued that there was still too much cricket being played, the schedule was somewhat better than the previous summer. First up was a three Test series against Sri Lanka, after which they would play them in one T20 and five ODIs. This was to be followed by four Tests against India, who they would then play in one T20 and a five-match ODI series to round off the summer.

Kevin knew that after a disappointing winter and the off-field controversies, it was important he consistently made decent contributions with the bat. However, in the first innings of the opening Test against Sri Lanka in Cardiff, he made just three before he was out LBW to Rangana Herath. Umpire Billy Doctrove didn't think it was out, but the review categorically proved that the ball hit Kevin's pad first. He hung around for a few moments before finally accepting the decision. Kevin knew his critics were ready to pounce, and several broadsheet journalists dropped heavy hints that he was a liability in the following day's papers. As was often the case the previous winter in Australia, this was a dominant performance by England's batsmen and they won the match by an innings and 14 runs, so Kevin wasn't given a chance to make up for it in the second innings. Indeed, England declared on 496/5 in the first innings, so the lower order and tail end weren't required to bat at all.

In the next Test at Lord's, England batted first and made an abysmal start, and were on 18/2 when Kevin came out to bat. He knew this was a golden opportunity to make a big innings and silence his growing army of critics, but with just two runs against his name, he was out thanks to a superb catch at gully by Tillakaratne Dilshine off the bowling of Suranga Lakmal. A man of Kevin's experience should have exercised better judgement and timing – he got an outside edge on the ball but it was a poor shot.

England were all out for 486 in the first innings and the visitors posted 479 in response. For once, Kevin would have an opportunity to make a decent contribution in the second innings. Andrew Strauss, who was having all sorts

of problems with his own batting, was out for a duck
after just two balls, but Cook and Trott built up a 117
partnership before the latter went for 58. Kevin knew this
was his chance to put in a big score at an important time.
He made a promising start, playing some sensible, yet
attacking shots, and this led him to a half-century. He was
eager to push on but when he reached 72 he was bowled
by a terrific delivery from Herath. It was pitched well
outside leg stump, and Kevin got forward and half-
heartedly tried to defend it, but the ball turned sharply and
went on to hit off stump. Kevin was initially looking to pad
it away, but he had to do something when the ball changed
direction so dramatically. Nevertheless, this was a positive
contribution that could help England win the match.
They declared on 335/7, with Strauss and Morgan the
only batting specialists who didn't make at least 50.
Unfortunately, there wasn't enough time left to bowl Sri
Lanka out and a draw was declared with them on 127/3.
The match would be remembered for Dilshin's 193 in the
first innings, and it turned out he broke his thumb while
batting, and he was subsequently ruled out of the third and
final Test. On a sourer note, Matt Prior was reprimanded
by the ICC after he broke a window in the dressing room
after he was run out after scoring just four runs in the
second innings.

The final Test saw Kevin return to the Rose Bowl, his
former home with Hampshire, which was hosting its first
ever Test match. Kevin knew he had to keep things
professional and avoid reopening old wounds. The county

had moved on and seemed to be coping well without him, while his loyalties were very much with Surrey. Chris Tremlett took six wickets as Sri Lanka were bowled out for 184 in the first innings. Kevin came in to bat with England on 14/2. Kevin knew this wicket well, and it was usually one that favoured the bowlers, but with Strauss still having major problems with form and Trott having made just four, this was a chance for him to shine. He and Alastair Cook formed an impressive partnership and took the score up to 120 before Cook was out for 55, but Kevin then formed a successful partnership with Ian Bell and took the score up to 191, having made 85 runs and chasing a century.

Kevin's innings up to this point had been patient and mature, however, he ran short of the former quality as he lunged into an extravagant drive to a full, wide delivery, giving Thisara Perera his first Test wicket. This was deeply frustrating, both for Kevin's supporters and his critics. He had shown just how good he could be, and if he'd carried on batting the way he had been, there was no reason why he couldn't have gone on to make at least a century. It was as though he had become bored with playing sensible shots and wanted to try something more adventurous.

England eventually declared on 377/8, but Sri Lanka successfully batted out the remaining time, with a century from captain Kumar Sangakkara helping them to 334/5, when the clock ran down. England had won the series 1-0 and this could be considered a successful series against a middle-ranking Test nation. For Kevin, it was once again a case of occasional glimpses of brilliance, but he could be terribly inconsistent, and he gave his wicket away in an irresponsible manner far too often for some people's liking.

Next up came a one-off T20 match in Bristol. England were the reigning World T20 champions, and this status inevitably meant Sri Lanka would raise their game. The home side batted first, and when Michael Lumb was out early on, Kevin came out to bat knowing this was a chance to rescue his side with a big innings. His first partner at the other end, Craig Kieswetter soon went, but he and Eoin Morgan got England up to 95, before Ravi Bopara helped them reach 101. Kevin was on 41 when he was bowled by Sanath Jayasuriya. To be fair to Kevin, it was a superb quick ball, which he was looking to run down to third man, but he simply missed the ball. In the T20 form of the game, this was a forgivable mistake. Others gave their wickets away far more cheaply and England were fortunate not to be bowled out before the 20 overs were up, as they reached 136/9. Sri Lanka raced to 40 before Kevin caught Jayasuriya at mid-off, giving Jade Dernbach his first international wicket, but this was a rare high for England as Sri Lanka recorded a nine wicket victory.

Sri Lanka rounded off their tour with a five-match ODI series against the hosts. This was by far England's weakest format of the game, and there had been some truly humiliating defeats in recent times. However, there were signs of hope during the recent World Cup, but they had, in many ways, shown that they were more than capable of getting decent results without Kevin. The pressure was very much on him as he returned to the ODI fold following a controversial period of absence. For the wider team, this was an opportunity to gain revenge for the 10 wicket victory Sri Lanka had over England in the quarter-finals of the World Cup. Andrew Strauss had stepped down as ODI captain following the World Cup and had retired from this format, and new skipper Alastair Cook was keen to get his reign off to a strong start.

The first four matches were shared at 2-2, but for Kevin, this had been a series to forget, as he made a highest score of just 41, which was well short of the standards he set himself, although it should be noted that he wasn't required to bat in the fourth match as England romped to a 10 wicket victory.

With the series level at 2-2, Kevin knew that the final match at Old Trafford was an opportunity for him to show he was capable of making a big innings at an important time, and deserved his place in the ODI side. England batted first and were going steadily on 87-2 when Kevin came out to bat. However, he lasted just 11 balls, making five runs, before he was caught by wicketkeeper Sangakkara from the bowling of Dhammika Prasad. The delivery had some extra bounce to it and was pitched outside off, and Kevin aimed a back foot drive but could only succeed in edging behind. For him, this was a most disappointing end to a generally poor series, but half-centuries from Trott and and Morgan helped England to 268/9. England's bowlers, particularly Tim Bresnan, were the real stars of the game as they contained the Sri Lankan batsmen and bowled them out for 252 to give England a 16 run win and a 3-2 series victory.

For Alastair, this was a solid start to his ODI captaincy.

There were certainly areas to work on, but he had impressed people with his leadership and by this stage he was being talked about as the natural successor to Andrew as Test captain. The spotlight was very much on Kevin following an indifferent series and he knew as much as anyone that he would have to pull his weight in this format of the game, because, frankly, he was giving his wicket away too cheaply too often, and competition for places was healthy.

There was less than a fortnight's break before the main business of the summer began – a four Test series against giants India. It was a shame in some ways that this wasn't a full five Test series, but nowadays that only happened in the Ashes. These were two evenly-matched teams and it would have been more sensible to invite one of the weaker nations to play two Tests against England at the start of the summer before playing a full five Tests against India. This was another series that would help this generation of England players cement their reputations as one of the all-time great Test sides.

In the opening Test at Lord's, England batted first and made a wobbly start, reaching 62/2 by the time Kevin came out to bat. At the close of play on a rain-affected first day, Kevin was 22 not out, but on day two, he made a spectacular return to form. Kevin batted for the majority of the day, and showed why he deserved his status as one of the greatest batsmen of all time. On this occasion, his judgement was spot on and he got the balance right between protecting his wicket and playing some attacking shots. He made a century, but he didn't rest on his laurels and pushed on to reach 202 not out. By this time, England were 474/8 and Andrew Strauss made the decision to declare, as pushing on for victory was his first priority. Who knows how far Kevin would've gone if there was more time in hand, and if he had more batting partners to come. For Kevin, this was a remarkable innings – it took him past 6,000 Test runs in exactly six years, which was the fastest in terms of time taken, although it's only fair to point out that he had played far more cricket than those of previous generations, with a total of 128 innings.

Broad and Tremlett were the star bowlers as India were all out for 286 towards the end of the third day. With plenty of time left in the match, this was a great opportunity to go 1-0 up in the series. When Strauss was out for 32 (he was still badly struggling for form), Kevin understood the importance of building on his first innings performance. However he lasted just three balls and made just one run when he was caught by wicketkeeper MS Dhoni from the bowling of Ishant Sharma. This was extremely disappointing for Kevin, as it gave some credence to the argument he was an all—or-nothing batsman. He either made massive scores, or barely got going. There was very little in between, and frankly, there had been too many single figure innings in recent times. Matt Prior's century helped them to 269/6 when they declared, giving themselves around a day and a session to bowl India out, as they chased a target of 458. Jimmy Anderson got his name on the Lord's honours board with a five wicket haul, and Broad took three as India were all out for 261, giving England victory by 196 runs. Kevin had rightly earned the Man of the Match award, but there were still those who questioned his lack of consistency with the bat.

In the second Test at the batsman-friendly Trent Bridge, Kevin made just 29 when he played a ball he should have left, bowled by his old friend 'Harry Potter' Sreesanth (as he was nicknamed by Kevin at the same venue four years earlier). The ball was an outswinger, just short of a length, outside off, and Kevin tried to withdraw late, but an edge had been taken and third slip Suresh Raina took an easy catch. This looked like being a disastrous innings for England, and they were 124/8 at one point, but Broad and Swann put together a 71 partnership and they were eventually all out for 221.

Broad was then the hero with the ball as he took six wickets as India were bowled out for 288. With more than three days still left in the match, England had every chance of fighting back from a poor start. Kevin and Ian Bell put together a superb 162 run third wicket partnership to put England in a strong position, before Kevin played a loose shot and was caught by wicketkeeper Dhoni, once again from the bowling of Sreesanth for 63. Kevin had made a solid contribution but it was still very frustrating to see him give his wicket away like this. He would have been well advised to think back to those very early days in his career here at Trent Bridge when Clive Rice drilled in to him the importance of protecting your wicket at all costs, as he was of no use to anyone sitting in the pavilion. Bell eventually made a superb 159 and excellent innings from Morgan (70), Prior (73) and Bresnan (90) saw England all out for 544 mid-way through day four. A five wicket haul by Tim Bresnan saw India bowled out for 158, handing England a 319 run victory.

England were now two up in the series with two to play, but this had been an important victory for another reason: Andy Flower was quick to remind them that they had shown in this match that they had recovered well from that batting collapse in the first innings, and that going forward, they should never just accept defeat as inevitable if they got off to a poor start. England had shown great mental strength in this match, even if some of the batsmen, including Kevin, had work to do in the nets with Graham Gooch in the days ahead. Great credit was also due to fast bowling coach David Saker who had really brought out the best in England's attack during the 15 months he had been in the job.

There was one sour note to the match. In the years since his retirement, Michael Vaughan had earned a reputation as a superb analyst for BBC Radio and the highlights programme on Channel 5. During the first session of play, India batsman VVS Laxman was on 27, with his side on 48/1, when the last delivery of Jimmy Anderson's over passed his bat. The bowler and the rest of the England field promptly went up in appeal for a catch behind the stumps and began gathering around the batsman. Umpire Asad rauf ruled in Laxman's favour and Andrew Strauss went for the

Decision Review System, which ruled in the batsman's favour. Kevin and Laxman were seen getting into an argument, and Vaughan tweeted, 'Has Vaseline on the outside edge saved Laxman?' He was implying that Laxman had put Vaseline on his bat so that 'hot spot' wouldn't pick up slight nicks. Vaughan wasn't alone in his thinking. Kevin and the rest of the England field were absolutely convinced Laxman had nicked it, but Stuart Broad later confirmed that he had gone and felt Laxman's bat and could find no evidence of Vaseline. Vaughan received a great deal of criticism for his accusation, not least from former India captains Sunil Gavaskar and Sourav Ganguly, indeed, the former suggested Laxman should take Vaughan to court for questioning his integrity as a cricketer. In response, Vaughan tweeted, 'Taken to court? Sense of humour required for many, I think. I might get an invite into Big Brother in India at this rate!' Indeed, the boffins behind the 'hot spot' technology soon insisted their device couldn't be nobbled by Vaseline.

Moving forward to the third Test at Edgbaston, India were bowled out for 224, with Broad and Bresnan once again the top bowlers, taking four wickets each. Kevin came in to bat with England on a very strong 252-2. Andrew Strauss had found some form, making 87, while Alastair Cook was on his way to making a mammoth innings. Kevin had been walking across his stumps all innings and his luck eventually ended when he was out LBW to Praveen Kumar for a respectable 63. Alastair went on to make 294 as England declared on 710/7. Kevin wasn't required to bat again as a four wicket haul by Anderson saw India all out for 244, handing England victory by an innings and 242 runs.

This was a massive win, and while Kevin hadn't been a stand-out player on this occasion, he had nevertheless made a worthwhile contribution. The series was England's, and the win had put them at the top of the Test rankings. This really was the best test side in the world, and Kevin could legitimately claim to be a major cog in the wheel, despite the problems he had with giving his wicket away on occasions.

A 4-0 whitewash would be the icing on the cake for England, and Kevin went into that final Test at The Oval believing he still had another big innings left in him. England won the toss and batted first, but rain curtailed play on the first day, and Kevin came in with the side on a steady 97/2 on day two. He built up a massive third wicket partnership worth 350 runs with Ian Bell, which put the side in a very strong position, but it was Kevin who was out first when he was caught and bowled by Suresh Raina after making 175. Just like in the first Test, this had been a positive and attacking, yet mature innings, and Kevin had exercised sound judgement throughout. Bell was eventually out for 235 and England declared on 591/6.

India were desperate to bring some respectability to the series. After all, their side contained an array of established, big-name players, but once again England's bowlers performed brilliantly and they were bowled out for exactly 300. England enforced the follow-on, and this time Graeme

Swann took six wickets as England won by an innings and six runs. The whitewash was complete, and Kevin ended the series as the highest England run scorer. Despite some of the valid criticisms of the way he gave away his wicket on occasions, the statistics didn't lie. Kevin was the best batsman in the best Test side in the world.

A few days later, it was announced that while Kevin was to play in the imminent one-off T20 match, he was being 'rested' for the ODI series against that followed. While Kevin had evidently recovered his Test form, the reality was that in ODIs he had made just two half centuries since November 2008. England selector Geoff Miller emphasised that Kevin was being rested rather than dropped, and this was part of their policy of 'sensibly managing player workloads'. Durham allrounder Ben Stokes was called into the squad as Kevin's replacement.

Kevin's final England innings of the summer came in the one-off T20 at Old Trafford. India batted first and were all out for 165 with two balls to spare. Kevin came in to bat for England when Alex Hales was out for a duck on his second ball, and made a respectable 33 before he came too far out of his ground and was stumped by MS Dhoni in a flash. Eoin Morgan top scored with 49 as England reached the target with three balls to spare and six wickets in hand.

In Kevin's absence, England won the ODI series 3-0, to end a hugely successful summer on a high, and to complete a humiliating whitewash over one of the great nations of world cricket. English cricket was on a high, and the side was performing in all three forms of the game. Tensions

THE CRACKS BEGIN TO APPEAR

still existed between Kevin, the England management and some of his teammates, but for as long as the side was performing as well as this, it was possible to paper over these cracks.

23
THE GULF WIDENS

Being a father to Dylan had a profound effect on Kevin, and he was in many ways a very different person to the one he had been a few years earlier. Marriage to Jess had curtailed much of his night clubbing, and, despite the visits to The Box earlier in 2011, these sorts of nights out were now quite rare. Cricket was no longer the be-all-and-end-all to Kevin's life, and he didn't really enjoy the long tours away to quite the same extent that he once did. He had been a frequent critic of the ICC's scheduling of tours, and he continued to air his views on the matter during interviews.

As the summer of 2011 drew to a close, attentions quickly turned to the upcoming winter's tours. First up, in only a matter of weeks, was a trip to India where they would play a five-match ODI series, followed by a T20 international. They would then travel to the United Arab Emirates for a Test, ODI and T20 series against Pakistan, who were still unable to play home matches due to security concerns. This would be followed by a short tour of Sri Lanka where they would play two Test matches.

Many people could see Kevin's point about the scheduling. It was perhaps easier for younger, care-free cricketers to handle this amount of travelling, but for older players, who often had family responsibilities, it was far harder. Was it really any wonder that so many cricketers complained of burnout or psychological problems? For Kevin, leaving for India was especially hard. Dylan was now around 16 months old and was increasingly aware of his surroundings. Now, whenever Kevin went to say goodbye before leaving, Dylan would grab his fingers, as though he knew his father was going away. In this case, he wasn't just going to another part of the country for a few days – he was looking at spending months away from his son, and saying goodbye was especially difficult.

His relationship with the England dressing room wasn't an especially major issue at this time, and it was easy to put differences to one side as the team was doing so well. It is always worth keeping these kinds of issues in perspective. Players not always getting along was nothing new, and there had been personality clashes of one sort or another in most cricket teams over the years. This is no different to any other walk of life. In most workplaces, especially large ones, colleagues fit into three categories: There are those who become good friends inside and outside work, there are those with whom you have a good working relationship, but wouldn't choose to have much to do with beyond the workplace, and there are those you don't especially like, but have to do your best to get along with for the greater good of the company.

Sports teams are no different, but winter cricket tours are so long, and so intense, it's easy to see why personality clashes can be more of an issue. If a person working in an office doesn't particularly get along with a colleague, they can go home at the end of the day and put it to the back of their minds. With cricket tours, you are away from home, and are around these people almost constantly for weeks, or even months on end. If somebody isn't your cup of tea, or if there is a side to their personality you didn't particularly like, it is far more likely to cause a problem than in a conventional workplace.

Kevin's core group of friends from when he started playing for England were now off the scene: Ashley Giles and Darren Gough were now long retired, while Paul Collingwood had bowed out of Test cricket, and didn't look like featuring in the ODI or T20 squads again. At this time, Andrew Strauss had a professional respect for Kevin for the most part – he admired his strong work ethic and he appreciated the way he tried to install these values into the younger members of the squad.

There was one point of tension around this time that couldn't be ignored. Graeme Swann had published his autobiography, titled *The Breaks Are Off*, in which he stated that he thought Kevin was 'never the right man' to captain England. He wrote: 'There is no doubt that Kev is a good player, a really fine batsman, but he was never the right man to captain England in my opinion. Some people are better leaders of men and Kev, for all his abundant talent, is not one of those natural leaders. I wouldn't say he was a useless captain, but he wasn't my sort of captain and we've ended up with the right man. I can't really work out why Strauss demands respect, but he does.' Swann also told the story of the Test match in Chennai in 2008 when India comfortably chased down 387 to secure a famous win. According to Swann, Kevin angrily instructed his bowlers to 'fucking bowl fucking straight'.

Kevin kept quiet for the time being, but during the period home between tours a few months later, he said that it was 'not a clever book' but that things were now 'absolutely fine' between the two, and that it was not affecting team spirit.

The tour of India began with two warm-up matches, in which Kevin produced disappointing scores, which were swiftly followed by the ODI series. India was a spinner's paradise, and Kevin knew this would be an opportunity to repair his reputation as someone who struggled with spin, especially left-arm spinners. For England, this would be an opportunity to build on their huge success against India the previous summer. Good teams won home series, but great teams could also win consistently overseas.

In the first ODI (all of which were day/nighters) at Hyderabad, the home side reached a promising total of exactly 300, but Kevin had a big job on his hands as he came out to bat after Craig Kieswetter fell when England had just seven runs on the board. Kevin started sensibly as he nudged the ball to mid-on and mid-off to run ones and twos, but with 19 runs to his name he was run out after Ravichandran Ashwin threw the ball at the stumps, and Kevin made no real effort to dive and save his wicket. It was a ghastly way to get out, and set the precedent as England collapsed to 174 all out.

Kevin was moved to fourth in the batting order for the next match in Delhi. England batted first, and he came in with his side two wickets down with no runs on the board. This was turning into a nightmare tour, and Kevin had to act fast to turn it around. He batted steadily and did a decent job at repairing the innings with the help of his partners, Jonathan Trott and Ravi Bopara, but on 46 he drove a wide delivery and got a thin edge through to wicketkeeper Dhoni from the bowling of Umesh Yadav. This was a reasonable innings but the damage was largely done by the time Kevin came out, and disappointing performances from England's lower order did further damage as they were bowled out for just 237. A century from Virat Kohli helped India to an eight wicket victory and saw them go 2-0 up in the series.

This was already turning into a disastrous series, and a defeat in the third ODI would put India 3-0 up with two to play, handing them a series win with a whitewash a very real possibility. In the next match at Chandigarh, England batted first and got off to a promising start, reaching 53/2 before Kevin came to the crease. Kevin reached a respectable 64 before falling LBW to Ravindra Jadeja for 64, meaning that once again, he had lost his wicket to a left-arm spinner.

Jonathan Trott was the star of the innings and reached 98 not out as England ended their 50 overs on 298/4. For once, they had given themselves a fighting chance of winning a match. England's bowlers, especially Bresnan and Finn, did an impressive job in containing the India attack, but India took the game by five wickets, with four balls remaining. India had won the series, but the real damage had already been done in the first two matches, and although there were certainly areas to work on for certain players, this was by no means a humiliating defeat.

The series was lost, but captain Alastair Cook and Kevin both emphasised the need to remain positive and build on the momentum of the third ODI. After all, a 3-2 series defeat would look far better in the record books than a 5-0 whitewash. In the fourth match at Wankhede Stadium, Mumbai, Kevin came out to bat with England on 39/2, having just lost the wickets of Cook and Kieswetter in consecutive balls. His 73 partnership with Trott was instrumental in rebuilding the innings, and he continued to make progress with Bopara. Kevin was out for 41 after he bent down low to play a slog sweep off the bowling of Ashwin. He connected well and then stood up to admire the shot, only for substitute fielder Manoj Tiwary to come charging across from midwicket before diving full length and clutching the ball with both hands while airborne. Kevin began to walk off the field but was stopped at the boundary's edge as the umpires checked for a no-ball. After a short delay, they realised the ball was fine and Kevin headed back to the pavilion. To his credit, nobody could

KP: BIOGRAPHY OF A REBEL

really accuse him of playing a bad ball – he was more the victim of an incredible catch on this occasion.

Although Trott and Bresnan made respectable scores, half the team lost their wickets before reaching double figures, and England collapsed to a miserable 200 all out. During India's response, Steven Finn was decent with the ball and debutant Stuart Meaker (who ironically also originally came from Pietermaritzburg) was impressive as he claimed opener Ajinkya Rahane's wicket, but the home side won the match by six wickets with more than five overs to spare, and the series whitewash was still very much on. Alastair Cook was especially downbeat in the post-match press conference, expressing his frustration with the way things had gone, but he appeared to offer little by way of solution.

A fractured left thumb kept Kevin out of the side for the final ODI in Kolkata, where, chasing a total of 271, England were bowled out for 176 in exactly 37 overs, with no fewer than seven England batsmen failing to reach double figures. The whitewash was complete, and England had lost four of the five matches in the series by humiliatingly large margins. In the ODI format of the game at least, they had shown that they were by no means a great side when overseas, and, although still a young team, there was a huge amount of work to be done in the nets and with regards to their psychological preparations.

Alastair admitted that, although he didn't think his men had thrown the towel in, their overall game wasn't up to the required standard. He was modest and polite, and paid tribute to the India team, but didn't go as far as some people would've liked when acknowledging that there was a great deal of work to be done both in the nets and psychologically if England were going to compete away from home.

One feature of this ODI series was that the matches were often sparsely attended. Alastair suggested that the reason for this was that the two sides had been playing each other for a long time by this stage (since mid-summer), and that perhaps people were starting to get a bit bored of it as a contest. In a sense, it appeared that Alastair had at least some sympathy with Kevin's criticisms of the ICC's scheduling of tours. It must be said that back-to-back home and away ODI series against India wasn't the smartest of scheduling, and a tour of such a prestigious cricketing nation as this without Test matches did seem rather odd. Ideally, England would have had October off, to give the players a sensible, and headed somewhere else to play a full series in all forms of the game during the winter months.

Kevin returned to action just four days after that last ODI as England played India in a one-off T20 match at the same venue – Eden Gardens, Kolkata. Many people didn't see the logic in playing just a single, one-off T20 game at the end of the tour, but nevertheless it was an opportunity for England to end their time in India on a positive note and to give a much-needed lift to team morale. As World T20 champions, all the England players realised that theirs was quite a scalp wherever they played.

India won the toss and batted first, but England's bowlers had them well contained from the start, especially Finn, Bresnan and Bopara, and they ended their innings on 120/9.

Kevin came in to bat with England on 21/1, and he formed useful partnerships, firstly with Alex Hales, then with Samit Patel, before he was out LBW for 53 when he swivelled into a reverse sweep but missed the ball and was struck on the pad. It was a very useful innings and England were on course for victory when he was given out with his side on 106/4, but the reality was that once again he had lost his wicket to a left-arm spinner in Jadeja.

England completed a comfortable six wicket victory, and this was a significant morale boost to Kevin and the rest of the boys as they prepared to head home. Despite the disastrous ODI series, they were still entitled to call themselves the best T20 team in the world.

It was now the end of October, and England wouldn't be back in action until early January. This was an opportunity for everybody in the England setup to have a break from cricket, and indeed one another, after an extremely intense 12 months.

However, Kevin had only been home a matter of days when his antics on Twitter landed him in a spot of bother once again. Early in his career, Kevin had said that while he wasn't a massive football fan, he did have a soft spot for Manchester United. In recent years, he had changed his allegiance to Chelsea, largely due to his friendship with Frank Lampard, combined with the fact he was now living in the area. By now, Kevin fancied himself as a bit of a football expert, and made it clear he had little time for his team's new manager, Andre Villas-Boas. Shortly after arriving home, Kevin tweeted: 'Who is the muppet coaching

THE GULF WIDENS

Chelsea??? AVB??? Hmmm!! 25yrs for Ferguson, hopefully not even 6 months for this AVB geezer!!'

While AVB had got off to an indifferent start at Chelsea (and indeed was sacked a few months later), quite a few people considered Kevin's comments to be unhelpful and thought he was speaking out of turn. AVB had an impressive track record in his previous job as manager of FC Porto in Portugal, and didn't deserve to be labelled a 'muppet', even though he appeared to be somewhat out of his depth at Chelsea at such an early stage in his managerial career. Kevin's judgement on the coaching ability of others wasn't always the best. All those years ago at Nottinghamshire, he clearly had a very difficult relationship with Mick Newell and Kevin made it very clear, very publicly, that he didn't think Newell was very good. However, in Kevin's final year at Notts (2004), the side had been promoted to Division 1 of the County Championship as champions. The following year, when Kevin had moved on, Notts won the Division 1 title, and they did so again in 2010, all under Newell's guidance. Kevin and Newell didn't get on, but his earlier comments about Newell's abilities as a coach were now looking extremely foolish.

Kevin would also have done well to have learned to use Twitter more wisely earlier in the year. In May, he started a rumour that Real Madrid and Brazil star Kaka was about to join Chelsea. He tweeted: 'Hope I'm not being a snitch.. BUT, I had dinner a couple tables away from KAKA last night.. Are we gonna see the great man CFC?? Hmmm,'

The restaurant in question was Zuma in Knightsbridge,

but apart from an off-the-cuff remark from the player's mother a week earlier hinting at a move to Stamford Bridge, there wasn't much to go on. In the end, nothing came of it and he remains at Real Madrid to this day.

Outside cricket, Kevin was developing other business interests. He had been represented by Mission Sports Management for some years now, run by Sir Ian Botham and Adam Wheatley. During 2011, Sir Ian sold his stake to Kevin, which left him in the rather intriguing position of owning part of the company whose clients included England teammates Ian Bell and Ravi Bopara, along with a host of other sportsmen and women.

Being home for that Christmas meant a lot to Kevin. By now, Dylan was 18 months old, and, while still a bit young to fully appreciate what was going on, he was certainly aware of something special happening. Kevin understood that these were precious times, because Dylan would inevitably growing up quickly, so he made the most of what was a peaceful and happy family Christmas.

Early in the New Year, it was time for Kevin to say goodbye to Jess and Dylan, which was made somewhat easier by the length of time he had spent catching up with his wife and bonding with his son. The squad flew out to the United Arab Emirates for the tour against Pakistan. The entire tour was played at two venues – the Dubai International Cricket Stadium, and at Sheikh Zayed Stadium, Abu Dhabi. It was unfortunate that security concerns made playing matches in Pakistan unviable for the time being, but this was, in many ways, a trip to the unknown, or, at least, the unfamiliar, as Kevin and the squad had to get to grips with the balmy heat that characterised the region. One plus point was the unique lighting system in the Dubai stadium, which was known as the 'Ring of Fire'. Rather than there being huge floodlights in all four corners, there were lights right around the circumference of the stands in the oval-shaped stadium, which minimised shadows.

In the first Test in Dubai, England batted first and Kevin came to the crease with the side on a disappointing 31-2. Kevin struggled with the conditions and had made just two runs in 29 balls when Saeed Ajmal's delivery initially appeared to squeeze past Kevin's outside edge and ran away for leg byes, but the subsequent review proved that the ball had struck him on the back pad. Replays categorically proved that it would've gone on to hit middle and leg stump, and he was out LBW. All England's batsmen, with the exception of Matt Prior, struggled with the wicket and they were all out for a disappointing 192.

In response, Pakistan posted 338, with Graeme Swann taking four wickets, and it was already looking unlikely that England could save the match, as it was still only day two. England were on an awful 25/2 when Kevin came out to bat. He was out for a duck after 13 balls, but the manner of his dismissal was truly shocking. It was a good short delivery from Umar Gul, and Kevin played an awful short to square leg where he was caught by Abdur Rehman. This was the sort of dismissal that would embarrass even the most ordinary village cricketer. Only Trott and Swann posted respectable scores with the bat, as England were all out for 160, leaving Pakistan needing just 15 runs to win, which they duly got in just 14 minutes, with more than two days to spare.

This was an abysmal performance from England, and Kevin had to accept a very large share of the blame. It's true that the conditions took a bit of getting used to, and Pakistan were more familiar with them, but that was no excuse for a defeat of this magnitude by the number one Test nation in the world.

There were just four days before the next Test in Abu Dhabi and Kevin knew he had a lot of work to do with Graham Gooch in the nets. Pakistan batted first and made 257, with Broad taking four wickets. When England began their innings early on day two, they knew this was a chance to make up for the disastrous first Test. An innings of 94 by Cook helped England to 166/2 when Kevin came out, but he made just 14 before an inside edge saw Mohammad Hafeez take a well-judged catch off the bowling of Ajmal. Broad's 58 helped England to 327 all out, and with half the playing time still available, this was very much game on.

Six wickets from Monty Panesar saw Pakistan bowled out for 214 shortly after lunch on day four, meaning England needed 145 runs to win. Cook and Bell fell early and England were on just 26/2 when Kevin came to the crease. This was a chance for him to put together a match-winning innings, but he'd made just one run when he was given out LBW following a review, and Hawkeye showed it was clipping the top of the stumps. Kevin had lost his wicket to

Abdur Rehman, who, yes, was a slow left-armer. England then suffered an appalling collapse and were all out for 72, with no fewer than nine of the batsman failing to make it into double figures. This was a real horror show for England, and was one of the most embarrassing defeats in the country's long cricketing history. After the match, Andrew Strauss admitted he couldn't think of a more disappointing match, and he gave a cliché-ridden press conference, referring to how they needed to 'take it on the chin' and so on. Monty had been a star in the first innings and Stuart had played his part with both bat and ball, while Alastair had a decent first innings. Everybody else had fallen well short of the standards they had set themselves, and they looked a million miles away from being a leading Test nation as they went 2-0 behind with one to play.

In the third Test back in Dubai, England bowled out Pakistan for just 99 in the first innings. In response, England lost Cook and Trott early on and Kevin came out with the side on just 7/2. He managed 32 before he was out to left arm spin once again, this time in the shape of Abdur Rehman. This was one of those dismissals where in times past he would probably have been given the benefit of the doubt, but in this age of DRS he had to go. England were predictably bowled out for 141, allowing Pakistan right back into the match. Centuries from Azhar Ali and Younis Khan helped Pakistan to a second innings score of 365, meaning that England needed 324 to win with more than two days to go.

England were on a cautiously optimistic 85/2 when Kevin

came out, but he was out for just 18 when he misjudged Saeed Ajmal's off-spin. It was a disappointing end to a dreadful series for Kevin, but things got worse as England collapsed to 252 all out, to complete a humiliating series whitewash. The reality was that, for all their superb efforts at home and in Australia, they couldn't cope with Asian conditions. England's bowlers had been quite good overall, but the batsmen had failed to adapt. Even if some allowances were made for the differences in conditions, there was still little excuse for the sheer magnitude of England's batting collapses in the three Tests.

It was now less than a week until England played the first of four ODI matches, and they were keen to make amends both for the recent Test series, and for the whitewash they had suffered in India at this form of the game a few months earlier.

In the first two matches, both at Abu Dhabi, Kevin, who continued to open the batting in ODIs, made only small contributions as two centuries form captain Alastair Cook saw England surge into a 2-0 lead. By the time of the penultimate ODI in Dubai, it was the second half of February, and it had been some months since Kevin had made a sizeable innings. He knew the pressure was on to justify his place in the side. Pakistan reached 222 all out in exactly 50 overs, and, in response, Kevin made a magnificent 111 not out under the floodlights as England cruised to a nine wicket victory. This had been a vintage Kevin Pietersen innings with ten fours and two sixes. He had dominated the England innings from start to finish and had ensured they won the series.

THE GULF WIDENS

Some predictable things were written by Kevin's critics about how he was an all-or-nothing cricketer, saying things like that for every century he made, there were would be half a dozen innings where he wouldn't pull his weight. It would do Kevin's morale, and that of the England setup, if he was to put in another strong performance in the final ODI at the same venue, and, as England chased a target of 238, Kevin hit 12 fours and two sixes as he made 130, before being caught at point with England needing two more runs. There was a small amount of tension as England sought two more runs with four wickets remaining in the final over, but Bresnan and Patel saw them to victory with four balls to spare.

Kevin had made back-to-back centuries playing exciting, yet wise shots, and had taken few extravagant risks with his wicket. He had won the Man of the Match award in both the final matches, and was England's stand-out batsman. This was exactly why Kevin was rightly regarded as one of the greatest batsmen of all time, but the general consensus was that he needed to be a lot more consistent. It wasn't that often that he made innings between 40 and 80. It was either below 40 or a century and in many respects this was dangerous.

England's time in the UAE ended with, for once, a sensible series of three T20 matches, beginning in Dubai just two days after the final ODI. Kevin made 33 in the first match, in which England suffered a narrow eight run defeat, and in the second at the same venue, he made 17 as Jonny Bairstow's 68 not out helped England to a 38 run victory to take the series into a decider at Abu Dhabi.

In that final T20 match, England won the toss and elected to bat. Kevin opened the batting and remained there throughout England's innings, making 62 not out as they ended on 129/6. It looked like a fairly small total, but wasn't untypical compared to the previous two matches. If anything, Kevin had been slightly too conservative in this innings. England's bowlers, especially spinners Patel and Swann, contained Pakistan's attack and Pakistan ended on 124/6, handing England a five run victory and the series.

Kevin's innings earned him the Man of the Match award. After a hugely disappointing Test series, Kevin had ended his time in the UAE on a high, and success in the shorter formats had given both his, and the England squad's morale a much-needed boost.

Just two weeks later, England were to start their tour of Sri Lanka, where they would play two warm-up matches and two Tests. However, England's presence in Sri Lanka was controversial. The previous November, the Sri Lankan military had taken control of all three of the country's main cricket stadia after the game's governing body in the country (which faced numerous accusations of corruption) said it could no longer afford to run them. This was the same Sri Lankan military that had been accused of some of the most serious war crimes committed in the 21st century by Amnesty International, Human Rights Watch, the United Nations, and the US State Department.

Andy Flower's views on this matter were of particular interest. Back in 2000, his international career with Zimbabwe was brought to an abrupt end when, at Harare

THE GULF WIDENS

Sports Club, right next to the Presidential residence, he, along with Henry Olonga, took to the field wearing black armbands in protest at the death of democracy in the country brought about by Robert Mugabe. At the time, Flower was arguably the best batsman in the world and almost certainly the best player of spin. In relation to the Sri Lanka situation, Flower said: 'As I understand it, those investigations by the UN are still on-going, it is certainly not my position here to take a political stance. I know yours is a human rights question, but it's my position here not to take a political stance. I understand to a certain extent the history of Sri Lanka's troubles and have much sympathy with both sides. However we are going to Sri Lanka to play cricket and we will be limiting our focus to that.'

On this basis, Kevin and the rest of the team headed to Sri Lanka for the short series. Kevin failed to impress in the warm-up matches, and he disappointed in the first Test at Galle, making three and 30 as England suffered a 75 run defeat, caused mainly by indifferent batting by most of the lineup in both innings.

The second Test in Columbo was a very different story. Sri Lanka won the toss and elected to bat, but were all out for a disappointing 275 as Swann took 4/75. Kevin came out to bat with England on a healthy 213/2, and he knew this was his opportunity to put England in a match-winning position and restore his reputation in Test cricket. He didn't disappoint, and played a near-perfect modern Test innings, reaching 50 in 59 balls, before turning it into 100 off 109, earning him his 20th Test century. He kept going, and reached 150 off 162, before being given out having made 151 following a review on an LBW call by Rangana Herath. England's leading batsmen had all played well and they were eventually all out for 460 towards the end of day three.

England bowled Sri Lanka out for 278, meaning they required 98 to win, but with their 72 all out against Pakistan still fairly fresh in the memory, they weren't taking anything for granted. England lost Strauss for a duck and Trott for just five, and the side was on 31/2 when Kevin came in, and it's fair to say there were a few nerves around. However, he and Alastair Cook steadied the ship and their partnership saw England all the way to an eight wicket victory. England had levelled the series and Kevin thoroughly deserved his Man of the Match award. After an appalling start to the winter, Kevin had spectacularly returned to form with some career-defining innings in the early months of 2012. Little could he have known at the time of the drama that was about to unfold.

24
THINGS
FALL APART

The first signs of trouble came when it was announced that Kevin had signed for the Delhi Daredevils in the IPL, who paid his previous team, the Deccan Chargers, around £1.3 million for his services. Kevin would only be available for roughly the first three weeks of the IPL, before he was expected to return to England to play a county game to set him up for a summer on international duty. He was expected to earn approximately £750,000 playing in the IPL, which was huge money, even by Premier League football standards.

The problem was that Kevin was the only one of England's World Cup winning T20 team who had been offered an IPL contract. If Kevin was a total mercenary, he would have told England he was retiring from all forms of international cricket, and could play the full IPL schedule, which would earn him two to three times this figure, while spending the rest of the year making himself available for other T20 competitions around the world, as and when it suited him. But he didn't do this. Instead, he played in the early stages of the IPL, with the approval of the ECB, and would return for the summer's cricket in England. This told us a lot about his character, but it also helped sow the seeds for some petty jealousies further down the line. To put it politely, they had just come through a 'mixed' winter in terms of results and performances, so it wasn't as easy to put differences to one side as it would have been when things were going well.

Kevin's short time with the Delhi Daredevils was a successful one – he smashed nine sixes as he scored his maiden T20 century to give his side a five-wicket victory over his former side, the Deccan Chargers. This was a very special experience for Kevin – the pressure was certainly on, not only because he was being paid so much money, but also due to the size of the crowd and the massive following the tournament had in India and around the world. He said, 'This is absolutely amazing, this is what dreams are made of. You come here as an England player and it's very, very intimidating but to come here and have all these fans cheering for you is very special. That was my first Twenty20 100 so it will be pretty hard to beat.' Although his stay was short, it was clear that Kevin loved the IPL, and the IPL loved Kevin.

Kevin arrived home to prepare for another bafflingly-scheduled summer of cricket. First up came a three-match Test series against the West Indies, who they would then face in a three-match ODI series, followed by a one-off T20. Australia would then arrive for a five match ODI series, and would depart before South Africa touched down for a three-match Test series. Next came a one-off ODI against Scotland, followed by a five-match ODI series against South Africa, who they would then face in three T20 games to round off the summer. Just when fans thought the ICC's scheduling couldn't get any more ridiculous, they came up with something like this. Few people could see the point of the ODI series against Australia, as they were due to come to England the following summer for the Ashes, an ODI series and T20s, as well as taking part in the ICC Champions Trophy in the country beforehand. It would surely have been more sensible to have a full, five Test series against South Africa or the West Indies, play then in the shorter formats, while beginning the summer with a shorter series against one of the weaker nations. This scheduling was confusing to fans, and cheapened the overall product.

In the opening Test against the West Indies at Lord's, Kevin was disappointing as he made just 32 and 13, but England won the match by a comfortable five wicket margin, largely thanks to Broad's seven-wicket haul in the first innings.

The first Test was marred by a row between Kevin and Sky Sports commentator Nick Knight. Kevin tweeted: 'Can somebody please tell me how Nick Knight has talked his way into the commentary box for home Tests? Ridiculous.' This wasn't the first time the pair had clashed – the previous year, Kevin said that Knight was 'stealing a living' by commentating on England matches. There was a lot of mis-reporting as to what had prompted Kevin to lash out at Knight in this way. The truth was slightly more complex. Kevin wasn't especially bothered that Knight had called for him to be dropped from the ODI team, nor was there any truth in the rumour that there was bad blood between the two from the days when Knight was Warwickshire captain while Kevin was at Nottinghamshire. In fact, Kevin and a number of his England teammates had become increasingly irritated by the way in which Knight went about his job. Knight had a habit of approaching England players while they were on the outfield and would then broadcast the information he obtained during his commentary stint.

Following a meeting convened by Andy Flower and managing director Hugh Morris, Kevin's remarks were deemed 'prejudicial to ECB interests and a breach of the England conditions of employment', and he was fined £5,000, partly suspended for 12 months . The story was blown out of proportion by some in the media. Kevin and Knight met during the Lord's Test to clear the air, and the pair parted amicably. The ECB were understandably sensitive about any criticism of the Sky coverage, because just a few months earlier, they had agreed a further four-year broadcasting contract worth £260 million.

In the second Test, the visitors made 370 in their first innings on a Trent Bridge pitch that favoured batting. This was the venue that Kevin called home when he started his career, and one of the reasons he was keen to move on was that he found it too easy to make runs here and he felt that it wasn't helping him improve his game. He arrived at the crease with his side on 123/2, and made an impressive 80, before being given out LBW to Ravi Rampaul after asking for a review. Strauss made 141 and England were all out for 428. Anderson and Bresnan took four wickets each as the West Indies were bowled out for 165, and Kevin wasn't required to bat as England reached the 108 run target with nine wickets in hand, winning them the match and the series.

A few days after the second Test, Kevin made the surprising announcement that he was retiring from ODI and T20 internationals. He wanted to continue to play in T20 matches, especially the T20 World Cup, which England were defending this autumn, but the terms of his central contract meant that he had to retire from both forms of the game. His statement read: 'With the intensity of the international schedule and the increasing demands on my body, I think it is the right time to step aside and let the next generation of players come through to gain experience for the World Cup in 2015.'

This was taken as a sign by some that Kevin's commitment to England was waning, and that he had effectively chosen the IPL over England duty if he felt he needed to cut back on his workload. However, there were plenty of people who sensibly acknowledged that the career of a professional sportsperson is short and they are perfectly within their rights to make as much money as possible in the time available. His 'retirement' wasn't going to be the end of the matter.

The final Test at Edgbaston was heavily affected by rain

and a draw was almost inevitable when no play was possible on the first two days, but Kevin made 78 before being caught by Darren Sammy off the bowling of Marlon Samuels. This was by no means anything like as strong a squad as those the West Indies brought to England in the 1980s, but overall, the team could be proud of the start they'd made to the summer's Test cricket after the nightmare against Pakistan during the winter.

A week after the final Test, Kevin's life was struck by tragedy. He had been close to the Maynard family for some years by this stage. Matthew, the former Glamorgan and England batsman, had helped Kevin hugely when he was Duncan Fletcher's assistant coach until 2007. At Surrey, Kevin had got to know Matt's son, Tom, who had joined the county from Glamorgan at the start of the 2011 season.

Kevin made no secret of the fact he thought Tom had huge potential as a batsman, and even went as far as to say he considered him his natural successor. Tom's behaviour had given some cause for concern in recent times. He had damaged a shoulder after being hit by a car in Brighton, where the side was playing Sussex at Horsham. That breach of discipline led to Tom being left out of Surrey's first T20match against Essex. On the Saturday, Tom appeared on the TV programme *Cricket AM*, where he appeared to be happy and good-humoured. He returned to action the following day for the match against Kent at Beckenham, in which they had been defeated. That night, Tom went for a night out in London, and had been drinking with teammates Jade Dernbach and Rory Hamilton-Brown at the Ship Inn pub in Wandsworth before continuing to drink in the home he shared with Hamilton-Brown. They arrived later at the Aura nightclub in London before leaving with three sisters and returning home. Tom arrived home and phoned his girlfriend, Carly, in the early hours of the morning saying he was really depressed and was coming to see her. When he failed to turn up she panicked and rang his phone about 50 times, without answer.

Tom's car had been stopped by police around 4am, roughly half an hour after he left home, when they saw it being driven erratically. Tom fled the scene, and at approximately 5am he ran onto a railway line near Wimbledon Park Station in South London, where he touched a live electric line, before being hit by a train, causing his death. Police treated the death as non-suspicious, and in the subsequent inquest, it was revealed that Tom was four times over the legal drink drive limit, and had been using both cocaine and ecstasy. Hair samples suggested he may have been a 'habitual' user in the months before his death.

Kevin was devastated by Tom's death, as although he didn't condone his behaviour in the run-up to his death, he believed Tom was essentially a decent lad and a tremendous cricketing talent. Those who knew Tom well described him as likeable and charismatic, but a bit of a 'loveable rogue', who deserved to be remembered for far more than the wrong things he did in the final part of his life. This was yet another tragedy for Surrey, who in recent years had lost players Ben Hollioake and Graham Kersey in car accidents.

Kevin was one of a number of big-name cricketers who

attended the funeral at the beautiful Llandaff Cathedral in Cardiff. Along with Tom's father, other cricketing legends present included Andrew Strauss, Andrew Flintoff, Mike Gatting, and Alec Stewart. Family friend Lucy Jones, who had reached the finals of the *X Factor*, sang two songs during the moving service, which also included the Surrey team song, 'A Little Respect' by Erasure, along with some of Tom's favourite songs by Coldplay and The Calling, along with a rousing version of 'Bread of Heaven'. It was a tremendously sad day, but Kevin felt pleased that his friend was given such a strong send-off, and that people were keen to focus on the good he had done in his short life.

In Kevin's absence, England won the ODI series against the West Indies 2-0, both by comfortable margins, with the third match being abandoned due to rain, and won the one-off T20 game that followed by seven wickets. This showed that Kevin's presence in the squad was by no means essential to England's success, and that the batting lineup was strong enough to cope without him if it needed to, and this was reinforced by a 4-0 whitewash over Australia in the following ODI series (the third match in the series was rained off).

Kevin returned to action in mid-July for the three-Test series against South Africa. There had been some pre-series publicity in the press about Kevin and Graeme Smith doing battle again, but their feud was now long-over and there was only a bit of harmless banter between the two in the papers. Just days before the start of the series, Kevin offered to end his exile from the short formats of international cricket on the condition that he be allowed to play the entire IPL season, meaning he would miss the two-Test series against New Zealand at the start of the 2013 summer schedule. There was no way the ECB or Andy Flower was ever going to accommodate Kevin's requests. The ECB was desperate to defend the status of the May series, which struggled for attention and crowds as it clashed with the end of the football season. It would also have set a dangerous precedent for any other England players, either now or in the future, who were offered IPL contracts.

Kevin complained that he had 'never been looked after' and that 'everyone else' in the squad was rotated. However, he had been rested on occasions in recent years, and had been permitted to return from the Caribbean to witness the birth of his son. Kevin was gaining a reputation as something of an unreasonable complainer, and, in reality, he hadn't been treated any worse than the rest of the team. Yes, Kevin was entitled to criticise the ICC's scheduling, and many, many people shared his views on that, but it's hard to see that anything other than a desire to play the entire IPL schedule was behind his complaints at this time, which increased the strain on his relationship with the ECB.

Flower admitted Kevin was a 'very different' person to him, and that he thought a player still very much in his prime, which Kevin was, should make himself available to his country in all forms of the game. Flower added that he thought Kevin would regret not playing in the World Cup and World T20 when he looked back on his playing career in years to come. That said, the evidence at this time suggested that England would cope very well without Kevin in the shorter formats, and they had just become the top-ranked ODI nation in the world. Kevin was effectively asking to be given a 'special' contract that would elevate him in importance over the rest of the players, and this wasn't acceptable. The relationship between Kevin and the ECB had deteriorated considerably as a result of this episode.

In the first Test at The Oval, Kevin came in with England on 170/2 and made 42 before failing an attempted hook shot, and was caught by wicketkeeper AB de Villiers from the bowling of the great Jacques Kallis. England made a respectable 385, but the bowlers had a torrid time, and South Africa declared on 637/2 at tea on day four, with Hashim Alma making 311 not out, which included 35 fours. England had to bat out the remaining four innings to force a draw, but they got off to a poor start when Kevin arrived with the side on 32/2. Kevin fully understood that this was an occasion where he just had to play for time, defending his wicket at all costs, even if it wasn't particularly eye-catching stuff. However, he had made just 16 from 36 balls when he was caught on the back foot and bowled by Morne Morkel. The wickets fell steadily and England were all out for 240 shortly before tea on the final day, handing South Africa victory by an innings and 13 runs.

The second Test at Headingley was overshadowed by the fact that the 2012 Olympic Games in London were underway, and this was very much the focus of the British nation's sporting attention at this time. Cricket was struggling to get anything close to the amount of column

THINGS FALL APART

inches it would normally expect at this time of year, which in some ways was a good thing, because Kevin's recent arrogance wouldn't have been well-received by most of the British media. South Africa posted a total of 419 in the first innings, with Alviro Petersen, one of cricket's true gentlemen, making 182, while Kevin claimed the wicket of Jacques Rudolph during his seven over spell.

In response, England made a reasonable start and were on 85/2 when Kevin came out to bat, shortly after lunch on day three. What followed was a classic Kevin Pietersen innings, as he dominated the rest of the day, forming strong partnerships with Trott, Bell and debutant James Taylor. Mid-way through the final session of the day, Kevin reached his century, scoring 100 off 147 deliveries, and he continued to push on, reaching 149 by the close of play. Three balls into day four, and having added no further runs, Kevin was out LBW to a perfectly pitched delivery by Morne Morkel. This had been a magnificent innings at an important time, and it had contained 22 fours and one six. For all Kevin's attitude problems around this time, he showed he was still very much at the top of his game as far as his cricket was concerned. England were eventually all out for 425, meaning that there was everything to play for. Unfortunately, there had been rain on all four days so far, and on this occasion it forced an early lunch and delayed the start of the afternoon session. In South Africa's second innings, Kevin made an unusually large contribution with the ball, as he claimed the wickets of both openers, Jacques Rudolph and Graeme Smith, before adding Hashim Amla later on, arguably the greatest batsman in world cricket at that particular time. Kevin's efforts with the ball (3-52, his best bowling figures in Tests), along with Broad's five wicket haul, saw the visitors bowled out for 258. Time was very much against England as they chased the target of 253 to win from around 33 overs, and Kevin was out for just 12 as he played an attacking shot but was caught at mid-on by Imran Tahir. The victory wasn't very likely, and the clock was run down with the draw being declared when England reached 130/4. This had been a classic Test match in many respects, and it was a shame that it received so little attention as the British media focussed so heavily on the Olympics.

Kevin was named Man of the Match for his exploits with both bat and ball, but shortly after the match, it became clear that there were very serious problems with Kevin's relationship with the squad, the coaching staff and the ECB. Despite all the behind-the-scenes talks, he had been left out of the provisional World T20 squad, which was announced during the Test, in preparation for the tournament in Sri Lanka, starting in early October. Kevin dropped a strong hint in the post-match press conference that the third and final Test against South Africa at Lord's might be his last, and that there were 'certain issues' in the England dressing room that needed to be resolved.

In the days that followed, allegations were made that Kevin had sent text messages to members of the South African team in which he had made derogatory comments about England captain Andrew Strauss and team director Andy Flower. By the same token, Kevin was angry that a parody Twitter account had been set up, called 'KP Genius', that poked fun at his supposed arrogance and sense of superiority over his England teammates. Kevin was convinced that some people from within the England setup were behind it.

The story moved quite quickly, and by the Saturday, Kevin's management stable released an online video in which he was questioned, out of shot, by Adam Wheatley. The timing of the video's release onto YouTube was interesting – it happened on that famous Saturday night of athletics where British athletes enjoyed an extraordinary and unexpected level of success, so this development with Kevin's saga didn't receive the level of media attention it would have done under normal circumstances. In it, Kevin made the surprise announcement that he wasn't going anywhere and wanted to commit to all forms of cricket for England. Wheatley's line of questioning didn't exactly amount to a grilling, and it was clearly well-rehearsed, but he did reveal that he had had a long discussion with an unnamed England teammate the previous day, in which a range of issues were discussed, and that he left that meeting a happy man. On the back of that meeting, he was looking forward to meeting up with the team again.

Kevin went on to admit that he hadn't handled the press conference after the Headingley Test at all well, and said things he shouldn't have said, but added, 'I need to pull towards the team, and the team needs to pull towards me.' He also made it clear that he was still hoping to be selected for the upcoming World T20 Championship and did not insist on being released from England duty to play the full IPL season. Kevin made it clear that he'd been doing a lot of thinking and realised how happy playing for England made him feel.

However, it wasn't quite as simple as that. The squad announcement for the third and final Test against South Africa was delayed as the ECB gave Kevin more time to clarify exactly what had been said in these text messages. When he did not, he was dropped for the third Test, his place being taken by Jonny Bairstow.

The following day, it was revealed that the parody Twitter account 'KP Genius' was the work of Richard Bailey, a Nottingham-based friend of Stuart Broad and Graeme Swann, who normally tweeted under the account @Bailsthebadger. He counted Broad and Tim Bresnan amongst his followers, along with promising young duo Ben Stokes and Joss Buttler. Bailey released a statement in which he said he was closing the account, as he only ever intended it to be for humorous purposes, and stated that nobody in the England setup had colluded with him on this.

Kevin's friend Piers Morgan became something of an unofficial spokesman in the days that followed. He posted a series of messages on his Twitter account and gave a radio interview that raised some valid points about some of the double standards that appeared to be being practised by the England setup. Morgan pointed out that the people Kevin was alleged to have been texting had been very old friends, going back decades in some cases. On that basis, were Strauss and Flower willing to confirm that they had never texted derogatory comments about Kevin to third parties? Why was Stuart Broad allowed to collude with Richard Bailey on the parody Twitter account, and no action was taken? Similarly, why didn't Graeme Swann face any punishment for the comments he made about Kevin in his book the previous winter? These were all fair questions, and it didn't appear as though Kevin was being judged by the same standards as some of the others.

Events took another twist on the eve of the final Test when the ECB revealed they had received an apology from Kevin and an admission that he had sent 'provocative' texts to members of the South African team. He was quoted as saying, 'I did send what you might call provocative texts to my close friends in the SA team. The texts were meant as banter between close friends. I need to rein myself in sometimes. I apologise to Straussy and the team for the inappropriate remarks at the press conference and for the texts. I truly didn't mean to cause upset or tension particularly with important games at stake.'

England managing director Hugh Morris confirmed they were in receipt of Kevin's apology but that further discussions needed to take place to establish whether it was possible to regain the trust and mutual respect required to ensure all parties are able to focus on playing cricket. However, he made it clear that the upcoming Test was his priority for the time being and nothing would happen until after that.

In that final Test at Lord's, another century from Amla and a five wicket haul by Vernon Philander were the key factors in helping South Africa to a 51 run victory, winning them the series 2-0. Days later, Andrew Strauss announced his resignation and indeed his retirement from all forms of cricket, after having played exactly 100 Tests. He had gone through a poor summer and felt this was the right time to bow out of the game. Strauss, a known wine connoisseur, received 100 bottles from his England teammates as a token of appreciation for his years of service and leadership. Alastair Cook was named as the new England captain, having impressed as Strauss' deputy, and as skipper in the shorter formats.

With Kevin very much off the scene, England drew 2-2 with South Africa in the ODI series, and drew the T20 series 1-1. Things weren't going well for England, and a player of Kevin's stature in the side would've gone a long way towards putting things right.

During this period of isolation, Kevin had a reminder that no matter how crazy the circus around him appeared to be, there were far more important things in life than cricket. The Pietersens remained close to the Cole Edwards family, and Kevin had never forgotten the many happy hours he spent playing sports with their children when growing up. One of the Cole Edwards family, Jon, had been suffering from ocular melanoma, a type of cancer. He had undergone surgery, but in recent months at the time of writing, it has returned and is present in his liver, lungs and pelvic bone. This type of cancer is treatable, but it is not curable. Jon remains a very positive man and his strong Christian faith gives him a great deal of strength and encouragement. His wife, Sarah, has recently given birth to twins. Jon set up the JCE Trust as a means of raising money and spreading hope for cancer suffers.

Kevin was more than willing to do his bit to help, and so, with the help of his brother, Bryan arranged the Kevin Pietersen and JCE Trust Golf Day at Stocks Golf Club in Hertfordshire. Friends, businessmen and famous sportsmen had travelled long distances to take part in this day – Shane Warne had flown in from Australia, and Kevin's father, Jannie made the journey from South Africa, to name but two.

A fun day was had by all – Jannie hit the closest to the pin shot on the third, while Bryan's longest drive attempt had everyone amazed. The day ended with a few words from Kevin and Jon, which were extremely moving. For a moment, they just put everything to one side and put life into perspective, they all stood together, they all embraced and they all believed. It's hoped this will be the first of many such days organised by the Trust, as Jon continues to bravely battle his illness with optimism and hope. Kevin's troubles suddenly didn't seem so serious after all.

25

BUILDING BRIDGES

It was always going to be a long and tricky way back into the England setup for Kevin, but in many people's eyes, he didn't help his cause when it was announced that he would be going to the ICC World T20 after all – to work as a studio pundit for host broadcaster ESPN Star Sports. Many thought he should keep a low profile under the circumstances, and didn't think that he should be making any kind of comments about the performances of his England teammates when there was so much uncertainty about if and when he would return to the fold. The day before the opening match, he sat in the studio alongside Sourav Ganguly and Wasim Akram, immaculately dressed in his suit, and made some calm, measured and thoughtful points during the discussion.

There wasn't a hint of extravagance or hyperbole, and his only comment on the ongoing furore with regards to his future was that he was disappointed not to be playing in this tournament, but he had the next best thing with this job in the studio.

With Kevin far away from the England camp, the defending champions had a poor tournament by the very high standards they set themselves. They began with a comfortable victory over Afghanistan, but in their next match against India, they collapsed to 80 all out, which turned out to be the lowest score of the tournament, and was also England's lowest ever T20 score. They obviously lost that match, and were also defeated in the next against the host nation. They'd done enough to reach the Super Eight stage, where they suffered a narrow 15 run defeat to the West Indies, before going on to beat New Zealand by a comfortable six wickets. However, a 19 run defeat to Sri Lanka in their final Super Eight match sealed their fate, and they would be flying home without the trophy, and indeed without having made it to the knockout stages. In the final, the West Indies showed how far they had come in recent months as they beat the host nation by 36 runs.

Kevin's personal highlight came when, during his role as a studio pundit, he donned a pair of sunglasses and did a 'Gangnam Style' dance, which had colleagues Wasim Akram and Sourav Ganguly falling about in fits of laughter, but they reluctantly admitted they'd preferred one of Chris Gayle's dancing efforts during a match in the tournament.

No sooner had England landed home than the ECB issued a statement that read: 'The ECB and Kevin Pietersen confirm that agreement has been reached concerning a process for his re-integration into the England team during the remainder of 2012. Upon completion of the programme, the England selectors will consider Kevin for future matches.'

It is unclear what exactly this 'reintegration' process involved, but it essentially seemed to involve a rebuilding of trust and diplomatic relations with the entire England setup, with a view to them travelling on to India as a harmonious camp. Kevin had agreed to fly home for three days following the end of the World T20 and the start of his Champions League T20 campaign with the Delhi Daredevils in South Africa, where he would meet an unnamed senior England player for talks. There was a bizarre twist when his flight was delayed, pushing back his reintegration process by a day, but he did make the brief trip home. A number of England players had made positive noises about Kevin's potential return to the squad, but one thing remained unclear: England were due to fly out to Dubai for a training camp around 10 days later, in preparation for their tour of India. If the Daredevils reached the latter stages of the Champions League T20, he would face a dilemma as to whether to stay on and try to help them win the competition, or leave them early and join up with England, assuming his 'reintegration' was successful and he was named in the squad.

It was at around this time that Andrew Strauss gave an interview which shed a little more light on the episode. Andrew was now retired and could speak with considerably more freedom than those still active in the game. Andrew revealed that following his resignation, he had penned personal letters to every member of the squad, but not to Kevin, to whom he just sent a text.

Andrew said that while he was aware there were issues brewing with regards to Kevin's future involvement in the IPL, but the whole 'texting' saga had taken him by surprise – he found it baffling and they had become quite estranged for a while. Before the texting episode, Andrew hadn't had a single hint that Kevin had a problem with him. He also said that nine-tenths of the time, he found Kevin a good guy who set the right example in practice. He acknowledged that Kevin could have been quite resentful of him becoming captain following the earlier saga, but that was never an issue and they both got on with their jobs.

Andrew also pointed out that he and Kevin had since met, and his apology had been contrite and sincere. He also believed that nobody had really got to the bottom of the text messaging business, and that some of the other players were wrong to be following the spoof 'KP Genius' account. Andrew said he would welcome Kevin back to the England fold, but it would be in everyone's interests if he did so as a totally committed member.

Kevin made a slow start to his Champions League T20 campaign, making a highest score of just 14 in the group stages. He stayed on for the semi-finals, meaning he would be slightly late in joining up with the England squad in Dubai. In the last four, the Daredevils faced South African side the Highveld Lions. The Daredevils won the toss and elected to field. Chasing a target of 140, the Daredevils suffered an early blow when they lost Virender Sehwag for a duck after just three balls. Kevin was next in, and survived being dropped by Chris Morris as he made exactly 50, when Morris, now bowling, got revenge as he bowled a bouncer, which panicked Kevin into playing a pull, but he mistimed it and was caught by wicketkeeper Thami Tsolekile. Kevin departed with his side on 92/8, and they fell well short of their target, reaching 117/9 from 20 overs. Their tournament was over, the ECB had been happy with the progress made in the 'reintegration' process, and it was time for Kevin to focus on England duty.

The India tour saw England play four Tests and two T20s, which would end just two days before Christmas. The ODI squad would then fly out on January 2 for a five match series. Being at home over Christmas meant a lot to Kevin, as Dylan had now reached an age where he believed in Father Christmas and appreciated the magic of the season. Meanwhile, there had been some changes to the England coaching setup. It had been decided to ease Andy Flower's workload and for him to focus solely on Tests. Ashley Giles had been brought in to take charge of the T20 and ODI squads. As far as Kevin was concerned, this was great news. Ashley had been a mentor to Kevin when he first came into the England side, and they developed a firm friendship in the early years of Kevin's international career. As well as there being a genuine friendship between the pair, Kevin had a professional respect for Ashley and felt comfortable with him taking charge of the short formats. Ashley came into the England setup having recently guided Warwickshire to the County Championship title.

BUILDING BRIDGES

In India, Kevin made just 23 in the first warm-up, but in the next he showed signs of settling back in as he scored 110 before retiring hurt to give colleagues some batting practice. In his final warm-up game against India A, he managed just 19 before being caught by Abhinav Muknud off the bowling of 'Harry Potter' Sreesanth.

This was an important series on many fronts. Firstly and most obviously, the pressure was on Kevin to show he deserved a place in the side, in light of all that had gone on in the last few months. Secondly, new captain Alastair Cook would want to get his reign off to a positive start. Thirdly, and most importantly, this was a chance for the entire England squad to prove they had learnt from the disasters in Asia the previous winter, and had learnt to cope with these types of wicket in the year since.

In the first Test at Ahmedabad, England's batting lineup for the first time included Nick Compton, grandson of the great Denis Compton. India won the toss and elected to bat, and it quickly became clear that, as widely expected, this was a spinner's wicket. Graeme Swann claimed five wickets and Kevin one, but the pacemen struggled as the home side posted a massive total of 521/8 declared. Kevin came in with England on 30/3, but made just 17 when once again he fell to a slow left-armer as he was bowled by Pragyan Ojha, giving him his second of five wickets, as England collapsed to 191 all out.

India enforced the follow-on, and Kevin came to the crease with the side on an optimistic 156/2, but he had made just two runs from nine balls when he was once again bowled by Ojha. Captain Alastair Cook's 176 and Matt Prior's 91 were the key factors in helping England to a total of 406, but the damage was done in the first innings, and despite Kevin taking a well-judged catch near the boundary to dismiss Sehwag, India reached their target of 77 runs with nine wickets to spare. England were 1-0 down, and it was beginning to feel like last winter all over again.

There was just a four-day interval before the next Test at Wankhede Stadium in Mumbai, and England sensibly opted to play both Swann and Panesar. England had shown in their second innings of the first Test that they were capable of batting well in these conditions, and it was now up to them to build on that. In Mumbai, India won the toss and batted first. Cheteshwar Pujara top scored with 135, but Swann and Panesar took nine wickets between them, with the latter memorably claiming that of Sachin Tendulkar for just eight runs, as India were all out for a moderate 327.

Cook and Compton put together a strong opening partnership of 66, but Compton and Trott both fell to Ojha in quick succession, and Kevin needed to steady the ship with England on 68/2 as he began his innings shortly before tea on day two. What followed turned out to be one of the most important innings of his career. Kevin and his captain put together a superb partnership that built England up to 178/2 by the close of play, with Cook on 87 and Kevin on 62 overnight. The following morning, Cook reached his century, and Kevin followed not long afterwards, having made 100 off 127 balls, which included 15 fours.

Between them, they helped England to 374/3 before

Cook fell on 122, but Kevin formed partnerships with Jonny Bairstow and Samit Patel before he was eventually caught by wicketkeeper MS Dhoni, once again off the bowling of Ojha after making a magnificent 186, which had included an incredible 20 fours and four sixes. This had been a breath-taking innings that those who witnessed would never forget. He had played some thrilling shots, almost treating it as a one-day game, but all along he was in control, and didn't take any silly risks with his wicket. This took Kevin to 22 Test hundreds, level with the England record, although it should always be pointed out that he had far more opportunities to play than those of previous generations. There were those in the media who suggested that England should wash their hands of Kevin after the controversy of the previous summer, but after an innings like this, even his harshest critics would surely agree it was worth persevering with him. It's also worth pointing out that Kevin and Alastair had effectively carried the England innings, as none of the rest reached 30 before England were bowled out for 413.

Swann and Panesar once again dominated the bowling, taking all ten wickets as India crashed to 142 all out. England's openers reached the modest target of 57 without dropping any wickets to complete a memorable Test victory with much more than a day to spare. Nobody could argue that Kevin didn't thoroughly deserve his Man of the Match award. He'd just reminded the world that, even if he had competition for the status of being the greatest batsman on the planet, everyone surely agreed that on his day, he was the most entertaining. More importantly, he had shown that he could put in a major innings at a crucial time in the match and series.

Kevin knew he couldn't rest on his laurels, and was determined to make at least one more big innings in the series.

In the third Test at Eden Gardens, Kolkata, Tendulkar's 76 was the stand-out performance as India reached 316 in the first innings. Alastair made a magnificent 190 (meaning he'd gone ahead of Kevin with 23 Test centuries for England), but Kevin played a useful supporting role with 54 as England were bowled out for 523. In India's second innings, England's seamers had a rare chance to shine in Asia, as Anderson and Finn took three wickets each to help bowl the home side out for 247. England made heavy work of the 41 runs they required to win on the final morning. They lost Cook and Trott cheaply as Kevin came in with his team on 7/2, but this wasn't to be his day as he was out for a duck, caught Dhoni bowled Ashwin. It didn't matter too much as Compton and Bell saw England home for a seven wicket victory, leaving them 2-1 up with just one Test to play.

Joe Root made his England Test debut in the final Test at Nagpur. He was being talked about as a player who was, in some respects, very similar to Kevin, and was widely regarded as his eventual heir apparent. Root considered himself more similar in style and technique to Michael Vaughan, and considered the Ashes-winning former captain as the player he wanted to emulate.

England won the toss and batted first, but they got off to

a terrible start as Compton and Cook fell early on, meaning Kevin was left to pick up the pieces with the side on 16/2. Kevin once again looked to be in good shape as he and Trott put together an 86 partnership before Trott fell with England on 103/2, but Kevin battled on with Bell and Root. Once again, Kevin lost his wicket to a slow left-armer, as he was caught at midwicket by Ojha off the bowling of Ravindra Jadeja for a very respectable 73. Debutant Root also made 73, and half-centuries from Prior and Swann helped England to a first innings total of 337 all out.

In response, Virant Kohli's century and Dhoni's 99 before being run out helped spare India's blushes as most of the leading batsmen posted poor scores, but Jimmy Anderson put in another strong performance with the ball, claiming four wickets, while Swann took three as India were all out for 326, just four behind England. It was game on.

In the second innings, England were on a steady 81/2 when Kevin came in, but he managed just six runs before he once again lost his wicket to Jadeja. On this occasion, he completely misjudged the ball, and he decided to leave it before it went on to hit off stump. It was a shame to lose his wicket to a slow left-armer for the umpteenth time, but it didn't really matter as the match ended with an inevitable draw, but not before Trott and Bell had posted centuries.

England had won the series 2-1, and this looked like a very different England side to the previous winter. After a wobbly start in the first Test, England's batsmen had adapted to the conditions and all had, at one time or another in the series, pulled their weight. The spin bowlers had taken advantage of the favourable conditions, while Anderson had shown it was possible to use pace to your advantage on these wickets.

Kevin was rested for the two T20 matches that followed, with both sides winning one each, and as he prepared to fly home in time for Christmas Eve, he learned that the selectors had come around to his way of thinking with regards to squad rotation and the need to use players wisely with such an intense schedule. Once the ODI series against India was over towards the end of January, Kevin would be rested for the T20 and ODI matches at the start of the tour of New Zealand that followed, but would be expected to make himself available for the three-Test series which began in early March. As far as he was concerned, common sense had prevailed, as he knew that, at the age of 32, he couldn't put his body through the sheer relentlessness of the modern schedule, and it was now sometimes necessary to prioritise.

Kevin returned to India in the New Year for the five-match ODI series. His 44 in the opening game at Rajkot helped England to a narrow nine run victory, but it was to be a rare moment of joy in what was a largely disappointing series. In the next match at Kochi, Kevin top-scored with just 42 as England collapsed to 158 all out, chasing India's 285. India went 2-1 in front as England crashed to 155 all out in Ranchi with Kevin making just 17, and the home side went on to win with more than 20 overs to spare.

The fourth match at Mohali brought out the best in Kevin. England batted first and he came in with his side on 37/1 after losing the wicket of bell for 10. He put together a thrilling 95-run partnership with Cook, before batting on with Eoin Morgan and Samit Patel, and was eventually bowled by Ishant Sharma after making 76, with seven fours and one six. He and Cook had the equal top score as England ended their innings on 257/7, but India's batsmen chased down the target with 15 balls and five wickets to spare, meaning they had taken the series as they led 3-1 with just one more to play. Kevin and Alastair had done their part, but others had gone off the boil and had not really pulled their weight in the series. England managed to win the final match by seven wickets thanks largely to an Ian Bell century, but Kevin managed just six before he was caught by Ravindra Jadeja at deep mid- wicket off the bowling of Shami Ahmed.

This had been a disappointing series for Kevin. He, personally had posted some largely respectable scores, but he was anything but a selfish player in that sense – in his mind, it was better to make a 40 and be on the winning side than to make a century and lose. The main problem in this series had been England's batting collapses, and in the ODI format at least, they hadn't moved on much in the last 12 months when it came to handling pitches in Asia. Each batsman had to look at his game and make the necessary changes, using the expertise of Graham Gooch, while fielding coach Richard Halsall had to work on sharpening the players up in certain areas. Kevin also considered it important to make the most of the increasingly sophisticated computer technology that was available to them in this day and age, and had no time for technophobes who would rather live in the past. To be fair to the England batsmen, they knew they had under-performed in this series and knuckled down to some hard work before they took on New Zealand.

Kevin flew home to enjoy a month or so with Jess and Dylan before he made the long trip to New Zealand for the Test series at the end of the tour. In his absence, England returned to form in the T20 series, taking two of the three matches by comfortable margins, while also winning two of the three ODIs with plenty of breathing space. In a sense, Kevin was happy that they could win without him, as although he knew he would be defined as a cricketer by his ability to make big innings at important times, it was good that the side wasn't overly-reliant on one or two batsman. Any batsman could have an off day, but as long as those around you were in form, you could cover for one another and the side would still prosper. However, if four or five batsmen were out of form or had problems with technique, it was not going to be possible for the team to succeed. Unfortunately, this logic didn't extend to the Test side, as Kevin found out soon after his arrival.

In the first Test at the University Oval, Dunedin, no play was possible on day one due to rain and bad light, so even before a ball had been bowled, there was always a fair chance it was going to be a draw. England batted first and made a terrible start as Kevin came in to try and salvage the innings with the score at 18/2. Unfortunately for Kevin, he was out first ball as Neil Wagner delivered a full, straight delivery that swung in and was a plumb LBW. Kevin couldn't get his bat across in time and there was no doubt whatsoever that he was out. England collapsed to 167 all out, with Jonathan Trott top scoring on 45. In response, New Zealand reached 460/9 before declaring early on day four. England effectively had to bat out four-and-a-half sessions of cricket to save the match. This was a case of protecting your wicket at all cost. The score didn't matter – it was important to just keep batting.

England rose to the challenge as openers Cook and Compton put together a 231 run partnership, while nightwatchman Steven Finn stood his ground as he outlasted Compton and Trott, before teaming up with Kevin. Maybe he was still slightly rattled from his first innings duck, but Kevin didn't seem to settle in well, and he was out for just 12 when he played across Wagner's full ball, got a thin inside edge and was caught by wicketkeeper BJ Watling. On this occasion, Kevin had not played his part, and would have done well to have remembered the advice Clive Rice drilled in to him time and time again during those early years at Notts – protect your wicket at all costs.

Despite a few scary moments, not least Kevin's dismissal, England ran the clock down and the match ended with them on 421/6. In reality, they had been saved by the loss of the first day's play along with a sizeable chunk of day three. Kevin knew they had been let off the hook, and that truly great Test sides shouldn't have to rely on nature to bail them out. However, there had been some positives – Cook had made yet another hundred while Compton picked up his maiden Test century.

At the next Test in Wellington, the home side won the toss and put England in to bat, and Kevin came in with his side on a strong 236/2, with Compton having just been dismissed after making exactly 100. Kevin formed useful partnerships with Trott, Bell and Root, before being dismissed on 73 when he lofted the ball high towards mid-off, only to be caught by Peter Fulton from the bowling of Bruce Martin. This had been an impressive innings that had included seven fours and one six, but had also seen some good judgement as Kevin took precautions to ensure he maintained his wicket.

England reached 465 all out, and Stuart Broad took six wickets as New Zealand were bowled out for 254.

England enforced the follow-on, and New Zealand reached 162/2 in their second innings at the end of day four. It was the home side's turn to be saved by the elements, as no play was possible on day five due to rain. It was incredibly frustrating, as England had the Kiwis on the rope, but there was absolutely nothing they could do about it.

Shortly after the second Test, it became clear that all was not well with Kevin. He had first hurt his right knee training in Queenstown prior to the start of the series. At first, it seemed bearable, and any specialist treatment could wait until he was back in England, but as time went by, his discomfort increased, and he was forced to reluctantly accept that his tour was over.

With Kevin having flown home, England salvaged a dramatic draw in the final Test at Eden Park, Auckland. On the final day, they were nine wickets down, while Matt

Prior and Monty Panesar successfully defended their
wickets while the clock ticked towards a draw. It was an
incredible, defiant effort and ensured the three-Test series
ended a 0-0 draw. It also demonstrated in all sorts of ways
how Test cricket is the absolute pinnacle of the game, and
that it requires skill, endurance, patience, fitness and good
judgement to excel at it.

The following day, Kevin was pictured near his
Kensington home wearing a knee brace. Earlier in the
week, he had undergone scans which confirmed a bone
injury and bone bruising. At first, it was thought he would
be back for rehabilitation within a fortnight and would
play a full part in the English summer, which included
return Tests by New Zealand, the ICC Champions Trophy,
and, of course, the Ashes.

However, as the weeks went by, it became clear he would
miss the whole of the first part of the summer, and stood no
chance of featuring for the Delhi Daredevils in the IPL.

By late April, it was clear that Kevin would play no part
in the return series against New Zealand, which was the
curtain raiser to the English summer, and was also ruled out
for the ICC Champions Trophy in June. A realistic target for
a comeback was Surrey's County Championship match
against Yorkshire at Headingley, starting on 21 June, after
which he would join the England setup for their Ashes
warm-up match against Essex. It was hardly ideal
preparation, but it was the best they could hope for under
the circumstances. It was certainly going to be a very long
summer, with two T20s and five ODIs following the Ashes,

after which England would have to prepare to head Down Under for another Ashes series during the winter.

Meanwhile, at Surrey, things had got very interesting indeed. The club had announced that a certain Graeme Smith was joining the side as their new captain on a three year deal! In April, Kevin went to the Oval to take a look at things, and discovered that his and Smith's lockers were next to one another. Kevin took a picture of the lockers and tweeted: 'Pleasantly surprised by this on my arrival into the dressing this am! My new #BFF .. @GraemeSmith49'

BFF is Twitterspeak for 'best friends forever'. Relations between the two had certainly moved on a great deal in recent years. Nowadays, Kevin genuinely liked and admired Graeme. He saw him as a really good guy and although opportunities to play at Surrey would be limited, lining up alongside him was something to really look forward to. It therefore came as a considerable blow when, in early May, it was announced that Graeme would be out of action for a few months, as he was returning to South Africa for ankle surgery.

Also joining Surrey, for June and July at least, was Ricky Ponting, now aged 38. He was initially signed as cover for Graeme, who was expected to be needed by South Africa for the ICC Champions Trophy in June, but with him having called time on his international career, it's possible he may end up sticking around for longer. With Graeme out of action, it may well happen.

So what next for Kevin? He turns 33 in the summer of 2013, and nobody can say for sure what the future holds for him. We can be certain that we will see plenty more exciting innings from him, wherever and whoever he plays for in years to come. It's also probable that there will be further controversies, in some shape or form. There is no doubt that he epitomises everything a professional cricketer should be in terms of his dedication in training, his desire to constantly improve as a player and his overall work ethic. He has undoubtedly brought some refreshing honesty to the game. He isn't afraid to upset people who badly need upsetting, but sometimes he would benefit from expressing his views in a more tactful and subtle way, to keep himself out of trouble if nothing else.

People will have their views about Kevin Pietersen. Some people will love him, and some people will hate him. That has been absolutely clear for some years. But there are two statements upon which all serious cricket fans can surely agree. Firstly, there isn't a more naturally talented batsman playing anywhere in the world at present. Secondly, when Kevin comes out to bat, he makes you sit up and pay attention like no other batsman can. When he's out in the middle, you never quite know what's going to happen next, but it'll definitely be worth watching.